THE SPIRIT OF THE EAST

ALSO BY GERALD DE GAURY

Arabia Phoenix
Arabian Journey
Rulers of Mecca
The Grand Captain, Gonzalo de Cordoba
Three Kings in Baghdad
Faisal, King of Saudi Arabia
Through Wahhabiland on Camelback (*Editor*)
Travelling Gent: A Life of Alexander Kinglake

ALSO BY H. V. F. WINSTONE

Kuwait: Prospect and Reality (*with Zahra Freeth*)
Explorers of Arabia (*with Zahra Freeth*)
Captain Shakespear
Gertrude Bell

THE SPIRIT OF THE EAST

An anthology of prose
and verse inspired by
the people, places and
legends of the East

———◆———

*Edited by Gerald de Gaury
and H. V. F. Winstone*

QUARTET BOOKS
LONDON · MELBOURNE · NEW YORK

First published by Quartet Books Limited 1979
A member of the Namara Group
27 Goodge Street, London W1P 1FD

Foreword and introductions copyright © 1979
by Gerald de Gaury and H. V. F. Winstone

Designed by Mike Jarvis

ISBN 0 7043 2230 7

Set in Monotype Garamond
by Clerkenwell Graphics, London
Printed in Great Britain by
Billing & Sons Limited, Guildford, London and Worcester

CONTENTS

LIST OF ILLUSTRATIONS

FOREWORD

The pieces here selected are from works of fact or imagination written or translated into English after Europe's long medieval sleep. Rarity, elegance of style or simply entertainment value were considered suitable criteria for inclusion.

Visitors to the East are becoming increasingly great in number; most are on business bent or sent by their governments. Time for them is often limited and their journeys are usually swift. They may be provided with up-to-date information in modern books, but few can have time, even on their return, to delve into the past in order to learn something of how the East appeared to their forerunners.

Between the two World Wars westerners who went to the East expected to stay longer than most do today. They travelled slowly and had greater opportunity to buy and read old travellers' books. Some made notes of passages they liked and later added others; and this has been done here. They came to know the terms currently in use for regions of the East that have changed, some of them more than once. The title for this book, *The Spirit of the East*, is taken from one such book, issued in London in 1838 for David Urquhart; it had a subtitle explaining that it covered his adventures in a journey through Rumeli. Rumeli was the name used by the Turks for their possessions in Europe seized from the Byzantines of Rum (now Rome) or Constantinople, later called Istanbul. The word Rumi was employed by country Arabs until recently to describe an Eastern Christian.

Western usage has changed too. The lands of the former Ottoman Empire and of the Persian Empire were known in England as the Near East. The Middle East was used to describe India and her immediate neighbours. In 1946 a deputation from the Royal Geographical Society of England approached the Prime Minister with a request that the use of the *Middle East*, which had been taken up by certain Government departments instead of the Near East, might be dropped in favour of reversion to the old name. No action, however, was taken. Nevertheless it seemed right to employ 'nearer East' here, in dealing with an anthology ending about 1914.

Before leaving the subject of terminology it should be added that the 'Eastern Question', often written and spoken about in the nineteenth century, referred to matters arising from the relations of Ottoman Turkey, the Balkan States (those between the Adriatic, the Aegean and Black Seas) and Russia to each other and to Europe.

The extracts given here are brought to an end about the time of the beginning of the 1914-18 war because it was felt that most of the books published by travellers since then would be known, at least by name, to the general reader; for example T. E. Lawrence's *Seven Pillars of Wisdom* and those books by the last explorers of the then still unknown part of Arabia, Bertram Thomas, H. St. J. Philby and, above all, Wilfrid Thesiger.

We have chosen from works of chiefly literary merit, but sometimes we have been swayed by discovery or revelation. Occasionally one begets the other. In his book *The Road to Xanadu*, J. L. Lowes says that Coleridge, before writing his prose poem, had read Purchas on Persia, Bruce on his travels in Abyssinia and several other works, making a whimsical conjunction of Tartary, Florida, Kashmir and Greece for the conjuring up of thoughts used by him in the poem. This short dreamlike creation typifies the English Romantic Age, embodying the current view of the Spirit of the East.

We have eschewed in general translations into English from Oriental authors, since they are the province of an altogether different anthology; but we have made two small exceptions, single verses from Burton's translation of Al-Mutanabbi and Gertrude Bell's rendering of Hafiz.

The choice of illustrations has rested on the availability of material from the literary works represented here, and on a desire to supplement the text where possible with drawings which stand on their own merits.

Transliteration of oriental names and phrases has been left as given by the various authors, for to introduce a modern system would have led to a disturbing variety in the text between old and modern habits.

ACKNOWLEDGEMENTS

The authors would like to record their special thanks to the Royal Geographical Society, the British Library and the London Library for the loan of books and manuscripts without which this work could not have been compiled; and for permission to reproduce illustrations from some of the publications in their possession.

Front view of the Khasne, a temple cut in the rock at Petra,
from Labarde's *Journey through Arabia Petraea*, London 1836

THE WANDERING JEW

From the Itinerary of
Rabbi Benjamin of Tudela
(TWELFTH CENTURY)

———◆———

One of the earliest travellers from Europe to the East in the late Middle Ages, Rabbi Benjamin of Tudela in Navarre, son of Jonas the Jew, does not give the exact date of his voyage but it is known from the introduction to the early Hebrew edition that he returned with a report on his travels to Castile in the year 1173. Included in it was much about the peoples and places he had seen or heard of, geographical information, such as the distance between cities, and in particular the whereabouts of Jewish communities and their numbers with names of rabbis and synagogues. From the Near East he went on to Ceylon and China. His story was in manuscript until publication in Constantinople in 1543 as the *Massa'oth* or *Itinerary*, in the original rabbinic character; it was put into Latin and printed at Ferrara in 1556, the only known surviving copy of which is in the Bodleian Library at Oxford. The first English translation was published in *Purchas His Pilgrims* in 1625 as the Peregrinations of Benjamin son of Jonas a Jew.

His accounts of Baghdad before the Tartar and Ottoman occupations and of China at the time of the Sung Emperors are vivid.

———◆———

FROM THE PEREGRINATIONS OF BENJAMIN SON OF JONAS A JEW, TRANSLATED BY A. ASHER (1840)

. . . Two days from thence (Okbeyr) stands Bagdad, the large metropolis of the Khalif Emir al Mumenin al Abassi, of the family of their prophet, who is the chief of the mahomedan religion. All mahomedan kings acknowledge him and he holds the same dignity over them, which the Pope enjoys over the christians.

The palace of the Khalif at Bagdad is three miles in extent, it contains a large park of all sorts of trees, both useful and ornamental and all sorts of beasts, as well as a pond of water led thither from the river Tigris; and whenever the Khalif desires to enjoy himself and to sport and to carouse, birds, beasts and fishes are prepared for him and for his councillors, whom he invites to his palace.

This great Abasside is extremely kind towards the Jews, many of his officers being of that nation; he understands all languages, is well versed in the mosaic law and reads and writes the hebrew language.

He enjoys nothing, but what he earns by the labour of his own hands and therefore manufactures coverlets which he stamps with his seal and which his officers sell in the public market; these articles are purchased by the nobles of the land and from their produce his necessaries are provided.

The Khalif is an excellent man, trustworthy and kind-hearted towards every one, but generally invisible to the mahomedans. The pilgrims, which come hither from distant countries on their way to Mekha in Yemen, [A confusion between Mocha in the Yemen and Mecca, or so it seems] desire to be presented to him and thus adddress him from the palace: 'Our Lord, light of the mahomedans and splendor of our religion, show us the brightness of thy countenance', but he heeds not their words. His servants and officers then approach and pray: 'O Lord, manifest thy peace to those men, who come from distant lands and desire shelter in the shadow of thy glory' and after such petition he rises and puts one corner of his garment out of the window, which is eagerly kissed by the pilgrims. One of the lords then addresses them thus: 'go in peace, for our Lord, the light of the mahomedans, is well pleased and gives you his blessing.' This prince being esteemed by them equal to their prophet, they proceed on their way, full of joy at the words addressed to them by the lord, who communicated the message of peace.

All the brothers and other members of the Khalif's family, are accustomed to kiss his garments, and every one of them possesses a palace within that of the Khalif, but they are all fetter'd by chains of iron, and a special officer is appointed over every household to prevent their rising in rebellion against the great king. These measures are enacted in consequence of an occurrence, which took place some time ago and upon which occasion the brothers rebelled and elected a king among themselves; to prevent this in future it was decreed, that all the members of the Khalif's family should be chained, in order to prevent their rebellious intentions. Every one of them, however, resides in his palace, is there much honor'd and they possess villages and towns, the rents of which are collected for them by their stewards; they eat and drink and lead a merry life.

The palace of the great king contains large buildings, pillars of gold and silver, and treasures of precious stones.

The Khalif leaves his palace but once every year, viz. at the time of the feast called Ramadan. Upon this occasion many visitors assemble from distant parts, in order to have an opportunity of beholding his countenance. He then bestrides the royal mule, dressed in kingly robes, which are composed of gold and silver cloth. On his head he wears a turban, ornamented with precious stones of inestimable value, but over this turban is thrown a black veil, as a sign of humility and as much as to say: See all this wordly honor will be converted into darkness on the day of death. He is accompanied by a numerous retinue of mahomedan nobles, array'd in rich dresses and riding upon horses, princes of Arabia, of Media, of Persia and even of Tibet, a country distant three months journey from Arabia.

This procession goes from the palace to the Mosque on the Bosra gate, which is the metropolitan Mosque. All those who walk in procession are dressed in silk and purple, both men and women. The streets and squares are enliven'd by singing, rejoicings and by parties who dance before the great king, called Khalif. He is loudly saluted by the assembled crowd who cry: 'Blessed art thou our Lord and King' ...

Bagdad is inhabited by about one thousand Jews, who enjoy peace, comfort and much honor under the government of the great king. Among them are very wise men and presidents of the colleges, whose occupation is the study of the mosaic law ...

The authority of the Prince of the Captivity [in Baghdad] over [Jews in] the following countries viz: Mesopotamia; Persia; Khorassan; S'ba which is Yemen; Diarbekr; all Armenia and the Land of Kola near mount Ararat; over the country of the Alanians, which is shut in by mountains and has no outlet except by the iron gates, which were made by Alexander; over Sikbia and all the provinces of the Turkmans unto the Aspisian mountains; over the country of the Georgians unto the river Oxus ...

At the time of the installation of the Prince of the Captivity he spends considerable sums in presents to the king, or Khalif, his princes and nobles. The ceremony is performed by the act of the laying on of the hands of the king or Khalif, after which the Prince rides home from the king's abode to his own house, seated in a royal state carriage and accompanied by the sound of various musical instruments; he afterwards lays his hands on the gentlemen of the university.

Many of the Jews of Bagdad are good scholars and very rich, the city contains twenty-eight jewish synagogues, situated partly in Bagdad and partly in Al-Khorkh, on the other side of the river Tigris, which runs through and divides the city. The metropolitan synagogue of the Prince of the Captivity is ornamented with pillars of richly colour'd marble, plated with gold and silver; on the pillars are inscribed verses of the psalms in letters of gold. The ascent to the holy ark* is composed of ten marble steps on the uppermost of which are the stalls set apart for the Prince of the Captivity . . .

The circumference of the city of Bagdad measures three miles, the country in which it is situated is rich in palm-trees, gardens and orchards so that nothing equals it in Mesopotamia; merchants of all countries resort thither for purposes of trade and it contains many wise philosophers, well skilled in sciences, and magicians proficient in all sorts of witchcraft . . .

To Babylon one day; this is the ancient Babel and now lies in ruins but the streets still extend thirty miles. Of the palace of Nebuchad-netsar the ruins are still to be seen, but people are afraid to enter it on account of the serpents and scorpions, by which it is infested . . .

---

*The place where the rolls of the Pentateuch are deposited; it is generally elevated above the seats of the congregation.

THE WAY TO CATHAY

From Cathay and the Way Thither by Friar John of Monte Corvino
(c. 1247–1328)

———

That 'profound and melancholy silence' which according to Gibbon shrouded much of the East for several centuries after the fall of Acre in 1291, was by no means as complete as the great historian believed.

It was in the very year of the surrender of the last outpost of the Crusaders in the Holy Land that a Franciscan missionary, Giovanni di Monte Corvino, set out from Mongol Persia to visit India and China. There he hoped to enhance his earlier labours in the Near East on behalf of the Catholic Church, to seek the reconciliation of Greek and Latin churches, and to expose the 'perverted' works of the Nestorian Christians who had, nevertheless, carried the flag of the faith through the dark centuries of Arab and Tartar conquest. He went East as Papal legate to the court of the Great Khan and other important personages of the Mongol world; and he sent back to Europe accounts of his journeys which provided valuable and detailed information on the geography, the governments and peoples of the Near East and the Indies. He was made Archbishop of Peking by Pope Clement V, and according to Franciscan tradition he converted to Christianity the third ruler of the Yuen dynasty of China, the Great Khan Khaishan Kuluk. At his death he was honoured by 'heathen and believer alike'.

The Friar's letters, mostly to be found in the Laurentian Library at Florence and the National Library of Paris, were translated by Sir Henry Yule, soldier and Oriental scholar, and published by the Hakluyt Society in 1866 (Volumes 36 and 37). Much of John of Monte Corvino's work, and that of his fellow Christians in Persia and other parts of the East, was recorded in *Jami-ut-Tawarikh*, or The Historical Cyclopaedia of Fazl-ullah Rashid, otherwise Rashiddin, chief Wazir of the Persian Empire under Ghazan Khan and an exact contemporary of Friar John. Rashiddin was eventually accused of killing the Shah's brother and, though he was a practising Muslim, of secretly embracing the Jewish faith. He was executed and his head borne through the streets of his native Tabriz as that of a blasphemous Jew. It is to his painstaking book of history that we owe much of our knowledge of the East at that time when Europe was beginning to turn her eyes eastwards.

LETTERS AND REPORTS OF MISSIONARY FRIARS

No. 1. First Letter of John of Montecorvino

I, Friar John of Monte Corvino, of the order of Minor Friars, departed from Tauris, a city of the Persians, in the year of the Lord 1291, and proceeded to India. And I remained in the country of India, wherein stands the church of St. Thomas the Apostle, for thirteen months, and in that region baptized in different places about one hundred persons. The companion of my journey was Friar Nicholas of Pistoia, of the order of Preachers, who died there, and was buried in the church aforesaid.

I proceeded on my further journey and made my way to Cathay, the realm of the Emperor of the Tartars who is called the Grand Cham. To him I presented the letter of our lord the Pope, and invited him to adopt the Catholic Faith of our Lord Jesus Christ, but he had grown too old in idolatry. However he bestows many kindnesses upon the Christians, and these two years past I am abiding with him.

The Nestorians, a certain body who profess to bear the christian name, but who deviate sadly from the christian religion, have grown so powerful in those parts that they will not allow a christian of another ritual to have ever so small a chapel, or to publish any doctrine different from their own.

To these regions there never came any one of the Apostles, nor yet of the Disciples. And so the Nestorians aforesaid, either directly or through others whom they bribed, have brought on me persecutions of the sharpest. For they got up stories that I was not sent by our lord the Pope, but was a great spy and imposter; and after a while they produced false witnesses who declared that there was indeed an envoy sent with presents of immense value for the emperor, but that I had murdered him in India, and stolen what he had in charge. And these intrigues and calumnies went on for some five years. And thus it came to pass that many a time I was dragged before the judgement seat with ignominy and threats of death. At last, by God's providence, the emperor, through the confessions of a certain individual, came to know my innocence and the malice of my adversaries; and he banished them with their wives and children.

In this mission I abode alone and without any associate for eleven years; but it is now going on for two years since I was joined by Friar Arnold, a German of the province of Cologne.

I have built a church in the city of Cambaliech, in which the king has his chief residence. This I completed six years ago; and I have built a bell-tower to it, and put three bells in it. I have baptised there, as well as I can estimate, up to this time some 6,000 persons; and if those charges against me of which I have spoken had not been made, I should have baptised more than 30,000. And I am often still engaged in baptising.

Also I have gradually bought one hundred and fifty boys, the children of pagan parents, and of ages varying from seven to eleven, who had never learned any religion. These boys I have baptized, and I have taught them Greek and Latin after our manner. Also I have written out Psalters for them, with thirty Hymnaries and two Breviaries. By help of these, eleven of the boys already know our service, and form a choir and take their weekly turn of duty as they do in convents, whether I am there or not. Many of the boys are also employed in writing out Psalters and other things suitable. His Majesty the Emperor moreover delights much to hear them chaunting. I have the bells rung at all the canonical hours, and with my congregation of babes and sucklings I perform divine service, and the chaunting we do by ear because I have no service book with the notes.

A certain king of this part of the world, by name George, belonging to the sect of Nestorian christians, and of the illustrious family of that great king who was called Prester John of India, in the first year of my arrival here attached himself to me, and being converted by me to the truth of the Catholic faith, took the lesser orders, and when I celebrated mass he used to attend me wearing his royal robes. Certain others of the Nestorians on this account accused him of apostacy, but he brought over a great part of his people with him to the true Catholic faith, and built a church on a scale of royal magnificence in honour of our God, of the Holy Trinity, and of our lord the Pope, giving it the name of the Roman Church.

This King George six years ago departed to the Lord a true christian, leaving as his heir a son scarcely out of the cradle, and who is now nine years old. And after King George's death his brothers, perfidious followers of the errors of Nestorius, perverted again all those whom he had brought over to the church, and carried them back to their original schismatical creed. And being all alone, and not able to leave his Majesty the Cham, I could not go to visit the church above-mentioned, which is twenty days' journey distant.

Yet, if I could but get some good fellow-workers to help me, I trust in God that all this might be retrieved, for I still possess the grant which was made in our favour by the late King George before mentioned. So I say again that if it had not been for the slanderous charges which I have spoken of, the harvest reaped by this time would have been great!

Indeed if I had had but two or three comrades to aid me 'tis possible that the Emperor Cham would have been baptized by this time! I ask then for such brethren to come, if any are willing to come, such I mean as will make it their great business to lead exemplary lives, and not to make broad their own phylacteries.

As for the road hither I may tell you that the way through the land of the Goths, subject to the Emperor of the Northern Tartars, is the shortest and safest; and by it the friars might come, along with the letter-carriers, in five or six months. The other route again is very long and very dangerous, involving two sea-voyages; the first of which is about as long as that from Acre to the province of Provence, whilst the second is as long as from Acre to England. And it is possible that it might take more than two years to accomplish the journey that way. But, on the other hand, the first-mentioned route has not been open for a considerable time, on account of wars that have been going on.

It is twelve years since I have had any news of the Papal court, or of our order, or of the state of affairs generally in the west. Two years ago indeed there came hither a certain Lombard leech and chirurgeon, who spread abroad in these parts the most incredible blasphemies about the court of Rome and our Order and the state of things in the west, and on this account I exceedingly desire to obtain true intelligence. I pray the brethren whom this letter may reach to do their possible to bring its contents to the knowledge of our lord the Pope, and the Cardinals, and the agents of the Order at the court of Rome.

I beg the Minister General of our Order to supply me with an Antiphonarium with the Legends of the Saints, a Gradual, and a Psalter with the musical notes, as a copy; for I have nothing but a pocket Breviary with the short Lessons, and a little missal: if I had one for a copy, the boys of whom I have spoken could transcribe others from it. Just now I am engaged in building a second church, with the view of distributing the boys in more places than one.

I have myself grown old and grey, more with toil and trouble than with years; for I am not more than fifty-eight. I have got a competent knowledge of the language and character which is most generally used by the Tartars. And I have already translated into that language and character the New Testament and the Psalter, and have caused them to be written out in the fairest penmanship they have; and so by writing, reading and preaching, I bear open and public testimony to the Law of Christ. And I had been in treaty with the late King George, if he had lived, to translate the whole Latin ritual, that it might be sung throughout the whole extent of his territory; and whilst he was alive I used to celebrate mass in his church according to the Latin ritual, reading in the before mentioned language and character the words of both the preface and the Canon.

And the son of the king before mentioned is called after my name, John; and I hope in God that he will walk in his father's steps.

As far as I ever saw or heard tell, I do not believe that any king or prince in the world can be compared to his majesty the Cham in respect of the extent of his dominions, the vastness of their population, or the amount of his wealth. Here I stop.

Dated at the city of Cambalec in the kingdom of Cathay, in the year of the Lord 1305, and on the 8th day of January.

A ROMAN AT MECCA

From *The Navigation and Voyage of Ludovico di Varthema*

(SIXTEENTH CENTURY)

------●------

'*There have been many before me, who to know the miracles of the worlde, have with diligent studye read dyvers authors which have written of such things.*'
So, in the language of the Elizabethan translation of his book of travel, wrote Ludovico di Varthema, Gentleman of Rome, who made the first recorded visit by a non-Muslim to the holy shrines of Islam at Mecca and Al Madina. Varthema was not content merely to read of the miracles of the world. In the last days of the year 1502, at an undisclosed age, he left his native Italy with 'prosperous winds' which took him and his companions from Venice to Alexandria. Thus began one of the most remarkable journeys by land and sea of the sixteenth century, or for that matter of any other time. His was a rumbustious, impudent progress through hot and dangerous lands; across Arabia, around the coast of India, through Asia Minor, to the East Indies and Africa, observing peoples and places, manners and customs keenly, sometimes exaggerating or understating his escapades, for he travelled as Yunus (Jonah) and swore the Muslim faith. When he returned to Rome and his home town of Bologna in the year 1508 to write an account of his eventful five years at large, he was under the watchful eye of the Papal Saviour Julius II. He did not seek to hide his apostacy or some of his outrageous behaviour, but he was doubtless as circumspect as his cavalier temperament allowed. Above all, he must be given credit for discoveries of real significance in Arabia, where he was the first European to record the Meccan pilgrimage and the first to describe Jebel Kheybar, the mountain of the Jews; and in regions east of Java in the Indonesian archipelago. As Sir Richard Burton said, he 'stands in the foremost rank of the old Oriental travellers'.

His book was entitled *The Navigation and Voyage of Ludovico di Varthema, Gentleman of the City of Rome*, to the regions of Arabia, Egypt, Persia, Syria, Ethiopia and East India, both within and without the River of Ganges, etc., in the Year of Our Lord 1503, containing many notable and strange things, both historical and natural, first published in Rome, 1510. It was translated into English by Richard Eden in 1576.

———

THE JOURNEY FROM DAMASCO TO MECHA, AND OF THE MANERS OF THE ARABIANS

After that I have largely spoken of Damasco, I wyll proceede to the rest of my voyage. Therefore in the yeere of our Lorde, 1503, the eight daye of the moneth of Apryll, when I had hyred certayne Cammelles (which they call Caravanas) to go to Mecha, and beyng then ignorant of the customes and maners of them in whose companye I shoulde go, I entred familiartie and friendshyppe with a certayne captayne Mamaluke, of them that had forsaken our fayth, with whom beyng agreed of the price, he prepared me apparell lyke unto that whiche the Mamalukes use to weare, and gevying me also a good horse, accompanyed me with the other Mamalukes. This (as I have sayde) I obtayned with great cost, and many gyftes which I gave hym. Thus enteryng to the jorney, after the space of three dayes, we came to a certayne place named Mezaris[1] where we remayned three dayes, that the Merchauntes which were in our company myght provide thynges necessarie, as specially Camels . . .

OF A MOUNTAIN INHABITED WITH JEWES, AND OF THE CITIE OF MEDINATHALHABI,[2] WHERE MAHUMET WAS BURIED

In the space of eyght dayes we came to a mountayne which conteyneth in circuite ten or twelve myles. This is inhabited with Jewes, to the number of fyve thousande or thereabout. They are very little stature, as of the heyght of five or sixe spannes, and some muche lesse. They have small voyces lyke women and of blacke colour, yet some blacker then other. They feede of none other meate then Goates fleshe. They are circumcised, and deny not them selves to bee Jewes. If by chaunce any Mahumetan comes into their handes, they flay him alyve. At the foot of the mountayne, we founde a certayne hole, out of whiche flowed aboundance of water. By fyndying this opportunitie, we laded sixtiene thousand Camels: which thyng greatly offended the Jewes. They wandred in that mountayne, scattered lyke wylde Goates or Prickettes, yet durst they not come downe, partly for feare, and partly for hatred agaynst the Mahumetans. Beneath the mountaine are seene seven or eyght thorne trees, very fayre, and in them we founde a payre of Turtle Doves, which seemed to us in maner a miracle, havyng before made so long journeyes, and sawe neyther beast nor foule. Then proceedyng two dayes journey, we came to a certayne citie named Medinathalhabi: foure myles from the said citie, we founde a well. Heere the Caravana (that is, the whole hearde of Camelles) rested. And remayning here one day, we washed our selves, and chaunged our shertes, the more freshely to enter into the citie: it is well peopled, and conteyneth about three hundred houses, the walles are lyke bulwarkes of earth, and the houses both of stone and bricke. The soile about the citie, is utterly barren, except that about two myles from the citie, are seene about fyftie palme trees that beare Dates. There, by a certayne garden, runneth a course of water fallying into a lower playne, where also passingers are accustomed to water theyr Camelles. And here opportunities now serveth to confute the opinion of them whiche thynke that the Arke or Toombe of wicked Mahumet in Mecha, to hang in the ayre, not borne up with any thyng. As touching which thyng, I am utterly of an other opinion, and affirme this neyther to be true, not to have any lykenesse of trueth, as I presently behelde these thynges, and sawe the place where Mahumet is buried, in the said citie of Medinathalhabi: for we taryed there three dayes, to come to the true knowledge of all these thynges. When wee were desirous to enter into theyr Temple (which they call Meschita, and all other churches by the same name) we coulde not be suffered to enter, without a companion little or great. They taking us by the hande, brought us to the place where they saye Mahumet is buried.

OF THE TEMPLE OR CHAPELL, AND SEPULCHRE OF MAHUMET, AND OF HIS FELOWES

His temple is vaulted, and is a hundred pases in length, and fourescore in breadth: the entry into it, is by two gates: from the sydes, it is covered with three vaultes, it is borne up with 4 hundred columnes or pillars of white brick, there are seene hanging lampes about the number of 3 thousande. From the other part of the Temple in the first place of the Meschita, is seene a Tower of the circuite of fyve pases, vaulted on every syde, and covered with a cloth of silke, and is borne up with a grate of copper curiously wrought, and distant from it two pases: and of them that goe thyther, is seene as it were through a lattesse. Towarde the lefte hande, is the way to the Tower, and when you come thyther, you must enter by a narrower gate. On every side of those gates or doores, are seene many bookes in maner of a Librarie, on the syde 20, and on the other syde 25 . . .

CONCERNING THE UNICORNS IN THE TEMPLE OF MECCA, NOT VERY COMMON IN OTHER PLACES

In another part of the said temple is an enclosed place in which there are two live unicorns, and these are shown as very remarkable objects, which they certainly are. I will tell you how they are made. The elder is formed like a colt of thirty months old, and he has a horn in the forehead, which horn is about three *braccia* in length. The other unicorn is like a colt of one year old, and he has a horn of about four *palmi* long. The colour of the said animal resembles that of a dark bay horse, and his head resembles that of a stag; his neck is not very long, and he has some thin and short hair which hangs on one side; his legs are slender and lean like those of a goat; the foot is a little cloven in the fore part, and long and goat-like, and there are some hairs on the hind part of the said legs. Truly this monster must be a very fierce and solitary animal. These two animals were presented to the Sultan of Mecca as the finest things that could be found in the world at the present day, and as the richest treasure ever sent by a king of Ethiopia, that is, by a Moorish king. He made this present in order to secure an alliance with the said Sultan of Mecca.

Varthema went on to the Yemen.

CONCERNING SOME PEOPLE CALLED BADUIN

Departing from the said city Gezan, we went for five days always in sight of land, that is to say, the land was on our left hand; and seeing some habitations on the sea shore, we disembarked fourteen of our people to ask for some provisions in exchange for our money. They answered our request by beginning to throw stones at us with slings, and these were certain people who are called Baduin: they were in number more than one hundred, and we were only fourteen. We fought with them for about an hour, so that twenty-four of them remained dead on the field, and all the others took to flight; for they were naked, and had no other arms than these slings. We took all that we could, namely, fowls, calves, oxen, and other things fit to eat. In the course of two or three hours the disturbance began to increase, as did also the inhabitants of the said land, so that they were more than six hundred, and we were obliged to withdraw to our ship.

HOW THE WOMEN OF ARABIA, ARE GREATLY IN LOVE WITH WHYTE MEN

After the army was departed, I was incontinent commytted to pryson, as I have sayde. Harde by the prysone was a long entrie in maner of a cloyster, where somtyme we were permitted to walke. Ye shall further understand, that in the Soltan's place remayned one of his three wyves, with twelve young maydes to wayte uppon her, very fayre and comely, after theyr maner, and of coloure inclynyng to blacke. The favoure that they bore me, helped me very much, for I with two other, beyng in the same pryson, agreed that one of us should counterfyte hym selfe to be mad, that by this device, one of us myght helpe an other. In fine it was my lotte to take uppon me the mad man's part, and therefore stoode me in hande to do suche follies as pertayne to madnesse. Also the opinion whiche they have of mad folkes, made greatly for my purpose: for they take mad men to be holy, and therefore suffered me to run more at large, untyll the Eremites had geven judgment whether I weare holy, or ragyng mad, as appeareth hereafter. But the fyrst three dayes in which I began to shew my madnesse, weryed me so muche, that I was never so tyred with laboure or greeved with payne, for the boyes and rascall people sometyme to the number of 40 or 50 hurled stones at me almost without ceassing, while in the meane tyme againe I paid some of them home with lyke wages. The boyes cryed ever after me, callying me mad man. And to shewe it the more, I caryed always stones with me in my shyrt, for other apparel had I none. The queene hearyng of my follies looked oftentymes out of the wyndowes to see me, more for a secrete love she bore me, then for the pleasure she tooke in my follyes, as afte-warde appeared.

Therefore on a tyme, when some of them, muche madder then I, played the knaves with me in the syght of the queene (whose secrete favour towardes me I somewhat perceyved) that my madnesse myght seeme more manifest, I cast off my shyrt, and went to the place before the wyndowes, where the queene myght see me all naked: wherein I perceyved she tooke great pleasure, for she ever founde some occasion that I myght not goe out of her syght: and would sometymes with all her damoselles ·vayting on her, spend almost the whole daye in beholdyng me: and in the meane season divers tymes sent me secretly muche good meate by her maydens, and when she saw the boyes or others doe me any hurt, she baddye me kyll them, and spare not, revyling them also, and callyng them dogges and beastes.

The Italian at last persuaded the Sultana to secure his release and he went on to Persia and the Indies. The Portuguese Viceroy of India conferred on him the Order of Chivalry at the recommendation of Tristan da Cunha and he returned home in 1508. 'I came to my long desyred and native countrey, the Citie of Rome, by the Grace of God, to whom be all honour and glory.'

Editors' Notes
1. AL MAZARIB.
2. MEDINA. EDEN MISTOOK VARTHEMA'S ARABIC-ITALIAN TRANSLITERATION; IT SHOULD OF COURSE READ 'MEDINAT-EL-NABI', CITY OF THE PROPHET.

TWO NOBLEMEN IN THE INDIES

Sir Thomas Roe and Pietro della Valle

———◆———

Within fifteen years of Queen Elizabeth's royal charter, granted in December 1600, the English East India Company had established factories at Musulipatam and Pettapoli in the Bay of Bengal. In 1609 James I had renewed the Company's charter 'forever', subject only to the proviso that it could be revoked at three years' notice if trade proved unprofitable. Thus was laid the foundation of Britain's Indian Empire.

In 1615 Sir Thomas Roe, scholar, diplomat and politician, intimate of Henry, Prince of Wales, and his sister Elizabeth, later Queen of Bohemia, went to India to the court of the Great Mogul, charged with the task of preserving and extending the Company's interests, and of securing a factory at Surat. On the completion of that mission he went to Constantinople as ambassador to the Porte, where even in the early seventeenth century he was able to observe that the Turkish imperial power was 'irrevocably sick'. The Czar of Russia was to make the same observation two hundred years later! Roe produced a journal of his visit to the Mogul and his letters have appeared in many places.

Some of the most interesting of his correspondence on the India of the Great Mogul was, however, included as an appendix to the letters of another nobleman traveller in the same regions and at much the same time, Pietro della Valle. His purpose in travelling East was very different from Roe's. He went 'to escape the pangs of unrequited love, an alternative to suicide'; yet the letters he wrote home to Italy, to his distinguished friend Mario Shipano, professor of medicine at Naples, were of great perception, and nicely balanced between learning and acute and witty observation of people and everyday matters. He travelled through Arabia, Iraq and Persia, and was the first modern voyager to send to Europe a sensible account of the mounds and debris of ancient Babylon as he passed along the Euphrates. But it was India that he observed most colourfully.

———◆———

Sir Thomas Roe
(1581–1644)

A Voyage to East-India

WITH
A DESCRIPTION OF THE LARGE TERRITORIES UNDER THE SUBJECTION OF THE GREAT MOGOL

Apologies do more question than strengthen Truth, which Truth hath such power in prevailing, that she doth not know, and much less needs, the use of Preface or words of Perswasion to get her credit; for though she appear simple and naked unto open view, yet dares the encunnter with armed falshood, and is sure last to overcome; which Truth being the best ornament of this ensuing Discourse, looks to be credited, in what is here faithfully related.

So to make a re-entry upon a long-since finished Voyage; The third of February 1615. our Fleet consisting of six good Ships, three great, viz. the *Charles*, Admiral of that Company, then a New-built goodly ship of a Thousand Tuns, (in which I sayled); the *Unicorn* a new ship likewise, and almost of as great a burden; the *James*, a great ship too: Three lesser, viz. the *Globe*, the *Swan*, the *Rose*, (all under the Command of Captain Benjamin Joseph) fell down from Graves-end into Tilbury-Hope, where we continued till the eighth day following, when we weighed Anchor, and by a Slow, that we might have the safer passage, the twelfth came into the Downs, where an adverse wind forced our abode till the ninth of March, on which day it pleased God to send us, what we had much desired, a North-East wind, which made us leave that weary Road, and set sail for East-India . . .

From Lahore to Agra it is four hundred English miles, and that the Country betwixt both these great Cities is rich, even pleasant and flat, a Campania; and the rode-way on both sides all this long distance planted with great Trees which are all the year cloathed with leaves, exceeding beneficial unto Travellers for the shade they afford them in those hot Climes. This very much extended length of way 'twixt these two places, is called by Travellers the Long Walk, very full of Villages and Towns for Passengers every where to find provision.

At Agra our Traveller made an halt, being there lovingly received in the English Factory, where he stayed till he had gotten, to his Turkish and Morisco or Arabian Languages, some good knowledge in the Persian and Indostan Tongues, in which study he was always very apt, and in little time shewed much proficiency. The first of those two, the Persian, is the more quaint; the other, the Indian, the vulgar Language spoken in East-India: In both these he suddenly got such a knowledge and mastery, that it did exceedingly afterwards advantage him in his Travels up and down the Mogol's Territory; he wearing always the Habit of that Nation, and speaking their Language . . .

The Elephant, though he be vast, and terrible, yea and cruel too, when he set to do mischief, or when he is mad; yet otherwise is a tame gentle Creature, so that the dread of this huge beast, most appears to the eyes. But notwithstanding his terribleness, I once there saw a Creature compared with an Elephant, not much bigger than a small Fish compared with a Whale, boldly to encounter one of them. The occasion by which this so came to pass offers it self thus: that year I went for East-India, the Merchants here (as from the King of England, in whose name they sent all their Presents) amongst many other things, then sent the Mogol some great English Mastives, and some large Irish Greyhounds, in all to the number of eight, dispersed in our several Ships; one of those high spirited Mastives in our Voyage thither, upon a day seeing a great Shoal or company of Porpisces (before described) mounting up above the waves, and coming toward that Ship wherein he was, suddenly lept overboard to encounter with them; before any did take notice of that fierce creature: to prevent that engagement, wherein he was irrecoverably lost, the Ship then having such a fresh gale of wind, that she could not suddenly slack her course, whereby that poor creature might have been preserved. Another, one of the Irish Greyhounds had his head shot off in our fight. The Mange was the destruction of four more of them; only two of the Mastives came alive to East-India, and they were carried up, each of them drawn in a little Coach, when I went up to the Embassador, that he might present them to the Mogol. The fiercest of these two, in our way thither, upon a time breaking loose, fell upon a very large Elephant that was hard by us, fastning his teeth in the Elephants Trunk, and kept his hold there a good while, which made that huge beast extremely to roar; and though the Elephant did swing the Mastive up and down above ground many times (as not feeling his weight) that he might throw him off; yet he could not suddenly do it, but at last freeing himself from the dog by throwing him a good space from him, there came a Mungril Curr of that Countrey towards our Mastive, who then lost this his most unequal match, fell upon that dog and kill'd him, by which means we recovered our Mastive again into our custody, he having not received any apparent hurts; by which we may see how much Courage and Mettle there is in those right fierce Mastives.

These vast Creatures, though the Countrey be exceeding fruitful, and all provisions in it cheap, yet by reason of their huge bulk, if they well be kept and fed, are very chargeable in keeping; they are kept usually under the shade of great Trees, where by a strong chain of iron upon one of their hind-legs they fasten them. And as they stand, the abundance of Flies vex them, and therefore with their fore-feet they make dust, (the ground usually being very dry) and with their Trunk cast the dust about their bodies to drive away those Flies from them.

The King allows every one of those great male-Elephants four femals, which in their language they call their wives. These brutes (as they say) will not endure any to behold them when they are coupling together; which may condemn many who call themselves men and women, but have so lost all modesty, that they are not ashamed when they commit any act of filthiness, no they are not ashamed, neither can they blush. The Female Elephants (as they further say) carry their young, one whole year ere they bring them forth; Thirty years expire ere they come to their full growth; and they fulfill the accustomed age of men ere they die. And lastly, notwithstanding the great Number there of those vast Creatures, and the excessive charge in keeping them well, they value them at exceeding high rates.

For this people, when as they journey from place to place, the men of the inferiour sort go all on foot, their women that cannot so travel, ride on little Oxen, inured to carry burdens, or on Asses, which carry their little children with them; the women like the men astride. Others that are of better quality ride on Horses, Mules, Camels, Dromedaries, or else in Slight Coaches with two wheels covered on the top and back-end, but the fore-part and sides open, unless they carry women. Those Coaches will carry four persons beside the driver, but two may lie at ease, and at length in them upon quilts,

The lively Portrait of the great MOGOL

Portrait of the Great Mogul from Thomas Roe's *A Voyage to East India*, etc., London 1665 (with *The Travels of Sig. P. della Valle*)

that lie in the body of them, upheld by girt-web, with which they are
bottom'd, which makes them by far more easie. These Coaches are
covered for men of quality with some thing that is costly; much of our
English broad cloth that is died red, is there bought from us and
imployed for that use. At the back-end of this Coach they have a long
round bolster, that reacheth both sides, stuffed with Cotten-wool, and
covered with Velvet or Sattin, or with some other thing that is rich.
These Coaches are drawn by Oxen, one yoke to a Coach; some of
which Oxen have their short horns neatly tipped with silver plate,
and some others with brass; and they have each of them a fine Collar
of large round bells, some of them made of Silver. They are pared and
suted as our Coach-horses for stature and colour; most of them thus
imployed are white, and some pide, or spotted all over with several
colours. They are guided with small cords which go through the
parting of their Nostrils, and so twixt their horns into the Coach-
mans hand, who by these restrains them when, and guides them how
he pleaseth; and when he would have them go on, pricks them forward with a small and short staff he keeps in his hand pointed like a
goad. These Oxen there, are very neatly made, slender, strait-limb'd
and not very large, but naturally very nimble, and by daily use made so
fit to perform that labour, (being kept well shod) as that they go
twenty miles a day and more, with good speed. They keep those Oxen
for this service, as their horses, well-dressed, and so well fed, that they
be plump and fat, and consequently very handsom to behold.

The men there of the greatest rank and quality, ride sometimes in
those Coaches, and sometimes on their curious Horses, and sometimes on their brave Elephants, but however they are carried, they
have their horses, which wait upon them when they go abroad, that
they may bestride them when they please. And at other times they ride
on mens shoulders, in a slight thing they call a Palankee, made
somewhat like a Couch or standing Pallat, covered with a Canopy,
wherein a man may lie at his full length, as many of those Grandees do,
when they are removed from place to place, giving themselves up to
ease, and over unto those sins which follow it; and while they are thus
carried, they make the shoulders and joints of those that feel their
heavy weight, to bow and buckle under their burdens . . . But,
Vae nobis miseris ad quos Paganorum vitia transierunt. Wo to us wretched
people of this Nation, unto whom the vices of Pagans are derived. It
was a curse that the old Cretans were wont to wish might fall upon
their greatest enemies, that they might fall in love with evil customs.

This doubtless is one, amongst many more, fallen upon us of this Nation, when some, not out of necessity, but choice, make other men their Packhorses to ride upon them, a thing (as I conceive of it) most unworthy of a man, as he is a man, so to do . . .

———◆———

Pietro della Valle
(1586–1652)

Pietro della Valle sailed from Venice on 8 June 1614 for Constantinople. He left there a year later armed with a good command of Turkish, a little Arabic and nine attendants, for he always travelled in a style appropriate to his position, bound for the Holy Land. He went on to Baghdad (where he married a Syrian Christian girl, Sitti Maani), to Persia (where he fought with Shah Abbas and visited Shiraz and Persepolis), and finally India. He set sail from Persia in January 1623. His wife had died two years before, but he enjoyed the company of an orphan girl whom Maani had adopted during their brief marriage. The girl, Mariuccia, was of noble Georgian stock and he married her at the end of their journeys together. She bore him fourteen sons. They travelled with the decomposing remains of Maani, and della Valle published on his return to Rome *A Funeral Oration* delivered at her burial.

He wrote Shipano long and detailed letters as he went, the first posted at Surat on 22 March 1623.

From *The Travels of Sig. Pietro della Valle, A Noble Roman, into East-India and Arabia Deserts*. In which, the several countries, together with the Customs, Manners, Traffique, and Rites both Religious and Civil, of the Oriental Princes and Nations, are faithfully described, In Familiar Letters to his Friend Signior Mario Shipano. Whereunto is Added A Relation of Sir Thomas Roe's Voyage into the East-Indies. Printed by J. Macook, for John Place, and are to be sold at his Shop at Furnivals-Inn-Gate in Holborn. 1665.

FROM ONOR, 30 OCTOBER, 1623

October the five and twentieth, came News to Onor how on Thursday night last, October the nine and twentieth, Venk-tapa Naieka lost his

chief Wife, an aged Woman, and well belov'd by him; her name was
Badra-Ama, Daughter of a noble-man of the same Race of Lingavant,
which Venk-tapa himself is of. Badra was her proper name, Ama, her
Title, denoting Princess or Queen. We stay'd all this while at Onor,
because as soon as we arriv'd there, Vitula Sinay writ to Venk-tapa
Naieka his Master, giving him an account of our arrival; and so it was
necessary to stay for his Answer and Orders from the Court: we also
waited for men to carry us upon the way, (the whole journey being to
be made in Litters or Palanchinoes) together with our Goods and
Baggage, which were likewise to be carry'd by men upon their
shoulders. And the Davali, or Feast of the Gentiles, falling out in the
mean time, we were fain to stay till it was pass'd; and I know not
whether the Queens Death and Funerals may not cause us to stay some
time longer. I will not supress one story which is reported of this Lady.
They say, that twelve or thirteen years since, when she was about five
and thirty years old, it came to her ears that Venk-tapa Naieka her
Husband, being become fond of a Moorish Woman, kept her secretly
in a Fort not farr from the Court, where he frequently solac'd himself
with her for two or three dayes together; whereupon Badra-Ama,
(first complaining to him not onely of the wrong which he did thereby
to her, but also more of that which he did to himself, defiling himself
with a strange Woman of impure Race, (according to their superstition) and of a Nation which drank Wine and eat Flesh, and all sort of
uncleannesses in their account) told him that if he had a mind to other
Women, he need not have wanted Gentile-Women of their clean Race,
without contaminating himself with this Moor, and she should have
suffer'd it with patience; but since he had thus defil'd himself with her,
she for the future would have no more to do with him; and thereupon
she took an Oath that she would be to him as his Daughter, and he
should be to her as her Father: After which she shew'd no further
resentment, but liv'd with him as formerly, keeping him company in
the Palace, tending upon him in his sickness, and other things with the
same love as at first, helping and advising him in matters of Government, wherein she had always great authority with him; and, in
short, excepting the Matrimonial Act, perfectly fulfilling all other
Offices of a good Wife. Venk-tapa Naieka, who had much affection
for her, notwithstanding the wrong he did her with his Moor,
endeavor'd by all means possible to divert her from this her purpose,
and to perswade her to live a Matrimonial Life still with him, offering
many times to compound for that Oath by the alms of above 20000

Pagods, (Pagod is a gold coin, near equivalent to a Venetian Zecchine, or English Angel) but all in vain, and she persever'd constant in this Resolution till death; which being undoubtedly an act of much Constancy and Virtue, was the cause that Venk-tapa Naieka lov'd her always so much the more . . .

FROM GOA, 31 JANUARY, 1624

Having seen the Bazar, and stay'd there till it was late, we were minded to see the more inward and noble parts of the City, and the out-side of the King's Palace; for to see the King at that hour we had no intention, nor did we come prepar'd for it, but were in the same garb which we wore in the Ship. Accordingly we walk'd a good way towards the Palace, for the City is great, and we found it to consist of plots beset with abundance of high Trees, amongst the boughs whereof, a great many of wild Monkies; and within these close Groves, stand the Houses, for the most part at a distance from the common Wayes or Streets; they appear but little, few of their outsides being seen, besides the low walls made of a black stone surrounding these plots, and dividing them from the Streets, which are much better than those of the Bazar, but without any ornament of Windows; so that he that walks through the City, may think that he is rather in the midst of uninhabited Gardens, than of an inhabited City: Nevertheless it is well peopled, and hath many Inhabitants, whose being contented with narrow buildings, is the cause that it appears but small. As we walked in this manner, we met one of those Men who had been at Goa with the Vice-Roy; and because he saw us many together, and imagin'd there was some person of quality amongst us, or because he knew our General, he invited us to go with him to his King's Palace; and going before us as our guide, conducted us thither. He also sent one before to advertise the King of our coming, and told us, we must by all means go to see him, because his Highness was desirous to see us and talk with us: Wherefore, not to appear discourteous, we were constrein'd to consent to his Request, notwithstanding the unexpectedness of, and our unpreparedness for, the visit.

The first and principal Gate of the Palace opens upon a little Piazza, which is beset with certain very great Trees, affording a delightful shadow. I saw no Guard before it, it was great and open; but before it, was a row of Balisters, about four or five foot from the ground, which serv'd to keep out not onely Horses and other Animals, but

also Men upon occasion. In the middle was a little pair of Stairs without the Gate leading into it, and another within on the other side. Yet,
I believe, both the Stairs and the Balisters are moveable, because 'tis
likely that when the King comes forth, the Gate is clearly open;
otherwise it would not be handsome, but this is onely my conjecture.
We enter'd this Gate, ascending the Stairs upon the Rails, where we
were met by the Messenger whom the above-said person had sent to
the King, and who again invited us into the Palace by the Kings Order.
Within the Gate we found a great Court, of a long form, without any
just and proportionate figure of Architecture; on the sides, were many
lodgings in several places, and in the middle, were planted divers great
Trees for shadow: The King's chief apartment, and (as I believe, by
what I shall mention hereafter) where his Women were, was at the end
of the Court, opposite to the left side of the Entrance. The Edifice, in
comparison of ours, was of little consideration; but, according to
their mode, both for greatness and appearance, capable of a Royal
Family. It had a cover'd porch in that form, as all their structures
have, and within that was a door of no great largeness leading into
the House. Here we found Cicco the Portugal youth, become an
Indian in Habit and Language, but, as himself told us, and as his
Portugal Name, which he still retain'd among the Gentiles, demon-
strated, no Renegado but a Christian . . . With the said Cicco we
found many other of the King's Courtiers who waited for us, and
here we convers'd with them a good while before the Gate, expecting
a new Message from the King, who, they told us, was now bathing
himself, according to their custom, after supper. Nor was it long
before Order came from the King for us to enter, and accordingly we
were introduc'd into that second Gate; and passing by a close room
like a chamber, (in which I saw the Image of Brahma upon his Peacock, and other Idolets) we enter'd into a little open Court, surrounded with two rows of narrow and low Cloysters, to wit, one
level with the ground, and the other somewhat higher. The pavement of the porch was also something rais'd above the plane of the
Court, so much as might serve for a Man to sit after our manner. The
King was not in this small Court, but they told us we must attend
him here, and he would come presently . . .

No sooner were we seated in this place, but two Girls about twelve
years old enter'd at the same Gate whereat we came in; they were all
naked, (as, I said above, the Women generally go) saving that they
had a very small blew cloth wrap'd about their immodesties, and their

Arms, Ears and Necks, were full of ornaments of Gold and very rich Jewels. Their colour was somewhat swarthy, as all these Nations are, but in respect of others of the same Country, clear enough; and their shape no less proportionable and comely, than their aspect was handsome and wel-favour'd. They were both the Daughters, as they told us, of the Queen, that is, not of the King but of his Sister, who is styl'd, and in effect is, Queen; for these Gentiles using to derive the descent and inheritance by the line of the Women, though the Government is allow'd to Men, as more fit for it, and he that governes is call'd King; yet the King's Sister, and, amongst them, (if there be more then one) she to whom, by reason of Age, or for other respects it belongs, is call'd and properly is Queen and not, any Wife or Concubine of the King, who has many. So also when the King, (who governes upon the account of being Son of the Queen-Mother) happens to dye, his own Sons succeed him not, (because they are not the Sons of the Queen) but the Sons of his Sister; or in defect of such, those of the nearest Kins-women by the same Female line: So that these two Girls, whom I call the Nieces of the Samori, were right Princesses or Infantaes of the Kingdom of Calecut. Upon their entrance where we were, all the Courtiers present shew'd great Reverence to them; and we, understanding who they were, arose from our seat, and having saluted them, stood all the time afterwards before them bare-headed.

Pietro della Valle returned to Rome on 18 March 1626 where he was received with honour and ceremony; he was appointed by Pope Urban VIII a gentleman of the Papal bedchamber. In a letter dated 25 July 1626, he described the burial of Sitti Maani, '*my wife (which I had brought with me so many voyages) in our Chappel of St. Paul*'. She was placed in a lead coffin, her head wasted away and without flesh when he looked upon it for the last time.

THE SERAGLIO

From Description of the Grand Signior's Seraglio by Robert Withers

(SEVENTEENTH CENTURY)

———◆———

In the early editions of Withers' book on the Seraglio no details are given as to how he came by all his information except that he was introduced by the British Ambassador, who, at that time, was Sir Paul Pindar (1565-1650), a man with considerable experience in the Near East.

———◆———

'Black-a-moor' girls, who for the most part come from Egypt by ship, being there collected or taken out of neighbouring countries for the Pasha of Cairo who sends them as presents to the Grand Signior, are, upon arrival, immediately brought into the women's quarters in the Seraglio, there to be trained and made fit for all kinds of service. And the more ugly and deformed they are the more they are esteemed and sought by the Pasha of Cairo for the purpose. They are therefore coal-black, blabber-lipped, flat-nosed and ill-favoured and the more so the more they are welcomed and acceptable. being given by the Grand Signior to his women in most favour . . .

First then I say that all they which are in the Seraglio, both men and women, are the Grand Signior's slaves (for so they style themselves) and so are all they which are subject to his Empire. For besides that he is their sovereign, they do all acknowledge that whatsoever they do possess, or enjoy, proceedeth merely from his good will and favour: and not only their estate but their lives also are at his disposal . . .

This Seraglio may rightly be called the seminary or nursery of the best subjects. For in it all they have their education who are afterwards the principal officers of and the subordinate rulers of the state and affairs of the whole Empire, as hereafter I shall show.

Those that are within the third gate, called the King's Gate, are about two thousand persons, men and women; whereof the women, old and young may be about twelve hundred. Now those that are shut up for their beauties, all are young virgins taken and stolen from foreign nations; who after they have been instructed in good behaviour and to play upon instruments, to sing, dance and sew curiously are given to the Grand Signior as presents of great value. Their number increases daily as they are sent by the Tatars, the Pashas and the other great men of the State to the King and Queen. There may likewise be a decrease in numbers as for one reason or another; some are turned out and sent to the Old Seraglio. Those that are brought into the Seraglio are immediately made Turks which is done by holding up their forefinger and saying 'There is no God but God and Muhammad is his Messenger.' These girls have very large rooms to live in. Their bedchambers will hold almost a hundred of them a piece. They sleep upon sofas, which are built longwise on both sides of the room with a large space left in the middle of it. By every ten virgins lies an old woman and all the night long there are many lamps burning so that one may see plainly throughout the whole room; which doth keep the young women from wantonness and serve upon any occasion which may happen in the night. Near unto the said bedchambers are divers rooms where they may sit and sew and keep their boxes and chest in which they lay up their apparel. They eat in groups and are served and waited upon by other women, nor do they want anything that is necessary for them. They go to school, learn to speak and read the Turkish tongue and to play on divers instruments, some hours being left to them for recreation in the gardens and familiar sports.

The King does not see these virgins unless it be at the instant when they are first presented to him or he desires one of them for his bedfellow, or that he is prepared for a fresh mate. In that case he gives notice to the Woman in Charge of them, who like a crafty baud chooses from among them such as she judges to be the most amiable and fair of them and places them in a room in two ranks on either side like so many pictures; she forthwith bringeth in the King, who walking four or five times in the midst of them, and having viewed them well, and taken good notice within himself of who that he liketh the best but says nothing; only as he goes out again, he throweth a handkerchief into that virgin's hand, by which token she knoweth that she is to lie with him that night; so she being exceedingly joyful to be the object of so great a fortune, in being chosen out from among so many to enjoy the society of an Emperor, hath all the art that possibly may be shown upon her by the Chief Woman, in attiring, painting and perfuming her; and at night she is brought to the quarters of the women set apart for that purpose. They being in bed together, they have two great wax lights burning by them all night; one at the foot of the bed and the other by the door; besides there are appointed by the Chief Woman old black-a-moor women to watch by turns that night in the chamber two at a time, one of them at the foot of the bed and the other at the door, and when they change another two come without making the least noise imaginable, so that the King is not disturbed. Now in the morning when he rises, for he rises first, he changeth all his apparel from top to toe, leaving all that which he wore to her that he lay with, and all the money that was in his pockets were it never so much; and so departeth to his own lodgings; from whence also he sendeth her immediately a present of jewels, money and vests of value agreeable to the satisfaction he received. In the same manner he deals with all such as he maketh use of in such way but with some he continueth longer than with others and enlarges his bounty according to his humour and affection to them increases by their fulfilling his lustful desires.

And if it so fall out that any of them doth conceive and bring forth his first begotten child, then she is called a Sultana Queen; and if it be a son, she is confirmed and established Queen by great feasts and solemnities and forthwith has a dwelling apart and of many rooms assigned to her, one well furnished and having many servants to attend upon her. She is likewise given a large revenue that she may give away and spend as she wishes. As the mother of the Sultan to be, she alone will remain forever in the Seraglio, for on the death of the Sultan all the other women are moved out into the Old Seraglio, whereas her own standing as mother of the reigning King or Sultan is unharmed.

Women of the Seraglio are punished for their faults very severely and beaten extremely hard by their overseers, and if they prove incorrigible they are, by the King's order, turned out and sent into the Old Seraglio. Should they be found culpable of witchcraft or such abominations they are bound hand and foot and put into a sack and in the night are cast into the sea from the wall of the Seraglio. So it behoveth them to be very careful and obedient and to contain themselves within the bounds of honesty, chastity and good behaviour if they mean to prosper and come to a good end.

DON QUIXOTE THE CAPTIVE

Miguel de Cervantes Saavedra

(1547-1616)

Cervantes is known to have been taken prisoner by the Moors, and he was ransomed. The story in Don Quixote of the prisoner of the Moors is believed to be based on this event.

In fine, the Turkish fleet returned in triumph to Constantinople, where, not longer after, my master Vehali died, whom the Turks used to call Vehali Fartax, which, in Turkish signifies the renegade, as indeed he was; and the Turks give names among themselves, either from some virtue or some defect that is in them; and this happens because there are but four families descended from the Ottoman family; all the rest, as I have said, take their names from some defect of the body or some good quality of the mind. This slave was at the oar in one of the Grand Seignior's galleys for fourteen years, till he was four-and-thirty years old; at which time he turned renegade, to be revenged of a Turk, who gave him a box on the ear, as he was chained to the oar – forsaking his religion for revenge; after which he showed so much valour and conduct, that he came to be King of Algiers, and admiral of the Turkish fleet, which is the third command in the whole empire. He was a Calabrian by birth, and of a mild disposition towards his slaves, as also of good morals to the rest of the world. He had above 3,000 slaves of his own, all which, after his death, were divided, as he had ordered by his will, between the Grand Seignior, his sons, and his renegades.

I fell to the share of a Venetian renegade, who was a cabin-boy in a Venetian ship which was taken to Vehali, who loved him so, that he was one of his favourite boys; and he came at last to prove one of the cruellest renegades that ever was known. His name was

Azanaga, and he obtained such riches, as to rise by them to be King of Algiers; and with him I left Constantinople, with some satisfaction to think, at least, that I was in a place so near Spain, not because I could give advice to any friend of my misfortunes, but because I hoped to try whether I should succeed better in Algiers than I had done in Constantinople, where I had tried a thousand ways of running away, but could never execute any of them, which I hoped I should compass better in Algiers, for hope never forsook me upon all the disappointments I met with in the design of recovering my liberty. By this means I kept myself alive, shut up in a prison or house which the Turks call a bagnio, where they keep their Christian slaves, as well those of the King as those who belong to private persons, and also those who are called El Almacen, that is, who belong to the public, and are employed by the city in works that belong to it. These latter with great difficulty obtain their liberty; for having no particular master, but belonging to the public, they can find nobody to treat with about their ransom, though they have money to pay it. The King's slaves, which are ransomable, are not obliged to go out to work as the others do, except their ransom stays too long before it comes; for then, to hasten it, they make them work, and fetch wood with the rest, which is no small labour. I was one of those who were to be ransomed; for when they knew I had been a captain, though I told them the impossibility I was in of being redeemed, because of my poverty, yet they put me among the gentlemen that were to be ransomed, and to that end they put me on a slight chain, rather as a mark of distinction than to restrain me by it; and so I passed my life in that bagnio, with several gentlemen of quality who expected their ransom: and, though hunger and nakedness might, as it did often, afflict us, yet nothing gave us such affliction as to hear and see the excessive cruelties with which our master used the other Christian slaves. He would hang one one day, then impale another, cut off the ears of a third; and this upon such slight occasions that often the Turks would own that he did it only for the pleasure of doing it, and because he was naturally an enemy to mankind. Only one Spanish soldier knew how to deal with him; his name was Saavedra; who, though he had done many things which will not easily be forgotten by the Turks, yet all to gain his liberty, his master never gave him a blow, nor used him ill, either in word or deed; and yet we were always afraid that the least of his pranks would make him be impaled; nay, he himself sometimes was afraid of it too: and, if it were not for taking up too much of your time, I could tell such passages of him as would divert the company much better than the relation of my adventures, and cause more wonder in them.

But to go on. I say that the windows of a very rich Moor's house looked upon the court of our prison; which, indeed, according to the custom of the country, were rather peeping holes than windows, and yet they had also lattices or jalousies on the inside.

It happened one day that being upon a kind of terrace of our prison, with only three of my comrades, diverting ourselves as well as we could, by trying who could leap farthest in his chains, all the other Christians being gone out to work, I chanced to look up to those windows, and saw that out of one of them there appeared a long cane, and to it was a bit of linen tied; and the cane was moved up and down, as if it was expected that some of us should lay hold of it. We all took notice of it, and one of us went and stood just under it, to see if they would let it fall; but just as he came to it the cane was drawn up, and shook to and fro sideways, as if they had made the same sign as people do with their head when they deny. He retired upon that, and the same motion was made with it as before. Another of my comrades advanced, and had the same success as the former; the third man was used just as the rest; which I seeing, resolved to try my fortune too; and as I came under the cane it fell at my feet. Immediately I untied the linen, within which was a knot, which, being opened showed us about ten zianins, which is a sort of gold of base alloy used by the Moors, each of which is worth about two crowns of our money. It is not to be much questioned whether the discovery was not as pleasant as surprising: we were in admiration, and I more particularly, not being able to guess whence this good fortune came to us, especially to me; for it was plain I was more meant than any of my comrades, since the cane was let go to me when it was refused to them. I took my money, broke the cane, and, going upon the terrace, saw a very fine white hand that opened and shut the window with haste. By this we imagined that some woman who lived in that house had done us this favour; and, to return our thanks, we bowed ourselves after the Moorish fashion, with our arms across our breasts. A little after there appeared out of the same window a little cross made of cane, which immediately was pulled in again. This confirmed us in our opinion that some Christian woman was a slave in that house, and that it was she that took pity on us; but the whiteness of the hand, and the richness of the bracelets upon the arm, which we had a glimpse of, seemed to destroy that thought again; and then we believed it was some Christian woman turned Mahometan, whom their masters often marry, and think themselves very happy; for our women are more valued by them than the women of their own country. But in all this guessing we were far enough from finding out the truth of the case; however, we resolved to be very diligent in observing the window, which was our north star. There passed above fifteen days before we saw either the hand or cane, or any other sign whatsoever, though in all that time we endeavoured to find out who lived in that house, and if there were in it any Christian woman who was a renegade; yet all we could discover amounted to only this, that the house belonged to one of the chief Moors, a very rich man, called Agimorato, who had been Alcayde of the Bata, which is an office much valued among them. But when we least expected our golden shower would continue, out of that window we saw on a sudden the cane appear again with another piece of linen and a bigger knot; and this was just at a time when the bagnio was without any other of the slaves in it. We all tried our fortunes as the first time, and it succeeded accordingly, for the cane was let go to none but me. I untied the knot, and found in it forty crowns of Spanish gold, with a paper written in Arabic, and at the top of the paper was a great cross. I kissed the cross, took the crowns, and, returning to the terrace we all made our Moorish reverences; the hand appeared again, and I having made signs that I would read the paper, the window was shut. We remained all overjoyed and astonished at what had happened, and were extremely desirous to know the contents of the paper; but none of us understood Arabic, and it was yet more difficult to find out a proper interpreter. At last I resolved to trust a renegade of Murcia, who had shown me great proofs of his kindness . . .

Having finished his translation, he said, 'All I have here put into Spanish is word for word what is in the Arabic; only where the paper says Lela Marien, it means our Lady the Virgin Mary.' The contents were thus:

When I was a child my father had a slave who taught me in my tongue the Christian worship, and told me a great many things of Lela Marien. The Christian slave died, and I am sure she went not to the fire, but is with Allah, for I have seen her twice since; and she bid me go to the land of the Christians to see Lela Marien, who had a great kindness for me. I do not know what is the matter; but though I have seen many Christians out of this window, none has appeared to me so much a gentleman as thyself. I am very handsome and young, and can carry with me a great deal of money and other riches. Consider whether thou bring it to pass that we may escape together, and then thou shalt be my husband in thy own country, if thou art willing; but if thou are not, it is all one, Lela Marien will provide me a husband. I wrote this myself. Have a care to whom thou givest it to read; do not trust any Moor, because they are all treacherous. And in this I am much perplexed, and could wish there were not a necessity of trusting any one; because, if my father should come to know it, he would certainly throw me into a well, and cover me over with stones. I will tie a thread to a cane, and with that thou mayest fasten thy answer; and if thou canst not find any one to write in Arabic, make me understand thy meaning by signs, for Lela Marien will help me to guess it. She and Allah keep thee, as well as this cross, which I often kiss, as the Christian slave bid me do.

You may imagine, gentlemen, that we were in admirtion at the contents of this paper, and withal overjoyed at them, which we expressed so openly that the renegade came to understand that the paper was not found by chance, but that it was really written by some one among us; and accordingly he told us his suspicion, and desired us to treat him entirely, and that he would venture his life with us to procure us our liberty. Having said this, he pulled a brass crucifix out of his bosom, and, with many tears, swore by the God which it represented, and in whom he, though a wicked sinner, did firmly believe, to be true and faithful to us, with all secrecy in what we should impart to him; for he guessed that by the means of the woman who had written that letter, we might all of us recover our lost liberty; and he, in particular, might obtain what he had so long wished for, to be received again into the bosom of his mother the Church, from whom, for his sins, he had been cut off as a rotten member. The renegade pronounced all this with so many tears, and such signs of repentance, that we were all of opinion to trust him, and tell him the whole truth of the business. We showed him the little window out of which the cane used to appear, and he from thence took good notice of the house, in order to inform himself who lived in it. We next agreed that it would be necessary to answer the Moorish lady's note. So immediately the renegade wrote down what I dictated to him, which was exactly as I shall relate; for I have not forgot the least material circumstance of this adventure, nor can forget them as long as I live. The words then were these:

The true Allah keep thee, my dear lady, and that blessed Virgin which is the true mother of God, and has inspired thee with the design of going to the land of the Christians. Do thou pray her that she would be pleased to make thee understand how thou shalt execute what she has commanded thee; for she is so good that she will do it. On my part, and on that of the Christians who are with me, I do offer to do for thee all we are able, even to the hazard of our lives. Fail not to write to me, and give me notice of thy resolution, for I will always answer thee; the great Allah having given us a Christian slave who can read and write thy language, as thou mayest perceive by this letter; so that thou mayest, without fear, give me notice of all thy intentions. As for what thou sayest, that as soon as thou shalt arrive in the land of the Christians thou designest to be my wife, I promise thee, on the word of a good Christian, to take thee for my wife; and thou mayest be assured that the Christians perform their promises better than the Moors. Allah and his mother Mary be thy guard, my dear lady.

Having written and closed this note, I waited two days till the bagnio was empty, and then I went up on the terrace, the ordinary place of our conversation, to see if the cane appeared, and it was not long before it was stirring. As soon as it appeared I showed my note, that the thread might be put to the cane, but I found that was done to my hand; and the cane being let down, I fastened the note to it. Not long after the knot was let fall, and I, taking it up, found in it several pieces of gold and silver, above fifty crowns, which gave us infinite content, and fortified our hopes of obtaining at last our liberty. That evening our renegade came to us, and told us he had found out that the master of that house was the same Moor we had been told of, called Agimorato, extremely rich, and who had one only daughter to inherit all his estate; that it was the report of the whole city that she was the handsomest maid in all Barbary, having been demanded in marriage by several bassas and viceroys, but that she had always refused to marry. He also told us that he had learned she had had a Christian slave who was dead, all which agreed with the contents of the letter. We immediately held a council with the renegade about the manner we should use to carry off the Moorish lady, and go all together to Christendom; when at last we agreed to wait for the answer of Zoraida – for that is the name of the lady who now desires to be called Mary – as well knowing she could best advise the overcoming all the difficulties that were in our way; and after this resolution, the renegade assured us again that he would lose his life or deliver us out of captivity.

The bagnio was four days together full of people, and all that time the cane was invisible; but as soon as it returned to its solitude, the cane appeared, with a knot much bigger than ordinary; having untied it, I found in it a letter, and a hundred crowns in gold. The renegade happened that day to be with us, and we gave him the letter to read, which he said contained these words:

> I cannot tell, sir, how to contrive that we may go together to Spain; neither has Lela Marien told it me, though I have earnestly asked it of her. All I can do is to furnish you out of this window with a great deal of riches. Buy your ransom and your friends' with that, and let one of you go to Spain, and buy a barque there, and come and fetch the rest. As for me, you shall find me in my father's garden out of town, by the sea-side, not far from the Bab-Ayoun gate, where I am to pass all the summer with my father and my maids; from which you may take me without fear, in the night-time, and carry me to your barque; but remember thou art to be my husband, and if thou failest in that I will desire Lela Marien to chastise thee. If thou canst not trust one of thy friends to go for the barque, pay thy own ransom and go thyself; for I trust thou wilt return sooner than another, since thou art a gentleman and a Christian. Find out my father's garden, and I will take care to watch when the bagnio is empty, and let thee have more money. Allah keep my dear Lord.

These were the contents of the second letter we received. Upon the reading of it every one of us offered to be the man that should go and buy the barque, promising to return with all speed; but the renegade opposed that proposition, and said he would never consent that any one of us should obtain his liberty before the rest, because experience had taught him that people once free do not perform what they promise when captives, and that some slaves of quality had often used that remedy, to send one either to Valencia or Majorca, with money to buy a barque, and come back and fetch the rest, but that they never

returned; because the joy of having obtained their liberty, and the fear
of losing it again, made them forget what they had promised, and
cancel the memory of all obligations. To confirm which he related
to us a strange story, which had happened in those parts, where every
day the most surprising and wonderful things come to pass. After
this he said that all that could be done was for him to buy a barque
with the money which should redeem one of us; that he could buy
one in Algiers, and pretend to turn merchant, and deal between
Algiers and Tetuan; by which means he, being master of the vessel
might easily find out some way of getting us out of the bagnio, and
taking us on board; and especially if the Moorish lady did what she
promised, and gave us money to pay all our ransoms; for, being free,
we might embark even at noon-day; but the greatest difficulty would
be, that the Moors do not permit renegades to keep any barques but
large ones, fit to cruise upon Christians; for they believe that a renegade, particularly a Spaniard, seldom buys a barque but with a design
of returning to his own country. That, however, he knew how to
obviate that difficulty, by taking a Tagarin Moor for his partner
both in the barque and trade, by which means he should still be
master of her, and then all the rest would be easy. We durst not
oppose this opinion, though we had more inclination every one of
us to go to Spain for a barque, as the lady had advised; but were
afraid that if we contradicted him, as we were at his mercy, he might
betray us, and bring our lives to danger, particularly if the business of
Zoraida should be discovered, for whose liberty and life we would
have given all ours; so we determined to put ourselves under the
protection of God and the renegade. At the same time we answered
Zoraida, telling her that we would do all she advised, which was
very well, and just as if Lela Marien herself had instructed her; and
that now it depended on her alone to give us the means of bringing
this design to pass. I promised her once more to be her husband. After
this, in two days that the bagnio happened to be empty, she gave us,
by the means of the cane, two thousand crowns of gold, and withal a
letter, in which she let us know that the next Juma, which is their
Friday, she was to go to her father's garden, and that, before she
went, she would give us more money; and if we had not enough, she
would, upon our letting her know it, give us what we should think
sufficient; for her father was so rich that he would hardly miss it,
and so much the less, because he entrusted her with the keys of all
his treasure. We presently gave the renegade five hundred crowns to

buy the barque, and I paid my own ransom with eight hundred crowns, which I put into the hands of a merchant of Valencia, then in Algiers, who made the bargain with the King, and had me to his house upon parole, to pay the money upon the arrival of the first barque from Valencia; for if he had paid down the money immediately, the king might have suspected the money had been ready, and lain some time in Algiers, and that the merchant for his own profit had concealed it; and, in short, I durst not trust my master with ready money, knowing his distrustful and malicious nature. The Thursday preceding that Friday that Zoraida was to go to the garden, she let us have a thousand crowns more; desiring me, at the same time, that if I paid my ransom, I would find out her father's garden, and contrive some way of seeing her there. I answered in few words, that I would do as she desired, and she should only take care to recommend us to Lela Marien, by those prayers which the Christian slave had taught her. Having done this, order was given to have the ransom of my three friends paid also; lest they, seeing me at liberty, and themselves not so, though there was money to set them free, should be troubled in mind, and give way to the temptation of the devil, in doing something that might redound to the prejudice of Zoraida; for though the consideration of their quality ought to have given me security of their honour, yet I did not think it proper to run the least hazard in the matter; so they were redeemed in the same manner, and by the same merchant, that I was, who had the money beforehand; but we never discovered to him the remainder of our intrigue, as not being willing to risk the danger there was in so doing.

Our renegade had in a fortnight's time bought a very good barque, capable of carrying above thirty people; and, to give no suspicion of any other design, he undertook a voyage to a place upon the coast called Sargel, about thirty leagues to the eastward of Algiers towards Oran, where there is a great trade for dried figs. He made his voyage two or three times in company with the Tagarin Moor, his partner. Those Moors who were driven out of Arragon are called in Barbary Tagarins; as they call those of Granda Mudajares; and the same in the kingdom of Fez are called Elches, and are the best soldiers that prince has.

Every time he passed with his barque along the coast he used to cast anchor in a little bay that was not above two bow-shots from the garden where Zoraida expected us; and there he used to exercise the Moors that rowed, either in making the sala, which is a ceremony

among them, or in some other employment; by which he practised
in jest what he was resolved to execute in earnest. So sometimes he
would go to the garden of Zoraida and beg some fruit, and her father
would give him some, though he did not know him. He had a mind
to find an occasion to speak to Zoraida, and tell her, as he since
owned to me, that he was the man who by my order was to carry her
to the land of the Christians, and that she might depend upon it;
but he could never get an opportunity of doing it, because the Moorish and Turkish women never suffer themselves to be seen by any of
their own nation, but by their husband, or by his or their father's
command; but as for the Christian slaves, they let them see them, and
that more familiarly than perhaps could be wished. I should have been
very sorry that the renegade had seen or spoken to Zoraida, for it
must needs have troubled her infinitely to see that her business was
trusted to a renegade; and God Almighty, who governed our design,
ordered it so that the renegade was disappointed. He, in the meantime, seeing how securely and without suspicion he went and came
along the coast, staying where and when he pleased by the way, and
that his partner, the Tagarin Moor, was of his mind in all things;
that I was at liberty, and that there wanted nothing but some
Christians to help us to row, bid me consider whom I intended to
carry with me besides those who were ransomed, and that I should
make sure of them for the first Friday, because he had fixed on that
day for our departure. Upon notice of this resolution I spoke to
twelve lusty Spaniards, good rowers, and those who might easiest
get out of the city. It was a great fortune that we got so many in
such a conjuncture, because there were above twenty sail of rovers
gone out, who had taken aboard most of the slaves fit for the oar;
and we had not had these, but that their master happened to stay at
home that summer to finish a galley he was building to cruise with,
which was then upon the stocks. I said no more to them than only
they should steal out of the town in the evening upon the next
Friday, and stay for me upon the way that led to Agimorato's garden.
I spoke to every one by himself, and gave each of them orders to
say no more to any other Christian they should see than they stayed
for me there. Having done this, I had another thing of the greatest
importance to bring to pass, which was to give Zoraida notice of our
design and how far we had carried it, that she might be ready at a
short warning, and not to be surprised if we came upon the house on a
sudden, and even before she could think that the Christian barque

could be come. This made me resolve to go to the garden to try if it were possible to speak to her; so one day, upon pretence of gathering a few herbs, I entered the garden, and the first person I met was her father, who spoke to me in the language used all over the Turkish dominion – which is a mixture of all the Christian and Moorish languages, by which we understand one another from Constantinople to Algiers – and asked me what I looked for in his garden, and who I belonged to. I told him I was a slave of Arnaut Mami (who I knew was his intimate friend) and that I wanted a few herbs to make up a salad. He then asked me if I were a man to be redeemed or no, and how much my master asked for me. During these questions the beautiful Zoraida came out of the garden-house hard by, having descried me a good while before: and as the Moorish women make no difficulty of showing themselves to the Christian slaves, she drew near, without scruple, to the place where her father and I were talking; neither did her father show any dislike of her coming, but called to her to come nearer. It would be hard for me to express here the wonderful surprise and astonishment that the beauty, the rich dress, and the charming air of my beloved Zoraida put me in; she was all bedecked with pearls, which hung thick upon her head and about her neck and arms. Her feet and legs were bare, after the custom of that country, and she had upon her ankles a kind of bracelet of gold, and set with such rich diamonds that her father valued them, as she has since told me, at 10,000 pistoles a pair; and those about her wrists were of the same value. The pearls were of the best sort, for the Moorish women delight much in them, and have more pearls of all sorts than any nation. Her father was reputed to have the finest in Algiers, and to be worth, besides, above 200,000 Spanish crowns, of all which the lady you here see was then mistress, but now is only so of me. What she yet retains of beauty, after all her sufferings, may help you to guess at her wonderful appearance in the midst of her prosperity. The beauty of some ladies has its days and times, and is more or less according to accidents or passions, which naturally raise or diminish the lustre of it, and sometimes quite extinguish it. All I can say is, at that time she appeared to me the best dressed and most beautiful woman I had ever seen; to which adding the obligation I had to her, she passed with me for a goddess from heaven, descended upon earth for my relief and happiness.

As she drew near, her father told her, in his country language, that I was a slave of his friend Arnaut Mami, and came to pick a salad in his garden. She presently took the hint, and asked me, in lingua Franca, whether I was a gentleman, and if I was, why I did not ransom myself. I told her I was already ransomed, and that by the price she might guess the value my master set upon me, since he had bought me for 1,500 pieces of eight. To which she replied, 'If thou hadst been my father's slave, I would not have let him part with thee for twice as much; for,' said she, 'you Christians never speak truth in anything you say, and make yourselves poor to deceive the Moors.'

'That may be, madam,' said I, 'but in truth I have dealt by my master sincerely and honourably, and do intend to deal so by all those I shall have to deal with.'

'And when does thou go home?' said she.

'To-morrow, madam,' said I; 'for here is a French barque that sails to-morrow, and I intend not to lose that opportunity.'

'Is it not better,' replied Zoraida, 'to stay till there come some Spanish barque, and go with them, and not with the French, who, I am told, are no friends of yours?'

'No,' said I; 'yet if the report of a Spanish barque's coming should prove true, I would perhaps stay for it, though it is more likely I shall take the opportunity of the French, because the desire I have of being at home, and with those persons I love, will hardly let me wait for any other conveniency.'

'Without doubt,' said Zoraida, 'thou art married in Spain, and impatient to be with thy wife.'

'I am not,' said I, 'married, but I have given my word to a lady to be so as soon as I can reach my own country.'

'And is the lady handsome that has your promise?' said Zoraida.

'She is so handsome,' said I, 'that to describe her rightly and tell truth, I can only say she is like you.'

At this her father laughed heartily, and said, 'On my word, Christian, she must be very charming if she be like my daughter, who is the greatest beauty of all this kingdom; look upon her well, and thou wilt say I speak truth.'

Zoraida's father was our interpreter for the most of what we talked; for though she understood the lingua Franca, yet she was not used to speak it, and so explained herself more by signs than words.

While we were in this conversation, there came a Moor running hastily, and cried aloud that four Turks had leaped over the fence of the garden, and were gathering the fruit, though it was not ripe. The old man started at that, and so did Zoraida, for the Moors do naturally stand in awe of the Turks, particularly of the soldiers, who are so insolent on their side that they treat the Moors as if they were their slaves. This made the father bid his daughter go in and shut herself up close, 'whilst,' said he, 'I go and talk with these dogs; and for thee, Christian, gather the herbs thou wantest, and go thy way in peace, and God conduct thee safe to thy own country.' I bowed to him, and he left me with Zoraida to go and find out the Turks: she made also as if she were going away, as her father bid her; but she was no sooner hid from his sight by the trees of the garden, but she turned towards me with her eyes full of tears, and said, in her language, Atameji, Christiano, Atameji; which is, 'Thou art going away, Christian; thou art going.' To which I answered, 'Yes, madam, I am, but by no means without you; you may expect me next Friday, and be not surprised when you see us, for we will certainly go to the land of the Christians.' I said this so passionately that she understood me; and throwing one of her arms about my neck, she began to walk softly, and with trembling towards the house. It pleased fortune that as we were in this posture walking together (which might have proved very unlucky to us) we met Agimorato coming back from the Turks, and we perceived he had seen us as we were; but Zoraida, very readily and discreetly, was so far from taking away her arm about my neck, that, drawing still nearer to me, she leaned her head upon my breast, and, letting her knees give way, was in the posture of one that swoons; I at the same time made as if I had much ado to bear her up against my will. Her father came hastily to us, and, seeing his daughter in this condition, asked her what was the matter. But she not answering readily, he presently said, 'Without doubt those Turks have frightened her, and she faints away'; at which he took her in his arms. She, as it were, coming to herself, fetched a deep sigh, and, with her eyes not yet dried from tears, she said, in the language she had used before, 'Begone, Christian; begone.' To which her father replied, 'It is no matter, child, whether he go or no, he has done thee no hurt; and the Turks, at my request, are gone.'

'It is they who frightened her,' said I; 'but since she desires I should be gone, I will come another time for my salad, by your leave; for my master says the herbs of your garden are the best of any he can have.'

'Thou mayest have what and when thou wilt,' said the father, 'for my daughter does not think the Christians troublesome; she only wished the Turks away, and by mistake bid thee begone too.' With this I immediately took leave of them both; and Zoraida, showing trouble in her looks, went away with her father. I, in the meantime, upon pretence of gathering my herbs here and there, walked all over the garden, observing exactly all the places of coming in and going out, and every corner fit for my purpose, as well as what strength there was in the house, with all other conveniences to facilitate our business. Having done this, I went my ways, and gave an exact account of all that had happened to the renegade and the rest of my friends, longing earnestly for the time in which I might promise myself my dear Zoraida's company, without any fear of disturbance.

A VIEW OF CONSTANTINOPLE

Lady Mary Wortley Montagu
(1689–1762)

The eldest daughter of the Duke of Kingston, Lady Mary accompanied her husband when Ambassador in Turkey. Apart from her correspondence she is well known for having introduced inoculation against the smallpox, as carried out in Turkey, into England.

VERSES, WRITTEN IN THE CHIOSK OF THE BRITISH PALACE, AT PERA, OVERLOOKING THE CITY OF CONSTANTINOPLE, DEC. 26, 1718 (1717).

Give me, great God! said I, a little farm,
In summer shady, and in winter warm;
Where a clear spring gives birth to murm'ring brooks
By nature gliding down the mossy rocks.
Not artfully by leaden pipes convey'd,
Or greatly falling in a forc'd cascade,
Pure and unsullied winding through the shade.
All bounteous Heaven has added to my prayer,
A softer climate and a purer air . . .
Near them the violet grows with odours blest,
And blooms in more than Tyrian purple drest;
The rich jonquils their golden beams display,
and shine in glory's emulating day;
The peaceful groves their verdant leaves retain,
The streams still murmur undefil'd with rain,
And tow'ring greens adorn the fruitful plain.
The warbling kind uninterrupted sing,
Warmed with enjoyments of perpetual spring.

TO THE COUNTESS OF — (MAR).
ADRIANOPLE, APRIL 1, O.S.(1717).

I wish to God, dear sister, that you were as regular in letting me
have the pleasure of knowing what passes on your side of the globe,
as I am careful in endeavouring to amuse you by the account of all I
see that I think you care to hear of. You content yourself with telling
me over and over, that the town is very dull: it may possibly be dull
to you, when every day does not present you with something new;
but for me that am in arrear at least two months' news, all that seems
very stale with you would be fresh and sweet here. Pray let me into
more particulars, and I will try to awaken your gratitude, by giving
you a full and true relation of the novelties of this place, none of
which would surprise you more than a sight of my person, as I am
now in my Turkish habit, though I believe you would be of my
opinion, that 'tis admirably becoming – I intend to send you my
picture; in the mean time accept of it here.

The first piece of my dress is a pair of drawers, very full, that reach
to my shoes, and conceal the legs more modestly than your petticoats.
They are of a thin rose-coloured damask, brocaded with silver
flowers, my shoes of white kid leather, embroidered with gold. Over
this hangs my smock, of a fine white silk gauze, edged with embroidery. This smock has wide sleeves, hanging half way down the
arm, and is closed at the neck with a diamond button; but the shape
and colour of the bosom very well to be distinguished through it. The
antery is a waistcoat, made close to the shape, of white and gold
damask, with very long sleeves falling back, and fringed with deep
gold fringe, and should have diamond or pearl buttons. My caftan,
of the same stuff with my drawers, is a robe exactly fitted to my shape,
and reaching to my feet, with very long strait falling sleeves. Over
this is the girdle of about four fingers broad, which all that can afford
have entirely of diamonds or other precious stones; those who will
not be at that expense, have it of exquisite embroidery on satin; but
it must be fastened before with a clasp of diamonds. The curdee is a
loose robe they throw off or put on according to the weather, being
of a rich brocade (mine is green and gold), either lined with ermine
or sables; the sleeves reach very little below the shoulders. The
head-dress is composed of a cap, called talpock, which is in winter of
fine velvet embroidered with pearls or diamonds, and in summer of a
light shining silver stuff. This is fixed on one side of the head, hanging

a little way down with a gold tassel, and bound on, either with a circle of diamonds (as I have seen several) or a rich embroidered handkerchief. On the other side of the head, the hair is laid flat; and here the ladies are at liberty to shew their fancies; some putting flowers, others a plume of heron's feathers, and, in short, what they please; but the most general fashion is a large bouquet of jewels, made like natural flowers; that is, the buds of pearl; the roses, of different coloured rubies; the jessamines, of diamonds; jonquils, of topazes, &c., so well set and enamelled, 'tis hard to imagine any thing of that kind so beautiful. The hair hangs at its full length behind, divided into tresses braided with pearl or ribbon, which is always in great quantity.

I never saw in my life so many fine heads of hair. I have counted a hundred and ten of these tresses of one lady's all natural; but it must be owned, that every beauty is more common here than with us. 'Tis surprising to see a young woman that is not very handsome. They have naturally the most beautiful complexions in the world, and generally large black eyes. I can assure you with great truth, that the court of England (though I believe it the fairest in Christendom) cannot shew so many beauties as are under our protection here. They generally shape their eyebrows; and the Greeks and Turks have a custom of putting round their eyes (on the inside) a black tincture, that, at a distance, or by candlelight, adds very much to the blackness of them. I fancy many of our ladies would be overjoyed to know this secret; but 'tis too visible by day. They dye their nails a rose-colour. I own, I cannot enough accustom myself to this fashion to find any beauty in it.

As to their morality or good conduct, I can say, like Harlequin, that 'tis just as it is with you; and the Turkish ladies don't commit one sin the less for not being Christians. Now I am a little acquainted with their way, I cannot forbear admiring either the exemplary discretion or extreme stupidity of all the writers that have given accounts of them. 'Tis very easy to see they have more liberty than we have. No woman, of what rank soever, being permitted to go into the streets without two muslins; one that covers her face all but her eyes, and another that hides the whole dress of her head, and hangs half way down her back, and their shapes are wholly concealed by a thing they call a ferigee, which no woman of any sort appears without; this has straight sleeves, that reach to their finger-ends, and it laps all round them, not unlike a riding-hood. In winter 'tis of cloth, and in summer plain stuff or silk. You may guess how effectually this disguises them, [so] that there is no distinguishing the great lady from her slave. 'Tis impossible for the most jealous husband to know his wife when he meets her; and no man dare either touch or follow a woman in the street.

This perpetual masquerade gives them entire liberty of following their inclinations without danger of discovery. The most usual method of intrigue is, to send an appointment to the lover to meet the lady at a Jew's shop, which are as notoriously convenient as our Indian-houses; and yet, even those who don't make that use of them, do not scruple to go to buy pennyworths, and tumble over rich goods, which are chiefly to be found amongst that sort of people. The great ladies seldom let their gallants know who they are; and it is so difficult to find it out, that they can very seldom guess at her name they have corresponded with above half a year together. You may easily imagine the number of faithful wives very small in a country where they have nothing to fear from a lover's indiscretion, since we see so many that have the courage to expose themselves to that in this world, and all the threatened punishment of the next, which is never preached to the Turkish damsels. Neither have they much to apprehend from the resentment of their husbands; those ladies that are rich having all their money in their own hands, which they take with them upon a divorce, with an addition which he is obliged to give them.

Upon the whole, I look upon the Turkish women as the only free people in the empire: the very Divan pays a respect to them; and the Grand Signior himself, when a pasha is executed, never violates the privileges of the harem (or women's apartment), which remains unsearched entire to the widow. They are queens of their slaves, whom the husband has no permission so much as to look upon, except it be an old woman or two that his lady chooses. 'Tis true their law permits them four wives; but there is no instance of a man of quality that makes use of this liberty, or of a woman of rank that would suffer it. When a husband happens to be inconstant (as those things will happen), he keeps his mistress in a house apart, and visits her as privately as he can, just as it is with you. Amongst all the great men here, I only know the tefterdar (i.e. treasurer), that keeps a number of she slaves for his own use (that is, on his own side of the house; for a slave once given to serve a lady is entirely at her disposal), and he is spoken of as a libertine, or what we should call a rake, and his wife won't see him, though she continues to live in his house.

Thus, you see, dear sister, the manners of mankind do not differ so widely as our voyage writers would make us believe. Perhaps it would be more entertaining to add a few surprising customs of my own invention; but nothing seems to me so agreeable as truth, and I believe nothing so acceptable to you. I conclude with repeating the great truth of my being,

Dear sister, &c.

A PRINCE OF ABYSSINIA

From Rasselas by Samuel Johnson

(1709–1784)

———————◆———————

When he was very young, and very poor, as he was long to remain, Johnson wrote and published an abridged translation of Geronimo Lobo's *Voyage to Abyssinia*. It was not until 1759 that he wrote *Rasselas,* a moral allegory, with Abyssinia and Egypt as its background scenery. It is a short novel said by him to have been written at nights during one week in order to pay for his mother's funeral and debts. He was fifty years old, at the height of his ability, and the memory of Lobo's work would have provided him with sufficient Oriental landscape.

The tale begins in the 'happy valley' in Abyssinia where members of the Imperial family, with their followers and friends, were immured by impenetrable mountains and forest, most if not all of them being consoled by a constant succession of pleasures and varying delights. The Prince Rasselas, however, believing that he might be called upon to become the ruler of his country, desires to know about the outside world and is increasingly curious to learn what he can of it. Discovering that one of his companions had travelled abroad before settling in the valley, he persuades him to help in an escape and accompany him. They do eventually find a way out and the Prince with his sister, her lady-in-waiting and the followers of both of them emerge to take part in a series of adventures and misadventures in the countrysides of Abyssinia and Egypt and at last in Cairo itself.

Because incidents during their travels are by no means always happy, though affording lessons about the world and mankind, and man unkind, the Prince and his sister have high hope that their stay in Cairo will be rewarding. There they seek out the sages and religios, visit the catacombs and a pyramid, but all in all come to the conclusion if sadly, that they had better return to the 'happy valley', which they do.

———————◆———————

RASSELAS
DESCRIPTION OF A
PALACE IN A VALLEY

Ye who listen with credulity to the whispers of fancy, and pursue with eagerness the phantoms of hope; who expect that age will perform the promises of youth, and that the deficiencies of the present day will be supplied by the morrow; attend to the history of Rasselas, prince of Abyssinia.

Rasselas was the fourth son of the mighty emperor, in whose dominions the Father of Waters begins his course; whose bounty pours down the streams of plenty, and scatters over half the world the harvests of Egypt.

According to the custom which has descended from age to age among the monarchs of the torrid zone, Rasselas was confined in a private palace, with the other sons and daughters of Abyssinian royalty, till the order of succession should call him to the throne.

The place, which the wisdom or policy of antiquity had destined for the residence of the Abyssinian princes, was a spacious valley in the kingdom of Amhara, surrounded on every side by mountains, of which the summits overhang the middle part . . .

The palace stood on an eminence raised about thirty paces above the surface of the lake. It was divided into many squares or courts, built with greater or less magnificence, according to the rank of those for whom they were designed. The roofs were turned into arches of massy stone, joined by a cement that grew harder by time, and the building stood from century to century deriding the solstitial rains and equinoctial hurricanes, without need of reparation.

This house, which was so large as to be fully known to none but some ancient officers who successively inherited the secrets of the place, was built as if suspicion herself had dictated the plan. To every room there was an open and secret passage, every square had a communication with the rest, either from the upper stories by private galleries, or by subterranean passages from the lower apartments. Many of the columns had unsuspected cavities, in which a long race of monarchs had deposited their treasures: they then closed up the opening with marble, which was never to be removed but in the utmost exigencies of the kingdom; and recorded their accumulations in a book which was itself concealed in a tower not entered but by the emperor, attended by the prince who stood next in succession.

THE DISCONTENT OF RASSELAS
IN THE HAPPY VALLEY

Here the sons and daughters of Abyssinia lived only to know the soft vicissitudes of pleasure and repose, attended by all that were skilful to delight, and gratified with whatever the senses can enjoy. They wandered in gardens of fragrance, and slept in the fortresses of security. Every art was practised to make them pleased with their own condition. The sages who instructed them, told them of nothing but the miseries of public life, and described all beyond the mountains as regions of calamity, where discord was always raging, and where man preyed upon man.

To heighten their opinion of their own felicity, they were daily entertained with songs, the subject of which was the *happy valley*. Their appetites were excited by frequent enumerations of different enjoyments, and revelry and merriment was the business of every hour from the dawn of morning to the close of even.

These methods were generally successful; few of the princes had ever wished to enlarge their bounds, but passed their lives in full conviction that they had all within their reach that art or nature could bestow, and pitied those whom fate had excluded from this seat of tranquillity, as the sport of chance and the slaves of misery.

Thus they rose in the morning and lay down at night, pleased with each other and with themselves, all but Rasselas, who in the twenty-sixth year of his age began to withdraw himself from their pastimes and assemblies, and to delight in solitary walks and silent meditation. He often sat before tables covered with luxury, and forgot to taste the dainties that were placed before him; he rose abruptly in the midst of the song, and hastily retired beyond the sound of music. His attendants observed the change, and endeavoured to renew his love of pleasure. He neglected their officiousness, repulsed their invitations, and spent day after day on the banks of rivulets sheltered with trees, where he sometimes listened to the birds in the branches, sometimes observed the fish playing in the stream, and anon cast his eyes upon the pastures and mountains filled with animals, of which some were biting the herbage, and some sleeping among the bushes.

This singularity of his humour made him much observed. One of the sages, in whose conversation he had formerly delighted, followed him secretly, in hope of discovering the cause of his disquiet. Rasselas, who knew not that any one was near him, having for some time fixed his eyes upon the goats that were browsing among the rocks, began to compare their condition with his own.

'What,' said he, 'makes the difference between man and all the rest of the animal creation? Every beast that strays beside me has the same corporeal necessities with myself: he is hungry and crops the grass, he is thirsty and drinks the stream, his thirst and hunger are appeased, he is satisfied and sleeps; he arises again and is hungry, he is again fed and is at rest. I am hungry and thirsty like him, but when thirst and hunger cease I am not at rest; I am, like him, pained with want, but am not, like him, satisfied with fulness. The intermediate hours are tedious and gloomy; I long again to be hungry, that I may again quicken my attention. The birds peck the berries or the corn, and fly away to the groves, where they sit in seeming happiness on the branches, and waste their lives in tuning one unvaried series of sounds. I likewise can call the lutanist and the singer, but the sounds that pleased me yesterday weary me to-day, and will grow yet more wearisome to-morrow. I can discover within me no power of perception which is not glutted with its proper pleasure, yet I do not feel myself delighted. Man surely has some latent sense for which this place affords no gratification; or he has some desires distinct from sense, which must be satisfied before he can be happy.'

After this he lifted up his head, and seeing the moon rising, walked towards the palace. As he passed through the fields, and saw the animals around him, 'Ye,' said he, 'are happy, and need not envy me that walk thus among you, burdened with myself; nor do I, ye gentle beings, envy your felicity; for it is not the felicity of man. I have many distresses from which ye are free; I fear pain when I do not feel it; I sometimes shrink at evils recollected, and sometimes start at evils anticipated: surely the equity of Providence has balanced peculiar sufferings with peculiar enjoyments.'

IN HAPPY ARABIA

From Travels in Arabia
by Carsten Niebuhr
(1733–1815)

On 4 January 1761, Carsten Neibuhr and four explorer companions, together with their Swedish servant, set sail from Copenhagen bound for the Arabian peninsula on what was to prove one of the most tragically ill-fated yet singularly productive of all voyages of discovery. Niebuhr was German by birth, Danish by adoption. He was a brave, resourceful and intelligent man. Two of his companions were quarrelsome and intellectually arrogant. Professor Friedrich von Haven, a philologist, was lazy and conceited. Georg Baurenfeind, artist engraver, was an agreeable companion who played duets on the violin with Niebuhr to while away many a lonely hour. Dr. Christian Kramer, the medical officer, was young and inexperienced. The most brilliant member of the party Peter Forsskal, a pupil of Linnaeus, a corresponding member of the German Academy of Sciences at the precocious age of twenty-four, a scholar of classical and Oriental languages, proved the most difficult and assertive of travellers. Von Haven and Forsskal battled constantly for rank and supremacy.

The expedition was sponsored and paid for by King Frederick V of Denmark and was intended to bring prestige to its royal patron; its members shared at least the common objective of serious and planned study as they made their way to Alexandria. But dissension kept them in Egypt for eighteen months. It was not until October 1762 that they went on to Jidda on the Red Sea coast and thence by native craft to Luhaiyah, the northern port of Yemen, *Arabia Felix*. They spent almost a year travelling across the desert regions of southern Arabia, stopping now and then in towns and oases to listen to the chatter of the coffee houses and enjoy the hospitality of the sheikhs. As their work in the Yemen came towards its close in August 1763, Niebuhr, Kramer, Baurenfeind and the servant Berggren were all seriously ill after nightmare marches in hot and disease-ridden country between Sana and Mocha. All had malaria. Forsskal was already dead, the victim of a terrible fever. The rest of the party took ship for India but Baurenfeind and Berggren died at sea. Kramer and Niebuhr disembarked at Bombay on 13 September 1763, but Kramer did not recover and died a few months later. Niebuhr gathered together the notes of his companions and went on to tour and record his impressions of India. At the end of 1764 he went to Muscat and then, disguised as a humble Arab, he journeyed through southern Persia, Iraq and Syria. He returned to Copenhagen on 20 November 1767, and the first volume of his travels *Beschreibung von Arabien* was published in 1772. It was one of the most faithful and scholarly accounts ever written by an outsider on the Arabs and, along with the accounts of della Valle and the seventeenth-century French scholar Barthélemy d'Herbelot, it provided the substance of Gibbon's fiftieth chapter.

OF THE ARABIAN NOBILITY

The Arabs are accused of being vain, full of prejudices with respect to birth, and ridiculously attentive to records of genealogy, which they keep even for their horses. This reproach cannot affect the great body of the nation, who know not their family names, and take not the trouble of keeping a register of births. Most of those, even in the middle station of life, know not who were their grandfathers, and would often be as much at a loss to know their fathers, if it were not regulated by custom, that the son shall join his father's name with his own.

All those petty princes who govern in Arabia are, undoubtedly, very proud of their birth, and with some reason, since their families have, from time immemorial, enjoyed independence and sovereign power. The nobility, who are free, or dependent only on the chiefs of their tribes, are equally so. They enjoy privileges which the traditional history of the nation represents as having always belonged to certain families. The Schiechs are excusable, therefore, although they value themselves upon advantages which are peculiarly theirs.

What adds to the high conceit the Bedouin Schiechs have of their nobility, is its being incommunicable, and not to be conferred by any sovereign prince, or even by the Caliphs. As it is founded on the customs of a pastoral people, who know no distinction of rank, but that of the heads of families, no sovereign can augment the number of these chiefs. Nobles can be created only in countries where the nobility form a distinct class, enjoying certain civil privileges, which may be equally conferred on others. The Bedouin nobility may be compared to the chiefs of the clans among the Scotch highlanders, who are in a very similar condition with respect to their honours and authority.

The descendants of Mahomet hold, with some reason, the first rank among the great families in Arabia. Mahomet was sprung from one of the noblest families in the country, and rose to the rank of a potent prince. His first profession of a dealer in camels, proves him to have been a Schiech of the genuine and pure nobility of his nation. It may be inferred, however, from the singular veneration in which his family are held, that religious opinions have contributed to gain them the pre-eminence which they hold, above even the most ancient sovereign houses. A sect naturally respect the posterity of their founder, as a race bearing an indelible character of sanctity.

These descendants of Mahomet have received different titles. In Arabia they are called Sherriffes, or Sejids; in the Mahometan countries situate northward, Sherriffes, or Emirs; and in the Arabian colonies in the East, simply Sejids. The Prince of Havisa, on the frontiers of Persia, takes the title of Maula, which has, I believe, been assumed by the Emperor of Morocco. In some countries, this family are distinguished by a green turban. Nay, on the coast of Arabia, ships hoist a green flag, when fitted out by a Sejid. Yet the green turban is not invariably a distinctive mark of a descendant of Mahomet. Beggars sometimes wear turbans of this colour; and one of our servants did the same, and was blamed by nobody.

The Sherriffes of Hedjas are esteemed the noblest of Mahomet's descendants, because they have made fewer intermarriages with strangers than the rest of the Prophet's posterity. In that province they are treated with almost incredible respect. A Sherriffe may enter into the midst of a fray, without the smallest fear of being intentionally hurt or killed. He needs not shut his doors against thieves. In the Ottoman provinces, the family of the Prophet are less regarded. In my time, a Sejid, who had been guilty of diverse crimes, and although warned and reproved by an indulgent governor, had not corrected his bad habit, was condemned to suffer capital punishment.

Having heard a distinction frequently made between a Sherriffe and a Sejid, I made inquiry into its nature. I learned that Sherriffes are constantly devoted to a military life, and are descended from Hassan; but that the Sejids are the posterity of Hussein and follow the pursuits of trade and science, although they have sometimes risen to sovereign power in some parts of Arabia.

There are, in all Mahometan countries, an astonishing number of

Sherriffes. I saw whole villages peopled with this family solely. To those who know not in what manner this title is transmitted, the numbers of those who enjoy this high rank must undoubtedly appear surprising; but polygamy naturally multiplies families, till many of their branches sink into the most wretched misery. In my account of Jebid, I have mentioned my acquaintance with a Sherriffe in that city, who was in extreme poverty. A peculiar custom tends to the farther increase of the race of Sherriffes. The son of a woman of the family of Mahomet is esteemed a Sherriffe, and transmits the honour to all his posterity. I travelled through Natolia with a Turk, who was called simply Achmed, and wore the common turban, while his son was honoured with a green turban, and with the title of Sherriffe, because his mother was a Sherriffa. Other similar instances came within my knowledge in the provinces of Turkey; and, from various circumstances, I was led to infer, that many persons enjoy this title who are not at all connected with the Prophet's family. The genuine Sherriffes, to strengthen their party against the Caliphs, have acknowledged kindred with various powerful families who were entirely strangers to them . . .

Of all the titles in use among the Arabian nobility, the most ancient and most common is that of Schiech. The Arabian language, which is in other respects so rich, is however, poor in terms expressive of the distinctions of rank. The word Schiech has, in consequence of this circumstance, various significations. Sometimes it is the title of a prince or noble; at other times, it is given to a professor in an academy, to a man belonging to a mosque, to the descendant of a saint, to the mayor of a town, and in Oman, even to the chief of the Jewish Synagogue. Although thus seemingly prostituted, yet is not this title despised by the great. A Schiech of an ancient Arabian family would not change the name for that of Sultan, which has been assumed by some petty princes in the highlands of Hadramaut and Jafa.

The Schiechs of illustrious families among the Bedouins have reason for considering their genealogy as a matter of some consequence. Some of them are descended from ancestors, who were princes before the days of Mahomet, and the first Caliphs. As it would be difficult, among a people who have no public registers or historians, to make out regular tables of genealogy reaching farther than ten centuries backwards, the Arabians have contrived a compendious mode of verifying their lines of descent. From among their later ancestors, they select some illustrious man from whom they are universally allowed to be descended. This great man, again, is as universally allowed to be descended from some other great man; and thus they proceed backwards to the founder of the family. The Sherriffes and Sejids, by the same expedient, prove the origin of their family to have been with Mahomet, and thus abbreviate their genealogy, without rendering it doubtful.

Beside these Schiechs and princes there are at Mecca some families not less concerned to preserve their genealogies, with all possible exactitude. These are the families descended from the tribe of Koraisch, which have held certain employments, by hereditary right, since the days of Mahomet and his first successors. Their employments are, first, The office of keeper of the key of the Kaba, which was conferred by Mahomet on the family of Othman Ibn Taelha: second, That of Mufti of the sect of Schafei: third, That of Mufti of the sect of Hanbali: and lastly, That of a learned Schiech to attend in the holy mosque.

There are also in Mecca, twelve other families, descended from the illustrious tribe of Koraisch. If any where in the world, a faithful list of genealogy, for more than ten centuries, may be found, it is certainly among these families of Koraischites, who are constantly obliged to prove the genuineness of their descent, in order to preserve their envied privileges.

I never heard the distinction between the genuine and naturalized Arabs formally explained. Such a distinction is made, however, for the Bedouins value themselves so much on the purity of their descent, that they look very contemptuously on the Arabs who live in cities, as a race debased by their intermixture with other nations . . .

OF MARRIAGE AMONG THE ARABIANS

The Europeans are mistaken in thinking the state of marriage so different among the Mussulmans from what it is with Christian nations. I could not discern any such difference in Arabia. The women of that country seem to be as free and happy as those of Europe can possibly be.

Polygamy is permitted, indeed, among Mahometans, and the delicacy of our ladies is shocked at this idea; but the Arabians rarely avail themselves of the privilege of marrying four lawful wives, and entertaining at the same time any number of female slaves. None but rich voluptuaries marry so many wives, and their conduct is blamed by all sober men. Men of sense, indeed, think this privilege rather troublesome than convenient. A husband is, by law, obliged to treat his wives suitably to their condition, and to dispense his favours among them with perfect equality; but these are duties not a little disagreeable to most Mussulmans; and such modes of luxury are too expensive to the Arabians, who are seldom in easy circumstances. I must, however, except one case; for it sometimes happens that a man marries a number of wives in the way of a commercial speculation. I knew a Mullah, in a town near the Euphrates, who had married four wives, and was supported by the profits of their labour.

Divorce, the idea of which is also regarded as horrid by the fair sex in Europe, is not nearly so common as is imagined in the East. The Arabians never exercise the right of repudiating a wife, unless urged by the strongest reasons; because this is considered a dishonourable step, by persons who value their reputation, and throws disgrace on the woman and her relations. Wives are entitled to demand a divorce when they think themselves ill used by their husbands. Only profligate and imprudent men, who have married without consideration, will divorce their wives for slight causes.

An Arabian, in moderate circumstances, seldom marries more than one wife. And even the most considerable persons in the nation are often contented with one for life. Rich men, who are in a condition to maintain as many wives as they please, have often confessed to me, that although they had begun to live with several wives, they had at last found that they could be happy only with one.

The Arabian women enjoy a great deal of liberty, and often a great deal of power, in their families. They continue mistresses of their dowries, and of the annual income which these afford, during their marriage, and, in the case of divorce, all their own property is reserved to them. Hence it happens, that when a man in narrow circumstances marries a woman of fortune, he is entirely dependent on his wife, and dares not divorce her.

It is absurd to say, as some travellers have, that the Mahometan wives are all slaves, and so entirely the property of their husbands, that they are even inherited by his heirs. In this representation, slaves purchased with money have been confounded with women of free estate, who dispose of themselves in the East just as in Europe.

The opinion, that women are slaves in Arabia, seems to have arisen from the mistaken notion, that fathers there sell their daughters to the highest bidder. It many times happens, no doubt, that a poor man who has an handsome daughter, is pleased to match her with a rich man,

from whom he may receive occasional presents. And rich voluptuaries, who choose to marry more wives than one, are obliged to take
young women of low condition, who are compelled by interested
parents, or seduced by splendour, to accept a husband who associates
them with other wives, and at length divorces them.

Instead of selling his daughter, every man, in tolerably easy circumstances, strives to give her a dowry, which may continue her own
property. The marriage is made out by the Cadi, and signed in his
presence; and in it not only is her dowry secured to the wife, but also
a separate maintenance, in case of a divorce. The rich often give their
daughters, in preference, to poor men, and consider their children as
more likely to be happy, when thus settled, than if they were married
to rich men. The wife is then mistress of all the property, and even of
the house of her husband, and is not in danger of being sent away.

Many ridiculous stories have been told of the marks of virginity
which an Arab expects when he marries a young woman. But most of
these stories greatly exaggerate the truth. The Bedouins, and the
highlanders of Yemen, a rude and almost savage race, do indeed
regard the want of those marks as a proof of dishonour, and think
themselves obliged to send a woman back to her relations, when her
chastity cannot thus be evinced. But the inhabitants of the towns,
being more civilized, never concern themselves about such a trifle;
only, in case of such an accident, a son-in-law forces an addition to the
dowry from his father-in-law, by threatening to send his daughter
home again, although he never actually does so. At Basra I heard of a
single instance of divorce upon this ground, and the man was of the
lowest class of the people.

Many superstitious observances, respecting marriage, still prevail
in Arabia. The Arabs still believe in the virtue of enchantments, and
in the art of tying and untying the knots of fate. The miserable victim
of this diabolical art addresses some physician, or some old woman;
for the old women are always skilled in sorcery. The Christians of the
East have a still more certain remedy against the effects of witchcraft.
They say masses for the person afflicted; and when, at last, the
imagination of the poor patient has had time to recover, the honour
of the cure is always ascribed to the powerful influence of the masses.

We imagine in Europe, that the inhabitants of the East keep
eunuchs for the guardians of their harams; yet eunuchs are not common through the East, and in Arabia there are none. The Turkish
Monarch keeps more eunuchs in his seraglio at Constantinople than

are in all the rest of his dominions. The Pacha of Aleppo had two, and he of Mosul one, whom he kept, because he had belonged to his father. It is wrong, therefore, to regard Arabia as the seat of eunuchism. They are brought from Upper Egypt, but are mostly natives of the interior and little known provinces of Africa. The Arabians abhor the cruel operation which is requisite to render a man a fit guardian of the chastity of a haram.

Eunuchs born in a climate which has a tendency to inflame the blood, are not absolutely void of all passion for the fair sex. On the sea, between Suez and Jedda, I met with a eunuch who travelled with his seraglio; and at Basra I heard of another rich eunuch, who kept female slaves for his private amusement.

Much has been said in Europe concerning the origin of the practice of polygamy, so generally prevalent through the East. Supposing that the plurality of wives is not barely allowed by law, but takes place in fact, some of our philosophers have imagined, that, in hot countries, more women than men are born; but I have already stated, that some nations avail not themselves of the permission given by the Mussulman law for one to marry several wives. It would be unfair to judge of the manners of a whole people by the fastidious luxury of the great. It is vanity that fills seraglios, and that chiefly with slaves, most of whom are only slaves to a few favourite women. The number of female slaves in Europe, who are, in the same manner, condemned in a great measure to celibacy, is equal or superior to that of those who are confined in the harams of the East . . .

The Shiites are, by their law, permitted to live for a certain time, by agreement, but without a formal marriage, with a free Mahometan woman. The Persians frequently avail themselves of this permission; but the more rigid Sunnites think this an illicit connection, and do not tolerate it. In Turkey, a man who should cohabit with a free woman, without being married to her, would be punished by law.

CALIPH VATHEK

From The History of the Caliph Vathek by William Beckford

(1760–1844)

The following was written by Beckford at the age of eighteen, in 1778:

'Meanwhile my thoughts were wandering into the interior of Africa and dwelt for hours on those countries I love. Strange tales of Mount Atlas and relations of Travellers amused my fancy. One instant I imagined myself viewing the marble palaces of Ethiopean princes seated on the green woody margin of Lakes ... Some few minutes later after, I found myself standing before a thick wood listening to impetuous water falls ... I was wondering at the Scene when a tall comely Negro wound along the slopes of the Hills and without moving his lips made me comprehend I was in Africa, on the brink of the Nile beneath the Mountains of Armara. I followed his steps thro. an infinity of irregular Vales, all skirted with Rocks and blooming with an aromatic Vegetation till we arrived at the hollow Peak and ... a wide Cavern appeared before us ... We entered the Cavern and fell prostrate before the sacred source of the Nile which issues silently from a deep Gulph in the Rock.'

William Beckford's life spanned the Romantic Age, his birth having been in 1760 and his life long. The work by which he is best known, the fantasy called *The History of the Caliph Vathek,* was written by him in French and published in Paris and Lausanne in 1787. The first English version was issued by the translator, without Beckford's name or permission.

The style and content of the book are almost as astonishing as Beckford's life. At the age of eleven Beckford was left a million pounds in ready money and an income of £100,000 a year by his father who had been more than once Lord Mayor of London. He attended neither school nor university, but was educated by tutors and from travel on the continent of Europe. He married a daughter of the Earl of Aboyne; she died following the birth of his second daughter. He was believed to have been present, as a mounted spectator, at the Bastille. One of his hobbies was the building of large country houses to which he would retire with a few friends.

The history of the Caliph Vathek does not pretend to be based on fact, but is an amusing display of how Beckford, in the penultimate decade of the

eighteenth century, projected the East for the enjoyment of his readers.
An Indian sorcerer visiting the Caliph's Court has beguiled him into
believing that he could lead him to King Solomon's treasure if he follows his
advice. Thus the Caliph has given instructions for his Court to be ready to
move.

The expedition commenced with the utmost order and so entire a
silence, that even the locusts were heard from the thickets on the plain
of Catoul. Gaiety and good humour prevailing, six good leagues were
passed before the dawn; and the morning star was still glittering in the
firmament when the whole of this numerous train had halted on the
banks of the Tigris where they encamped to repose for the rest of the
day.

The three days that followed were spent in the same manner; but on
the fourth the heavens looked angry, lightnings broke forth in frequent flashes, re-echoing peals of thunder succeeded, and the trembling Circassians clung with all their might to their ugly guardians. The
Caliph himself was greatly inclined to take shelter in the large town of
Gulchisser, the Governor of which came forth to meet him, and
tendered every kind of refreshment the place could supply; but
having examined his tablets, he suffered the rain and camped where
he was.

When he woke Vathek was greatly disturbed, foodless and water-
less as they were in a land of dreadful rocks and dark valleys. His
people were repining at their journey and complaining for the lack of
water. He began to turn over the tablets he had been given by his
mother Carathis, who advised him to consult them in case of emer-
gencies. While he was doing so he heard a shout of joy and a loud
clapping of hands; the curtains of his pavilion were soon drawn back
and he beheld Bababalouk, followed by a troop of his favourites,
conducting two dwarfs, each a cubit high, who brought them a large
basket of melons, oranges and pomegranates. They were singing in
the sweetest tones, saying how much they loved the Caliph as did their
master the good Emir Fakreddin. Little as they were he knew their
hearts to be good as their bodies were contemptible and had placed
them here to aid those who are bewildered on these dreary mountains.
They had informed their master at once and he himself picked the
fruit they now brought, and was following them with a hundred
dromedaries, laden with the purest water of his fountains and is

coming to kiss the fringe of his, the Caplih's consecrated robe, and
implore him to enter his humble habitation. The dwarfs having ended
their address remained standing with hands crossed upon their
bosoms, preserving a respectful silence. In spite of finding warnings
in the tablets left with him by his mother, Vathek decided to accept
the Emir's invitation, to the delight of Bababalouk and of the ladies of
the harem. The dwarfs were entertained and caressed and seated with
ceremony on little cushions of satin. The symmetry of their persons
was the subject of criticism; not an inch of them was suffered to pass
unexamined.

The good Emir who was punctiliously religious and likewise a
great dealer in compliments, made an harangue five times more prolix
and insipid than his harbingers had already delivered. The Caliph
unable any longer to refrain, exclaimed: 'For the love of Mahomet,
my dear Fakreddin, have done! let us proceed to your valley and enjoy
that which heaven hath vouchsafed you.'

The hint of proceeding put all into motion, the venerable attendants
of the Emir set forward somewhat slowly, but Vathek, having ordered
his little pages in private to goad on the dromedaries, loud fits of
laughter broke forth from the cages, for the unwieldy curveting of
these poor beasts, and the ridiculous distress of their superannuated
riders, afforded the ladies no small entertainment.

The cavalcade soon entered a path which was skirted by flowering
shrubs, and extended to a vast wood of palm trees, whose branches
overspread a building of hewn stone. This edifice was crowned with
nine domes, and adorned with as many portals of bronze, on which
was engraven, 'This is the asylum of pilgrims, the refuge of travellers,
and the depository of secrets for all parts of the world.'

Nine pages, beautiful as the day, and clothed in robes of Egyptian
linen, very long and very modest, were standing at each door. They
received the whole retinue with an easy and inviting air. Four of the
most amiable placed the Caliph on a magnificent *taktrevan*; four others,
somewhat less graceful, took charge of Bababalouk, who capered for
joy at the snug little cabin that fell to his share; the pages that remained waited on the rest of the train.

When everything masculine was gone out of sight, the gate of a
large enclosure on the right turned on its harmonious hinges, and a
young female of slender form came forth; her light brown hair
floated on the hazy breeze of the twilight; a troop of young maidens,
like the Pleiades, attended her on tip-toe. They hastened to the pavi-

lions that contained the Sultanas, and the young lady, gracefully bending, said to them: 'Charming Princesses, everything is ready; we have prepared beds for your repose, and strewed your apartments with jasmine, no insects will keep off slumber from visiting your eyelids, we will dispel them with a thousand plumes: come then amiable ladies! refresh your delicate feet and your ivory limbs in baths of rose-water; and by the light of perfumed lamps, your servants will amuse you with tales.'

The Sultanas accepted with pleasure these obliging offers and followed the young lady to the Emir's harem.

Vathek, meanwhile, found himself beneath a vast dome, illuminated by a thousand lamps of rock crystal; as many vases of the same material, filled with excellent sherbet, sparkled on a large table, where a profusion of viands were spread; amongst others were sweetbreads stewed in milk of almonds, saffron soups, and lamb *à la crème*, of all of which the Caliph was amazingly fond.

He took of each as much as he was able, testified his sense of the Emir's friendship by the gaiety of his heart, and made the dwarfs dance against their will, for these little devotees durst not refuse the Commander of the Faithful: at last he spread himself on the sofa and slept sounder than he had ever before.

Beneath this dome a general silence prevailed, for there was nothing to disturb it but the jaws of Bababalouk, who had untrussed himself to eat with greater advantage, being anxious to make amends for his fast in the mountains. As his spirits were too high to admit of his sleeping, and not loving to be idle, he proposed with himself to visit the harem and repair to his charge of the ladies, to examine if they had been properly lubricated with the balm of Mecca, if their eyebrows and tresses were in order, and, in a word, to perform all the little offices they might need. He sought for a long time together, but without being able to find the door; he durst not speak aloud for fear of disturbing the Caliph, and not a soul was stirring in the precincts of the Palace; he almost despaired of effecting his purpose when a low whispering just reached his ear; it came from the dwarfs, who were returned to their old occupation, and, for the nine hundred and ninety-ninth time in their lives, were reading over the Koran. They politely invited Bababalouk be of their party, but his head was full of other concerns. The dwarfs, though scandalized at his dissolute morals, directed him to the apartments he wanted to find; his way thither lay through a hundred dark corridors, along which he groped as he went, and at last began to catch, from the extremity of a passage, the charming gossiping of the women, which not a little delighted his heart. 'Ah, ha! what, not yet asleep?' cried he; and taking long strides as he spoke, 'Did you not suspect me of abjuring my charge? I stayed but to finish what my master had left.'

Two of the black eunuchs, on hearing a voice so loud, detached a party in haste, sabre in hand, to discover the cause, but presently was repeated on all sides: 'Tis only Bababalouk! no one but Bababalouk!' This circumspect guardian, having gone up to a thin veil of carnation-coloured silk that hung before the doorway, distinguished by means of the softened splendour that shone through it, an oval bath of dark porphyry, surrounded by curtains festooned in large folds; through the apertures between them, as they were not drawn close, groups of young slaves were visible, amongst whom Bababalouk perceived his pupils, indulgingly expanding their arms, as if to embrace the perfumed water and refresh themselves after their fatigues. The looks of tender languor, their confidential whispers, and the enchanting smiles with which they were imparted, the exquisite fragrance of the roses, all combined to inspire a voluptuousness, which even Bababalouk himself was scarcely able to withstand.

He summoned up, however, his usual solemnity, and, in the peremptory tone of authority, commanded the ladies instantly to leave the bath. While he was issuing these mandates the young Nouronihar, daughter of the Emir, who was sprightly as an antelope, and full of wanton gaiety, beckoned one of her slaves to let down the great swing, which was suspended to the ceiling by cords of silk, and whilst this was doing, winked to her companions in the bath, who, chagrined to be forced from so soothing a state of indolence, began to twist it round Bababalouk and tease him with a thousand vagaries.

When Nouronihar perceived that he was exhausted with fatigue, she accosted him with an arch air of respectful concern and said: 'My Lord! it is not by any means decent, that the chief eunuch of the Caliph, our Sovereign, should thus continue standing; deign but to recline your graceful person upon this sofa, which will burst with vexation if it has not the honour to receive you.' Caught by these flattering accents, Bababalouk gallantly replied: 'Delight of the apple of my eye! I accept the invitation of thy honeyed lips; and, to say truth, my senses are dazzled with the radiance that beams from thy charms.' 'Repose then at your ease' replied the beauty; and placed him on the pretended sofa, which, quicker than lightning , gave way all at once. The rest of the women, having aptly conceived her design, sprang naked from the bath, and plied the swing with such unmerciful jerks, that it swept through the whole compass of a very lofty dome, and took from the poor victim all power of respiration; sometimes his feet grazed the surface of the water, and at others the skylight almost flattened his nose; in vain, did he pierce the air with the cries of a voice that resembled the ringing of a cracked basin, for their peals of laughter were still more predominant.

Nouronihar in the inebriety of youthful spirits, being used only to eunuchs of ordinary harems, and having never seen anything so royal and disgusting, was far more diverted than all of the rest; she began to parody some Persian verses, and sang with an accent most demurely piquant:

> 'O gentle white dove, as thou soar'st through the air,
> Vouchsafe one kind glance on the mate of thy love;
> Melodious Philomel, I am thy rose;
> Warble some couplet to ravish my heart!'

The Sultanas and their slaves, stimulated by these pleasantries, persevered at the swing with such unremitted assiduity, that at length the cord which had secured it snapped suddenly asunder, and Bababalouk fell floundering like a turtle to the bottom of the bath. This accident occasioned a universal shout; twelve little doors, till now unobserved, flew open at once, and the ladies in an instant made their escape, after throwing all the towels on his head and putting out the lights that remained.

The deplorable animal, in water to the chin, overwhelmed with darkness, and unable to extricate himself from the wrap that embarrassed him, was still doomed to hear for his further consolation the fresh bursts of merriment his disaster occasioned. He bustled, but in vain, to get from the bath, for the margin was become so slippery with the oil spilt in breaking the lamps that at every effort he slid back with a plunge, which resounded aloud through the hollow of the dome. These cursed peals of laughter at every relapse were redoubled; and he, who thought the place infested rather by devils than women, resolved to cease groping and abide in the bath . . .

The Caliph wondering at his absence had caused him to be everywhere sought for. At last, limping and chattering his teeth, he appeared before his master, who inquired what was the matter, and how he came soused in so strange a pickle? Of his garbled reply, full of invective about the women, the Caliph comprehended not a word and obliged him to relate what had happened to him minutely. When he did understand, instead of sympathizing he laughed immoderately at the device of the swing and the figure of Bababalouk mounting upon it. The stung eunuch could scarcely preserve the semblance of respect. 'Ay laugh my lord! laugh,' he said, but 'I wish this Nouronihar would play some trick on you, she is too wicked to spare even majesty itself.' These words made for the present but a slight impression on the Caliph, but they not long after recurred to his mind.

KUBLA KHAN
Samuel Taylor Coleridge
(1772–1843)

Ten years after the first issue of Beckford's history of the Caliph Vathek, Samuel Taylor Coleridge wrote his well-known unfinished verses beginning 'In Xanadu did Kubla Khan . . .' They were not, however, published until 1816, but when they did appear the author wrote as follows:

The following fragment is here published at the request of a poet of great and deserved celebrity (Lord Byron), and, as far as the Author's own opinions are concerned, rather as a psychological curiosity, than on the ground of any supposed poetic merits.

In Xanadu did Kubla Khan
A stately pleasure-dome decree:
Where Alph, the sacred river, ran
Through caverns measureless to man
Down to a sunless sea.
So twice five miles of fertile ground
With walls and towers were girdled round:
And there were gardens bright with sinuous rills,
Where blossomed many an incense-bearing tree;
And here were forests ancient as the hills,
Enfolding sunny spots of greenery . . .

A damsel with a dulcimer
In a vision once I saw:
It was an Abyssinian maid,
And on her dulcimer she played,
Singing of Mount Abora.
Could I revive within me
Her symphony and song,
To such a deep delight 'twould win me,
That with music loud and long,
I would build that dome in air,
That sunny dome! those caves of ice!

And all who heard should see them there,
And all should cry, Beware! Beware!
His flashing eyes, his floating hair!
Weave a circle round him thrice,
And close your eyes with holy dread,
For he on honey-dew hath fed,
And drunk the milk of Paradise.

ORIENTAL ROMANCE

From *Lalla Rookh* by *Thomas Moore*

(1779–1852)

Thomas Moore, born the son of John Moore who kept a small shop in Dublin, must seem a rather unlikely candidate for success as a poet and socialite in London. It was in 1817, the year after Coleridge's *Kubla Khan* came out, that Moore's *Lalla Rookh, An Oriental Romance*, was published and became an immediate and great success. Seven editions were demanded in the first year of its printed existence. It was exactly suited to the taste of the day. Moreover, Moore had little about him to rouse envy among contemporary authors and critics; he came from a very poor background and his appearance was not striking, except that he was noticeably short.

    Lalla Rookh is in four parts, all purporting to be stories told by one Feramorz, a minstrel from Kashmir appointed as a special concession to entertain Lalla Rookh, youngest daughter of Aurungzebe, the Emperor of India, when she is sent on her long way from Delhi as bride-to-be of the young King of Lesser Bukharia. The bridgeroom would come out to meet her at Kashmir.

Ne'er did the march of Mahadi display
Such pomp before; not even when on his way
To Mecca's temple when both land and sea
Were spoiled to feed the pilgrim's luxury;
When round him 'mid the burning sands, he saw
Fruits of the North in icy freshness thaw
And cooled his thirsty lip, beneath the glow
of Mecca's sun, with urns of Persian snow:
Nor e'er did armament more grand than that
Pour from the Kingdoms of the Caliphat.
First, in the van, the People of the Rock,
On their light mountain steeds of royal stock;
Then Chieftains of Damascus, proud to see
The flashing of their swords' rich marquetry;

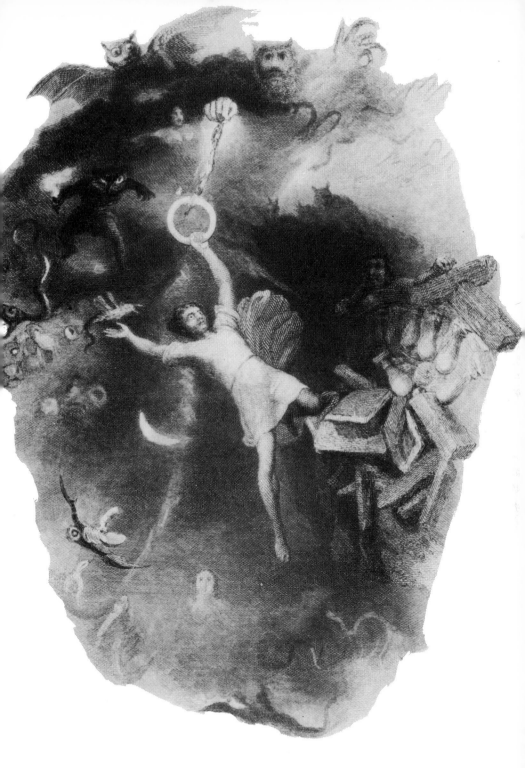

Engraving by E. Goodall for Thomas Moore's *The Epicurean*,
London, 1837. Made from a study for vignette by Turner, one
of thirteen such studies by the artist for Moore's book, nine of
which were deposited at the British Museum by Ruskin, bearing
the stricture 'Bad'

Men from the region near the Volga's mouth,
Mixed with the rude, black archers of the South;
And Indian lancers, in white turbaned ranks,
From the far Sinde, or Attack's sacred banks,
With dusky legions from the land of Myrrh,
And many a mace-armed Moor and Mid-sea Islander.

Nor less in number, though more new and rude
In warfare's school, was the vast multitude
That fired by zeal, or by oppression wronged,
Round the white standard of the Imposter thronged
Besides his thousands of believers, blind,
Burning, and headlong as the Samiel wind –
Many who felt and more who feared to feel
The bloody Islamite's converting steel,
Flocked to his banner:– Chiefs of the Uzbek race,
Waving their heron crests with martial grace;
Turkomans, countless as their flocks, led forth
From the aromatic pastures of the North;
Wild warriors of the turquoise hills, – and those
Who dwell beyond the everlasting snows
Of Hindoo Kosh, in stormy freedom bred,
Their fort the rock, their camp the torrent's bed.
But none, of all who owned the Chief's command,
Rushed to that battle-field with bolder hand
Or sterner hate than Iran's outlawed men,
Her worshippers of Fire-all panting then
For vengeance on the accursed Saracen;
Vengeance at last for their dear country spurned,
Her throne usurped, and her bright shrines o'erturned.
From Yezd's eternal Mansion of the Fire,
Where aged saints in dreams of heaven expire;
From Badku, and those fountains of blue flame
That burn into the Caspian, fierce they came,
Careless for what or whom the blow was sped
So vengeance triumphed, and their tyrants bled!

Such was the wild and miscellaneous host
That high in air their motley banners tost
Around the Prophet Chief – all eyes still bent
Upon that glittering veil, where'er it went.

AT THE PERSIAN COURT

From The Adventures of Hajji Baba by James Justinian Morier
(1780–1849)

Morier, a diplomatist, was British representative at the Persian Court from
1810 to 1816. Keenly observant and with a good sense of humour, he wrote
Hajji Baba of Ispahan (1824) and *The Adventures of Hajji Baba in England* (1828).
Some Persians are said to have believed that these satires so well displayed
the Persian mind that they could only have been written by a Persian. Five
years before he died at 24 Marine Parade, Brighton, Morier wrote and gave
in charity to the Sussex Hospital *An Oriental Tale,* its frontispiece by him
showing a galloping Turcoman.

It was just about this time, in September 1845, that three younger literary
men, W. M. Thackeray, W. E. Brookfield and Alexander Kinglake, author of
Eothen, were paying visits to Brighton. Thackeray had been in Constantinople
and Egypt in 1844, contributing to *Punch* about it; Kinglake's *Eothen,*
giving a light-hearted account of his own journey through Turkey a few
years earlier, had also come out in 1844.

It is not known that Morier met them, but it is quite possible as they were
staying not far away from him. Thackeray was engaged on *Vanity Fair* and,
according to Brookfield, was so pleased at finding that title for it that he
danced round his room.

In order to celebrate the success of the expedition, an entertainment
was given by the chief to the whole encampment. A large caldron
filled with rice, was boiled, and two sheep were roasted whole. Then
men, consisting of our chief's relations, who came from the surrounding tents, and most of whom had been at the attack of our
caravan, were assembled in one tent, whilst the women were collected
in another. After the rice and the sheep had been served up to the men,

Kurdish chiefs from James Morier's *A Second Journey through Persia*, etc., London, 1818

they were carried to the women, and when they had done, the shepherds' boys were served, and, after they had devoured their utmost, the bones and scrapings of dishes were given to us and the dogs. But, when I was waiting with great anxiety for our morsel, having scarcely tasted food since we were taken, I was secretly beckoned to by one of the women, who made me screen myself behind a tent, and setting down a dish of rice, with a bit of the sheep's tail in it, which was sent, she said, by the chief's wife, who pitied my misfortune, and bade me be of good courage, hurried away without waiting for my acknowledgments.

The day was passed by the men in smoking, and relating their adventures, and by the women in singing and beating the tambourine, whilst my poor master and I were left to ponder over our forlorn situation. The mark of favour which I had just received had set my imagination to work, and led me to consider my condition as not entirely desperate. But in vain I endeavoured to cheer up the spirits of my companion; he did not cease to bewail his hard fate. I brought to his mind that constant refuge of every true Mussulman in grief. 'Allah kerim! — God is merciful!' His answer was, 'Allah kerim, Allah kerim, is all very well for you who had nothing to lose; but in the meantime I am ruined for ever.' His greatest concern seemed to be the having failed to secure the profits which he had expected to make on his lamb-skins, and he passed all his time in calculating, to the utmost farthing, what had been his losses on this occasion. However, we were soon to be parted. He was sent off next day to the mountains, in charge of a string of fifty camels, with terrible threats from the chief that his nose and ears should pay for the loss of any one of them, and that if one died, its price should be added to the ransom-money which he hereafter expected to receive for him. As the last testimony of my affection for him, I made him sit down on a camel's pack-saddle, and, with some water from a neighbouring spring, and a piece of soap, which, together with my razors, I had saved from the wreck of our fortunes, shaved him in the face of the whole camp. I very soon found that this exhibition of my abilities and profession might be productive of the greatest advantage to my future prospects. Every fellow who had a head to scratch immediately found out that he wanted shaving, and my reputation soon reached the ears of the chief, who called me to him, and ordered me to operate upon him without loss of time. I soon went to work upon a large head that exhibited the marks of many a sword-cut, and which presented as rough a surface as that of the sheep-dogs aforementioned. He who had been accustomed to have his hair clipped, perhaps, with the same instrument that sheared his sheep, and who knew of no greater luxury than that of being mutilated by some country barber, felt himself in paradise under my hand. He freely expressed his satisfaction and his approbation of my services, said, on feeling his head, that I had shaved him two days' march under the skin, swore that he never would accept of any ransom for me, be it what it might, and that I should, henceforth, be entitled to the appointment of his own body barber. I leave the gentle reader to guess what were my feelings upon this occasion. Whilst I stooped down and kissed the knee of this my new master, with every appearance of gratitude and respect, I determined to make use of the liberty which the confidence reposed in me might afford, by running away on the very first favourable opportunity. From being so often near the person of the chief, I soon began to acquire great ascendency over him; and although I was still watched with care, yet I could already devise plans, which appeared to me to be practicable, for escaping from this hateful servitude into which I was thrown, and I felt in a less degree than another would have done the drudgery and wretchedness of my situation.

OF BEDOUINS AND WAHABYS

From Notes on the Bedouins and Wahabys by John Lewis Burckhardt
(1784-1817)

———◆———

Born in Lausanne and educated first in Germany and then at Cambridge, he became English by adoption; and so Jean Louis Burckhardt wrote in the English tongue and used the forenames John Lewis. He was a scholar among explorers, observing acutely and reporting with care. He went to the holy cities of the Hijaz in 1814, five years after leaving Cambridge for the Orient at the behest of the Association for Promoting the Discovery of the Interior of Africa.

———◆———

GHALEB, SHERIF OF MEKKA, AND THE TURKISH PASHA OF BAGHDAD, AT WAR WITH THE WAHABYS — THE HOLY CITIES, MEKKA AND MEDINAH, TAKEN BY THE WAHABYS

During my residence in Arabia I made repeated inquiries after a written history of the Wahabys, thinking it probable that some learned man of Mekka or Medinah might have composed such a work; but my search proved fruitless. Nobody takes notes of daily occurrences, and the dates of them are soon forgotten. Some few persons, well informed of what has passed in their own neighbourhood, know but little of distant transactions; and before a complete and satisfactory account of the Wahaby affairs could be compiled, it would be necessary to make a journey through every part of Arabia.

Baghdad, from its vicinity to Nedjd, the centre of the Wahaby dominion, is, under present circumstances, the place where probably the most accurate statements might be collected.

I shall here give but few details respecting the history of this extra-ordinary people before the Turks re-conquered Hedjaz; an event which I can describe with more accuracy, having myself resided in that country while the war still continued.

The Wahabys had for nearly thirty years established their doctrines, made numerous proselytes, and successively conquered Nedjd and subdued most of the great Bedouin tribes, who feed their cattle there in spring and retreat afterwards to the Desert. Yet war had not been declared, nor did the Wahabys encroach upon the rights of the two governments nearest to them; that of Baghdad on the north, and that of Hedjaz towards the south. The pilgrim-caravans passed from Damascus and from Baghdad without any molestation through their territory. Their increase of power, and the assiduity with which they propagated their doctrines, seem first to have excited the jealousy of Sherif Ghaleb. Under his authority, and partly under his influence, were placed all the tribes settled in Hedjaz, and several on the fron-tiers of that country. The attempts made by Abd el Azyz to gain over these latter to his party after he had subjugated their neigh-bours, could not be viewed with indifference by Ghaleb, whom we may consider rather as a powerful Bedouin sheikh than an eastern prince; and the same causes that produce constant wars between all great neighbouring tribes of the Desert, sowed the seeds of contest between him and the Wahabys. A few years after his succession to the government of Mekka, Ghaleb first engaged in open hostility with the Wahabys, about the year 1792 or 1793. This warfare he continued until the final surrender of Mekka . . .

When all the cats and dogs of Mekka had been devoured, and the Sherif's provisions became scarce, he left the town with his own people, carrying off the whole of his family and baggage, having previously set fire to such furniture of his palace as was not easily portable. He retired to Djidda, and Mekka was left to its fate. On the next morning the chief inhabitants went out to capitulate, or rather, to surrender at discretion; and Saoud entered on the same day. These events occurred in April and May, 1803. The Mekkans still remember with gratitude the excellent discipline observed by these wild Wahabys on their entering the town. Not the slightest excess was committed. On the next day all the shops were opened by order of Saoud, and every article which his troops required was purchased with ready money. Saoud declared that he might have taken the town by assault long before, but that he wished to avoid disorder and excesses; and he told the olemas in full council that he had seen Mohammed in a dream, who threatened him that he should not survive three days if a single grain of corn were forcibly taken from the holy city.

The people of Mekka now became Wahabys; that is, they were obliged to pray more punctually than usual, to lay aside and conceal their fine silk dresses, and to desist from smoking in public. Heaps of Persian pipes, collected from all the houses, were burnt before Saoud's head-quarters, and the sale of tobacco was forbidden. The brother of Ghaleb, Abd el Mayen, was placed by Saoud at the head of the Mekkan government; and a learned man from Derayeh, called Ibn Name, was appointed kady of the town. So upright was this Bedouin judge that his sentences have become almost proverbial, and the Mekkans now say in derision of their venal Constantinopolitan kady 'There goes Ibn Name!' At this time the prayers for the sultan, usually recited in the grand mosque, were abolished.

From Mekka Saoud turned his arms against Djidda, where Sherif Ghaleb had taken refuge. The town was besieged for eleven days, but the inhabitants fought bravely; and Saoud, despairing of being able to force the walls, retreated. Many persons affirm that Ghaleb, who had made preparations on board a large ship in the harbour, for escaping by sea, induced Saoud to retire, by a bribe of fifty thousand dollars. The Wahabys now moved back towards the Northern Desert. Ghaleb issued from Djidda, and resumed the government of Mekka (in July 1803), where the small Wahaby garrisons of the two castles capitulated, and Abd el Mayen, a man of peaceable character, again submitted to his brother; but Ghaleb himself, soon after, knowing that he could not defend the place for any time, compromised with Saoud, and surrendered to that Wahaby chief. The details of this war, although it had occurred only eleven years before my travels in Hedjaz, were related to me with different circumstances, by various persons.

Ghaleb enjoyed, on this occasion, more favourable conditions than those usually granted to other proselyte chiefs. He was left in possession of his towns and their incomes. Several Bedouin tribes were permitted to remain under his influence; and in consideration of his high station, and the respect due to those who inhabited the holy city, neither himself, nor the Mekkans, were required to pay tribute to the great chief. On the other hand, the Sherif renounced the custom duties at Djidda from all true Wahabys.

The capture of Mekka was the signal for other advantages in Hedjaz. The tribe of Harb was obliged to yield, but not without a severe contest, which so exasperated the Wahabys, that they treated them more rigorously than any other Bedouins of the country. A branch of the Harbs, called Beni Sobh, successfully maintained themselves in their steep mountains, and were never reduced to submission. Yembo surrendered when the Beni Harb and Djeheyny (another large tribe of that neighbourhood) had joined the Wahaby party; and Medinah soon after (early in the spring of 1804) followed its example. The principal man of this city, Hassan el Kaladjy, had usurped a despotic power, and been guilty of the greatest injustice during the general distress, while all supplies were withholden from the town by the Wahabys. He at last seized upon the treasure attached to the tomb of Mohammed, and divided part of it among his adherents; after which, he proposed to surrender. The inhabitants of Medinah who are much more inclined to the Turkish interest than the Mekkans, and live wholly upon the profits derived from those who visit their mosque, were not so leniently treated as the people of Mekka had been. The usual tribute was required, but private property was not plundered. The chief Turkish officer of the town, the Aga el Haram (appointed by the sultan), was obliged to leave Medinah, with many Turkish hadjys; and El Medheyan, whom the Wahaby chief had nominated sheikh of the whole tribe of Harb, was appointed governor of Medinah.

Here the Wahabys enforced, with great strictness, the regular observance of prayers. The names of all the adult male inhabitants were called over in the mosque after morning, mid-day, and evening prayers; and those who did not obey the call were punished. A respectable woman, accused of having smoked the Persian pipe, was placed upon a jack-ass, with the pipe suspended from her neck, round which was twisted the long flexible tube, or snake; in this state she was paraded through the town. Hassan el Kaladjy still retained some influence under the Wahabys, and continued to annoy the inhabitants.

Saoud soon after visited Medinah, and stripped Mohammed's tomb of all the valuable articles that it still possessed (the gold vessels had been previously taken away). He also endeavoured to destroy the high dome erected over the tomb, and would not allow Turkish pilgrims to approach Medinah from any quarter; and several of them, who attempted to pass from Yembo to the town, were ill treated; their beards also were cut off, as the Wahabys, who themselves have short scanty beards, declared, that the prophet did not wear so long and bushy a beard as those of the northern Turks. This was done by the low classes of Wahabys in derision of the Turks, and not in obedience to any law, or command.

The Wahabys, however, continued always to visit Medinah in honour of Mohammed; and they paid a devout visit also to the mosque of that prophet, but not, like other Muselmans, to his tomb, situated in that mosque. The tomb was left uninjured; but Saoud regarded as idolatrous any visits, prayers, or exclamations, addressed to it, and therefore he prohibited them. But it is false to assert, as the Turks have done, that the pilgrimage to Medinah was abolished by the Wahabys . . .

While Medinah was compelled to admit within its gates the northern Wahabys, those of the south were not idle in extending the influence of their arms . . .

Although Hedjaz was now conquered, the Sherif's power continued to be very great. His name and venerable office, his great talents for intrigue, and his personal influence over many Bedouin tribes, that still resisted the authority of Saoud, and the valuable presents made to the latter, whenever he visited Mekka, caused the Wahaby chief to connive at several of Ghaleb's proceedings. When Saoud approached Mekka for the annual pilgrimage (which he regularly performed, with great numbers of his Arabs), a whole caravan of camels, loaded with presents from the Sherif, came to meet him at Zeyme, two days distant from the city. The presents comprised all sorts of choice provisions, clothes, and other articles, besides several camel-loads of Indian muslin, to serve for the *ihram*, or mantle, in which the pilgrims enter the sacred territory. All his officers received similar presents. The women and children had all new suits of clothes, and quantities of sweetmeats. Such, indeed, was the liberality of Ghaleb on these occasions, that Saoud often said, it made him blush, and rendered it impossible for him to treat the Sherif as he otherwise should have done . . .

The Wahabys did not refuse to admit pilgrims from all quarters into the holy cities; they had often publicly offered to allow their peaceable passage should they behave with decorum, and not assume any airs of supremacy in these countries, which the natural disposition and character of their inhabitants, as well their geographical position, had made an Arabian and not a Turkish province. After Mekka and Medinah had yielded to the Wahabys, after the Sherif himself had become a proselyte to their faith, and acted in open hostility against the Porte, and all Hedjaz followed his example, the most natural measure that presented itself was to cut off any further supplies, by shutting the ports of Cosseir and Suez against all Hedjaz shipping. That such a step was not taken during the Mammelouk reign, when no general measure could ever be carried into effect in Egypt, where, besides, those Beys whose influence predominated, derived considerable profits from the Hedjaz trade, will not surprise us. But one might reasonably wonder at the neglect of this prohibitory system, under the government of Mohammed Aly, who, since 1805, possessed the port of Suez, and since 1808 that of Cosseir; and who had promised in the strongest terms, to his sovereign, that he would rescue Hedjaz from the Wahabys.

During all that time, and even in the beginning of 1810, when Mohammed Aly made serious preparations for attacking the Wahabys, there were daily arrivals at Suez and Cosseir of ships from Djidda and Yembo, which went back loaded with corn and provisions for the Sherif, as well as for private adventurers; nor was that traffic discontinued until a few months before the sailing of the first expedition from Suez against Arabia, when fears were entertained of the ships being seized in that port for the conveyance of troops. To withhold all supplies from Hedjaz for a single year, would have produced most alarming consequences in that country, where it is usual to lay by provisions for more than two months; and the scanty supplies brought from Nedjd and Yemen could not have prevented a famine. Had this actually occurred, the Wahaby chief would certainly have been induced to make terms with the governor of Egypt, highly in favour of the hadj, and of the whole Turkish empire.

RESIDENT
OF BAGHDAD

From Narrative of a
Residence in Koordistan
by Claudius James Rich
(1787-1821)

In 1783, seven years after Carsten Niebuhr had published his speculative
account of the ruins of Persepolis and of the indecipherable cylindrical seals
he had picked up on his travels, the Honourable East India Company
appointed a permanent agent in Baghdad. In 1808, galvanized by the
Napoleonic wars and the increasing interest of France in the Near East, the
Company sent one of the finest of its officers to occupy its Residency in the
ancient capital of the Abbasids at the heart of Turkish Arabia, Claudius
James Rich.

Rich was born near Dijon in Burgundy in 1787 and was taken as an infant
to Bristol in England. He had no formal schooling but was instructed in
Greek and Latin by a relative. He taught himself several modern languages
with the aid only of books, and at the age of eight or nine he saw some
Arabic manuscripts at the home of a friend of his family. Thus was born the
supreme enthusiasm of his life and he quickly learnt to read and write the
language with fluency, assisted in his studies by nothing more than a
dictionary and grammar. By the time he was fifteen he had mastered Hebrew,
Syriac, Chaldaean, Persian and Turkish, as well as Arabic, and had begun to
unravel the Chinese language. At the age of sixteen, courted by businessmen
and academics alike and with a number of careers open to him, he sought a
cadetship in the East India Company. 'Let me but get to India, leave the rest
to me,' he said.

He was recommended to the directors of the Company by the
distinguished linguist Sir Charles Wilkins as 'a person of such singular and
rare talents, as would amply justify and do honour to any exertion of your
patronage'. The young man left England in 1804 to join Sir James
Mackintosh, the Recorder of Bombay. He travelled by way of Cairo to the
Persian Gulf, passing through Palestine and Syria in the protective disguise
of a Mameluk, and sailed to Bombay from Basra in 1807. Soon after his
arrival Sir James wrote:

'He far surpassed our expectations, and we soon considered his wonderful oriental attainments as the least part of his merit. I found him a fair classical scholar, and capable of speaking and writing French and Italian like the best educated native. With the strongest recommendations of appearance and manner, he joined every elegant accomplishment and every manly exercise; and combined with them, spirit, pleasantry, and feeling. His talents and attainments delighted me so much, that I resolved to make him a philosopher . . .'

On his return from a brief journey Mackintosh discovered that the pupil in philosophy he had left behind in Bombay was desirous of the hand of his daughter Mary. *'He had no fortune, nor had he then even an appointment, but you will not doubt that I willingly consented to his marriage with my eldest daughter, in whom he had the sagacity to discover, and the virtue to value, the plain sense, modesty, purity, and good nature, which will, I hope, make her a source of happiness to him . . .'*

In January 1808 Rich and his wife set out for the Pashalik of Baghdad. He was twenty-one when he arrived at Basra to be received with ceremony by Samuel Manesty, the Company's Resident there, and thence to make his way to Baghdad with wife and retinue aboard the Residency yacht. He made his entry in style, with Sepoy guard, Mary carried on a mule-borne palankeen, a long line of Armenian servants bringing up the rear. Thus began an association of Britishers with Baghdad and the Asiatic dominions of Turkey which was to bring honour to them and their countrymen, and to command the respect of oppressed and oppressor alike.

He subdued Turkish Pashas and gave succour to the poor and ill-used among the subject people of the Porte. Turks, Kurds, Armenians and Arabs respected him equally for the force of his personality and the brilliance of his mind. He left to his successors a note on the handling of the Ottoman, and oriental despots in general:

'Nothing but the most decisive conduct will do; any other will increase the insolence of his disposition . . .'

In 1820 he set out with his wife and a massive caravan of soldiers and servants to tour the little-known territory of Kurdistan, noting as he went every detail of his long and arduous journey. He returned to Baghdad a year later but he was not to survive long enough to publish an account of his travels, which was issued posthumously in 1836 as the *Narrative of a Residence in Koordistan and on the Site of Ancient Nineveh* with a journal of a Voyage Down the Tigris to Baghdad, and an account of a visit to Shirauz and Persepolis.

———————

May 8.—We marched at forty minutes past five, and pursuing our way gently along the foot of the hills, with much ascending and descending, we arrived at our camp before Sulimania at forty minutes

past six, where I was received by several Koordish gentlemen belonging to Mahmood Pasha, who, having made their compliments,
immediately went away, except two who were left to attend on us.
We had anticipated some trouble from the crowd, the Koords being
celebrated starers, and we the first European party most of them had
ever seen here: not a soul, however, appeared, except those who were
on duty. This, I understood, proceeded from an order of Mahmood
Pasha's, strictly enjoining the Koords to give us no trouble. I had but
little rest to-day, and the draft on my spirits was rather more than
they could answer. I had scarcely sat down in my tent, when in came
an express Tartar from Constantinople. I had rather he had shown
himself at any other time; especially as, bringing the news of the
king's death, it was requisite to forward on the dispatches immediately.

I had scarcely recovered from the arrival of the Tartar, when my
old friend, Abdullah Pasha's chief officer, arrived; and he again was
succeeded by Mahmood Masraff, the prime minster of the Pasha of
Sulimania–a very celebrated character in Koordistan, of whom I
had often heard at Baghdad. He came with the information that his
master himself was coming at *aasser* [afternoon prayer], to pay me
the first visit, and welcome me himself to his country. This was quite
an unlooked-for honour, and was a great proof of his friendly and
hospitable disposition. I had not expected even that he would return
my visit; but coming himself to me in the first instance I had considered as totally out of the question.

I accordingly made the best preparations my situation would
admit of to receive Mahmood Pasha; and shortly after *aasser* his
approach was announced. The sight was a gay and barbaric one. He
alone was on horseback; and, being a very small man, was almost
hid by the crowd of tall Koords, habited in every colour of the
rainbow, but chiefly in pink, yellow, and scarlet, which hues especially
made up the tassels and fringes which covered their heads. The march
was silent, and yet their tread was heard from afar. When my guard
saluted, the Pasha immediately returned them the compliment, by
laying his hand on his breast with considerable dignity. I sent my
tchaoushes to meet him, and advanced myself beyond the door of the
tent to receive him. As soon as he saw me, he alighted from his
horse, his tchaoushes shouting out; and shaking hands with me with
both his hands, we came into the tent, and sat down together on
a shawl, which I had prepared for the occasion. It was with difficulty,

and only after some time, that I could persuade him to adopt the easier mode of sitting and crossing his legs; he wished to persist in the more respectful and difficult attitude of kneeling, resting on his heels. He welcomed me again and again to Koordistan, assured me that the country was mine, and many other such Eastern compliments. Many civil things, of course, passed – on his part in apologies for his country, and on mine in praise of it. I at least was sincere; for I really was charmed with the verdant hills, and delighted to be out of Baghdad. I then gave him the Pasha of Baghdad's message, which, being a very civil one, I took care to deliver audibly before all his attendants, and he seemed sensible of the attention. He spoke of the state of the country; exposed the difficulties with which he had to contend, in being placed on the frontiers of two rival powers, one of which never ceased persecuting him for contributions – the other, his natural sovereigns, that is the Turks, insisted that he should neither serve nor pay Persia; and yet Turkey was neither able nor willing to defend him, when the Shahzadeh of Kermanshah carried on his exactions by force. He pointed out the pernicious way in which this combination operated on the prosperity of the country, in a modest and sensible manner; and expressed his wish of adhering with fidelity to the cause of the Pasha of Baghdad. I believe, in fact, that personally he is well inclined to the Turks from religious prejudices; but it is easy to see that their cause is not very popular, and that the generality here have neither respect nor confidence in the Ottomans; nor do they deserve it. Their political conduct is blind, arrogant, and treacherous. With a little prudence and conciliation, and by a skilful application to the Sunite feelings of the bigoted Koords, who detest the Persian sect, they might have attached firmly to them a brave and numerous people – who possess the most important lines of their frontier – and who, at particular moments, might turn the scale in favour of the power whose cause they espoused. There is at present a game going on, the intricacies of which it would be difficult thoroughly to unravel; but it is evident that it is a kind of *ruse contre ruse* affair. The Pasha of Baghdad is endeavouring to cheat the Pasha of Koordistan and the Shahzadeh of Kermanshah – while the Shahzadeh is cheating both the Pasha of Baghdad and the Pasha of Koordistan; and all of them, both collectively and severally, are endeavouring to cheat the Porte, who will unquestionably come off worst of the whole set, and who in everything contrives to make herself the common enemy. With this, however, I had nothing to do.

The situation I held obliged me to uphold Turkey, at least negatively, which in my answer I endeavoured to do. The Pasha, after a short silence, and I thought as if he were really affected, then said, 'My father, of blessed memory, loved you much; he would have rejoiced to have seen this day, which he often anticipated; and I could have wished it had been he who received you, instead of me.' I answered, that Abdurrahman Pasha was a much-esteemed friend of mine, and that I greatly respected his memory; but that his place was worthily filled. A due allowance of callioons having been smoked, sherbet, incense, and rose-water were brought; and he retired in the same manner as he had come. Before he took his leave, he told me that, if it were agreeable to me, he would wish me to enter Sulimania the day after to-morrow, at 9 a.m. I perceived at once that he had an astrological superstition about this, which, of course, I indulged him in.

Six months later Rich approached the site of biblical Nineveh, near the modern city of Mosul. Here in Mesopotamia (Assyria) and at the southern sites of Babylonia earlier travellers had noted the mounds and bricks and plaster-work suggestive of great antiquity, but none had so far looked with as much precision or zeal as was shown by Mr Rich. Already scholars were at work in France, Denmark and Germany in an attempt to translate the wedge-shaped script with which the tantalizing bricks and tablets of Assyria and Babylon were inscribed. Rich intended to transmit his findings to the young Professor Grotefend who was working on the translation of the 'cuneiform' at Göttingen, but that was not to be. In October he arrived at the mound of Arbil:

October 27. – I was up by peep of day, and began my operations immediately. I first went to the old minaret, which is the most conspicuous object in this neighbourhood. The mosque to which it belonged is quite in ruins, and bricks are dug up on its site all around. The minaret is by measurement one hundred and twenty-one feet high. The circumference of the shaft is fifty-one feet. It stands on an octagonal base, each face of which is nine feet eleven inches, and the height of the base is between thirty and forty feet. Two stairs wind, without communicating, up to the gallery, which is destroyed, as well as all above it, except two small fragments of brick-work, the remains of the shaft which once rose above the gallery. It is in the style of the minaret at Taouk, and is apparently of the age of the Caliphs, or rather perhaps of the Sahibs of Arbil. All around are ruins, or rather heaps of rubbish, like those in the ruins of Old Baghdad. Remains of the wall and ditch are also traceable, especially on the side where our camp is situated, which is pitched close to it. The town was once evidently very large, probably about the size of modern Baghdad. Arbil is situated at the foot of the artificial mount, principally on the south side, and contains a bath, caravanserais, and bazaars . . .

From here we went on to the mosque which covers the tomb of Jonah, or Nubi Jonas, at Mosul. It is on the north and higher end of the mound, and is rather a considerable building. The principal dome is ribbed and of a conical shape; it stands on an octagonal base, eight feet each face, which is again placed on a square pediment, standing on the terrace that covers the building. The dome is of small circumference, whitened, and crowned with a spike. The terrace, or flat roof, is about fifteen feet above the level of the mound on the south side, but on the north it rises forty feet by measurement above the mound, about thirty feet perpendicular height of which remains between the foot of the wall, and level of the plain or area above Nineveh; so that the perpendicular height of the highest part of the mound above the level of the plain is about fifty feet . . .

From the terrace of the mosque is an admirable view of Mosul. The whole population of the town assembled to gaze at us, but none offered the least molestation, though some of them were heard opining that I was ascertaining if great guns would bear upon Mosul from that position.

We afterwards rode through the area of Nineveh to the first wall of the enclosure. It is a line of earth and gravel, out of which large hewn stones are dug, as out of all the walls of the area. Beyond this is a ditch, still very regular, and easily traceable, on the other side of which is another wall. Under this wall is the well of Damlamajeh, noticed before; and beyond it, leaving only a narrow ravine or ditch, there is still another, and, I believe, the largest wall . . .

The area of Nineveh, on a rough guess, is about one and a half to two miles broad, and four miles long, extending a little way south of Nebbi Yunus. On the river, or west side, there are only remains of one wall, and I observed the same at the north and south extremities; but on the east side there are the remains of three walls . . .

From Nebbi Yunus, Rich went to the neighbouring mound of Kouyunjik.

The Mount of Kouyunjik is, except at its west and part of its eastern face, of rather an irregular form. Its sides are very steep, its top nearly flat; its angles are not marked by any lantern or turret. The perpendicular height is forty-three feet; the total circumference 7691 feet.

The top of the mount does not wear the appearance of ever having been greatly higher than it is at present; but it evidently has had building on it, at least round its edges. Stones and bricks are dug or ploughed up every where. There were also other buildings farther in the mount; and at a place where they had been digging into it, we saw the same coarse stone and mortar masonry, and a piece of coarse grey stone, shaped like the capital of a column, such as at this day surmounts the wooden pillars or posts of Turkish or rather Persian verandahs; but there was no carving on it. We also saw, in many parts, a flooring, or pavement, on the surface of the mount, of small stones rammed down with earth. Pottery we also found, and other Babylonian fragments; also bits of brick, with bitumen adhering to them; and I am informed that many bricks with bitumen are found in these ruins. A piece of fine brick or pottery, covered with exceedingly small and beautful cuneiform writing, was found while we were looking about the mount. It is of the finest kind, yellowish, with a polished or hard surface, and apparently belonged to one of the large cylinders. On the north-east angle of the mound is the little village of Kouyunjik. Some part of the surface of the mound, probably where the buildings were either less solid or perhaps entirely wanting, is ploughed over ...

We now went along the wall in a north-west direction on horse-back, till we came to a part of it higher and broader externally than the rest. Here, some years ago, an immense bas-relief, representing men and animals, covering a grey stone of the height of two men, was dug up from a spot a little above the surface of the ground. All the town of Mousul went out to see it, and in a few days it was cut up or broken to pieces. I picked up at this place a piece of a cornice of gypsum, or what is called Mousul marble.

Hence we went along the wall to another high mount on the wall, like the one we had last observed. Here were some ruins, or inequalities of the ground, stretched north-west into the area of the city; but I am inclined to believe they are only inequalities. All the area from the commencement of this inequality up to the east wall is higher and not so smooth as the western part of it. We continued riding along the wall, which here was high and steep, to the place where the Khausser runs through it, and where is a mount on which

I fixed as one of my stations for observations. It does not seem to have been broken; and on the banks of the Khausser here, and also a little higher up, is some stone-work, which may have been part of a pier or bridge.

On the outside of the wall, as far round as the last mount but one, the country is hilly, or perhaps it would be more correct to say, unequal; and thereabouts it runs off to form the high bank of the river . . .

November 11. — There was some rain in the night but not enough to spoil my day's work. I therefore went out at the usual time . . . I went round the southern part of Nineveh, sketched the country, and took the remaining angles . . .

As I proposed to devote a day entirely to the inspection of Nineveh beyond the wall, and was besides anxious to take the angles at the base while there was good light to see my distant signals, I returned to the inclosure to take my last station, remarking on my way several stones which had been dug out of the wall or elevation under which the well is situated, between it and the inclosure wall. Most of these stones seem to be of the same kind, that is, a coarser kind of Mousul marble or gypsum, of a grey colour. I also observed sandstone cut into blocks. Most of the stones dug up were of enormous dimensions.

On 1 March 1821, after visiting the Nestorian Christians and the so-called 'devil worshippers' of Yezid in the Zakho mountains of Kurdistan, Rich noted in his diary:

Kosrou Effendi, who is most excellent authority, tells me to-day that Bekir Effendi, when digging for stones to build the bridge of Mousul, found on digging into the Koyunjuk a sepulchral chamber in which was an inscription; and in the chamber, among rubbish and fragments of bone, the following articles: a woman's khalkhal, or ankle bracelet, of silver covered with a turquoise-coloured rest; a hejil of gold; ditto a child's; a bracelet of gold beads quite perfect; some pieces of engraved agate. All these articles, and the chamber in which they were found, were seen and handled by Kosrou Effendi. The gold and silver were melted down immediately, the agates were thrown away, and the chamber broken up by the stones being taken out and then buried in the rubbish.

On his arrival back in Baghdad in 1821, Rich decided to take up an important post that had been offered him in Bombay. Before he left, however, the Turkish Pasha ordered his troops to make a sudden and unprovoked attack on the British Residency. Rich led his Indian troops in a counter attack and taught the Ottoman soldiers a salutary lesson. The Resident decided to complain to the government in London through the ambassador at Constantinople and to await Turkish reparation. Meanwhile he went down to Basra and saw his wife Mary off to Bombay. In the interval of diplomatic exchange he decided to visit Shiraz and the tomb of Cyrus at Persepolis. As he arrived in the old Persian capital an epidemic of cholera broke out. In a matter of a few days, 6,000 people had died. Every Persian nobleman and official left the place, but Rich stayed to comfort the sick and to calm the population, visiting the dying and administering drugs to those who might benefit from them. But by then the disease was in his own veins. He died on 5 October 1821, and was buried in the royal garden of Shiraz, where a grateful Persian population in a final tribute erected a monument to his memory. He was thirty-four years of age. His epitaph was written by a friend: '*Never did the British character attain so high a degree of eminence in Turkish Arabia, as when he presided in Baghdad.*'

A SAINT
IN BAGHDAD

From A Memoir of the late
A. N. Groves by Rev. A. J. Scott
(1795 – 1853)

———◆———

If faith and prayer and goodness are rewarded in that life which follows death, Anthony Norris Groves, nineteenth-century missionary of the Established Church, must surely occupy a privileged place in Heaven. A few pages from his diary of the year 1831 tell all that need be told of his ordeals, and of the conviction which supported him at a time of almost unimaginable adversity.

———◆———

The first entry Mr Groves makes in the Journal for 1831, the second year of his residence in Baghdad, is about the Lord's goodness in providing for their wants, he says, 'I have this day settled all my accounts, and find, after everything is paid, including the expenses of my baggage from Bushire, and of the house and school for another year, that our little stock will last us, with the Lord's blessing, two months longer, and then we know not whence we are to be supplied, but the Lord does not allow us to be anxious; He has so wonderfully provided for us hitherto, that it would be most ungrateful to have an anxious thought. Even for my baggage, Major Taylor only allowed me to pay half the charge, and he has, moreover, told me, that should I at any time want money, only to let him know and he will lend it me. Now, really to find such kind and generous friends, is more than we could have hoped, but thus the Lord deals with us, and takes away our fears. That we may many times be in straits, I have no doubt, but the time of our necessity will be the time for the manifestation of our Lord's providential love and munificence.'

'*March* 13*th*. – A Jew came to borrow an Arabic Bible from me which I let him have. Another Jew was with me yesterday who translated the Hebrew into Arabic very tolerably; but generally they only learn to read, without understanding the language.

'An Armenian Priest has just come to ask for four or five Armenian Bibles, to send to some villages between Hamadan and Teheraun. This is a plan we like better than sending many to one place, not only as spreading knowledge further, but also from the greater probability of their being read.'

Of the goodness of the Lord in appearing for them, and providing beforehand for their wants, Mr Groves writes:

'God our Father has most marvellously eased our way, and so great has been the kindness of our friend here, that he would do anything he could for us. He even told me the other day never to let our work stand still for want of funds, for should I want any he would gladly supply me, and lend me for my personal wants whatever I might need. Now when we consider there is but one English family now resident in Baghdad besides our own, how like the Lord's acting it is to make them willing to supply the necessary help. Not only does the Lord give us the necessary means, He does not even allow us, when our little fund gets low, to know the anxiety of expecting, or thinking what we should do. And surrounded as we have been these many months, by the alarm of war, and the fear of plague or cholera, even our dear native islands have not been without their anxieties; but I have been much struck of late with the peculiar dealings of God towards His chosen; as of old the pillar that was all darkness to the enemy was light to the church in the wilderness, so now this dark cloud, the darkness of which may be felt, which is spreading from one end of the Christian and Mohammedan world to the other, has towards the church in her pilgrimage its full, steady, bright light surmounted by "Behold he cometh!" Blessed assurance! But a little day of toil, and then we shall come with Him, or rise to join His assembled saints, dressed all anew with our house from heaven, that spiritual clothing meet for the new creature in Christ Jesus. O, what glorious liberty we are heirs to, as children of God, one day to love the Eternal Father, Son, and Spirit, with unalloyed affections, when our whole nature shall be again on the side of God, and not a place left for the enemy to put his foot to harass the heir of glory . . . '

'*April 7th.* – We thought the Lord had removed the sword from us, but we hear it is now near at hand; and the plague seems extending, or every one is running away. Sometimes, on looking round on our dear little circle, the old, heavy, faithless flesh would seek its quiet, sheltered retreat under the lofty elms at Exeter, but the Lord never allows the spirit for one moment to desire otherwise than to wait,

and see the salvation of our God, who will for His name's sake do
wonderfully for us that our hearts may rejoice in Him. We hear the
enemy is within three days of the city, and the Pasha is going out
with all his Harem, whether to contend or fly we do not know, but
we think from his character, the latter; but where will he fly? If
he flies with gold, there are those who will plunder him; if he flies
without, he cannot stir a step. In fact, in the moment his affairs are
actually sinking, all the miserable elements of his present compara-
tive strength turn against him.

'*April 9th*. – Stillness continues to prevail over the city, like the calm
which precedes a convulsion; our neighbours are preparing for defence, by getting armed men into their houses, but we sit down under
the shadow of the Almighty's wings, fully assured that in His name
we shall boast ourselves. The Pasha, however, has not gone out as
he intended yesterday. We have just heard that the reports of the
plague have stopped for a little the approach of his enemies; still
every thing is exceedingly unsettled. He is going to shut himself up
in the citadel till the answer to his overtures comes from Constantinople, but all those about him are against him, and wishing for the
arrival of his enemies. About fifty went out the other day and seized
on Hillah,* but they were driven out.

'*April 10th*. – The Lord has in many respects this day altered our
position here. One of Major Taylor's sepoys has died of the plague,
and now four of the servants are attacked. This has so alarmed Major
T. and the family, that they are immediately going off to a country
house, built by order of the Government of Bombay, for the Resident, in the neighbourhood of Bussorah, and they may or may not
return to this place. They have kindly offered us an asylum with
them, and a passage in their boat. Having no immediate occupation
here at present, I feel quite free to accept it, but there are considera-
tions that prevent us. Hitherto the Lord has kept us safe, and no
symptom of plague has appeared in our dwelling, though it is all

*Hillah is a small town on the river Euphrates, a little below the ruins of Babylon.
It was built in the year 495 of the Hegira, or 1115 of the Christian era, in a district
called by the natives El Aredh Babel; its population does not exceed six or seven
thousand, and consists of Arabs and Jews, there being no Christians, and only
such Turks as are employed in the Government. The inhabitants bear a very bad
character. The air is salubrious, and the soil extremely fertile, producing great
quantities of rice, dates, and grain of different kinds, though it is not cultivated to
above half the degree of which it is susceptible. — See Mr Rich's Memoirs on the
Ruins of Babylon.

around us. We cannot move without coming in contact with numbers of people for many days, and being shut up in a small boat with the Arab sailors; and even the very plague we may leave this city to avoid may have reached Bussorah before we could arrive there, as thousands have already set off from hence for that place; besides which, should it be the Lord's pleasure that the plague terminate soon, and we then wish to return, it may be many months before we may meet with an opportunity. The only advantage seems to be, that we should thus be apparently further removed from those troubles which seem likely to arise in the threatened attempt to depose this Pasha; yet, on the whole, we feel we may hold on with the Lord's blessing; but if we were once to leave our present post, it might be very difficult to regain it.

'As to the numbers of those who have died of the plague, on this side of the river alone, in little more than one fortnight, all agree in making it about 7,000. The poor inhabitants know not what to do: if they remain in the city, they die of the plague; if they leave it, they fall into the hands of the Arabs, who strip them of everything, or they are exposed to the effects of the inundation of the Tigris, which has now overflown the whole country around Baghdad, and destroyed, they say, 2,000 houses on the other side of the river, but I think this must be exaggerated: the misery of this place, however, is now beyond expression, and may yet be expected to be much greater. Dreadful as the outward circumstances of this people are, their moral condition is infinitely worse; nor does there seem to be a ray of light amidst it all. The Mohammedans look on those who die of the plague as martyrs, and no wailing is made for them, so that amidst all these desolations there is a stillness, which when one knows the cause, is very frightful.

'*April* 12*th*. – I have just taken leave of the kind T.'s. The accounts of the deaths are truly terrific; they say, the day before yesterday 1,200 died; and yesterday, Major T.'s man of business obtained a statement that they amounted to 1,040 on this side of the river. If this can be relied on, the mortality within and without the city must be truly appalling, and should it not please the Lord soon to stay the destroying angel's hand, the whole country must become one wide waste. Some very kind Armenians have offered to provide what is necessary for our journey to Damascus, if we will go with them. The possibility of meeting our dear brethren is a great temptation, but still we do not see clearly our permission to go, and the Lord has given us all such perfect peace in staying, and such perfect health, that we are even unwilling to go; we remain therefore and rest upon our Lord's love, which we feel assured will be manifested towards us amidst this scene of death; and afterwards we shall see why we remained more clearly perhaps than now.

'*April* 13*th*. – The plague has just entered our neighbour's dwelling, where they have collected together nearly thirty persons, not simply their own family. It seems as if a spirit of infatuation had seized them, for instead of making their number as small as possible, they seem to congregate as many as they can.

'O, what a blessed portion is ours, to have the God of Israel and His unchangeable promises for our sure and abiding place of rest – our little sanctuary unto which we may always resort! Yea, in the secret of His pavillion He will hide us.

'*April* 14*th*. – This is a day of awful visitation. The accounts of deaths yesterday vary from 1,000 to 1,500; and to-day, they say, is worse than any, and the increase in the numbers of deaths does not include the immense multitudes who are dying without the city. One of our schoolmasters is gone to Damascus, and has taken with him his little nephew who was boarding with us, so we are indeed now quite alone. In fact, nothing prevents the entire desertion of the city but the dangers of the way, and the poverty of the inhabitants.

'*May* 7*th* [flood water adding to the city's anguish] — The water is decreasing most rapidly, so that rice is beginning to be brought from the other side of the river; and as those who monopolised the sale of wood, and not only asked enormous prices, but cheated in the weight, are all dead, everyone now that needs wood takes it, so that the situation of the poor seems in this respect a little improved.

'There has not been among all the circumstances of this scene of complicated suffering, any one that has more painfully affected my own mind than the increasing number of infants and little children that have been left exposed in the streets, and the absolute impossibility of meeting such a state of things. We greatly desired to take one or two; but our own little baby was ill so that by night Mary had hardly any rest, and at best, not being strong in such a climate, we came reluctantly to the decision that we were not able to undertake such an additional charge.

'This is an anxious evening. Dear Mary is taken ill – nothing that would at any other time alarm me, but now a very little creates anxiety; yet her heart is reposing on her Lord with perfect peace, and waiting His will. A few hours, perhaps may show us that it is but a little trial of our faith to draw us nearer the fountain of our life. To nature it seems fearful to think of the plague entering our dwelling; in our present situation, nothing but the Lord's especial love could sustain the soul in the contemplation of a young family left in such a land at such a time, and in such circumstances; but we feel we came out under the shadow of the Almighty's wing, and we know His pavillion will be our sanctuary, let His gracious providence prescribe what it may. On His love, therefore, we cast ourselves with all our personal interests.

'*May* 8*th*. — The Lord has this day manifested that the attack of my dear wife is the plague, and of a very dangerous and malignant kind, so that our hearts are prostrate in the Lord's hand. As I think the infection can only have come through me, I have little hope of escaping, unless by the Lord's special intervention. It is indeed an awful moment, – the prospect of leaving a little family in such a country at such a time.

'*May* 9*th*. – My dearest, dearest wife still alive, and not apparently worse than yesterday.'

'*May* 10*th*. – Last evening my dearest wife was more herself than she had been till with a few hours of her being taken ill, which was manifested by her asking to see her dear little baby, the first thing she had voluntarily asked for, since her illness. She again mentioned her confidence in her Lord, and acquiescence in His will. She asked me what I thought of her situation. I said I had committed her to the Lord, who I knew, would deal graciously by her. She replied, "Yes, that He will." She continued in this state of improvement till today at about nine o'clock, when her mind again began to wander. When I quoted to her, that to the Lord's servants light should spring up in darkness, she said, "Yes, that it shall." She said, "I feel much better than yesterday – don't you see that I am." In fact, my hopes of her being really improving would have been complete, but from that peculiar look of the eyes which authors who have written on this subject all denote as most fatal; from this, therefore, my hopes never were very high, yet though I had yesterday been enabled, through the Lord's grace, to lie in His hands like a weaned child, today the disappointment of the dear hope, slight as it was, of having her restored to us, has brought my soul again into very deep waters. She also this morning expressed her anxiety about the dear children, and her fear, lest, in attending her, I should take the plague, and they be left orphans here.

'In every respect, certainly the Lord has been most gracious to her. She is about to be transplanted to her native soil, where tears and sorrows shall never enter, and in the way of her removal, since the Lord's time is come, nothing can be more compassionate to her peculiar weakness of heart than not allowing her anxiety to dwell on the dear children, and their probable situation here. To have been happy in quitting them, amidst such a scene as now surrounds us, and in such a country, perhaps no mortal faith could have been equal to; the Lord, therefore, suffered not her mind to possess its usual sensibilities; but took them from her, and left her only to return to His bosom in peace.

The plague has attacked two more of our household, – the schoolmaster's wife and our maid-servant, and how far it will go now, no one knows but He who guides it with His sovereign will. My dearest Mary's sufferings, for four or five hours last night, were very great; she was quite delirious, and her dear voice was so affected, that I could not make out two words connectedly. How mysterious are God's ways! O, my soul, learn the lesson of patient submission to His holy will! I have cast myself upon Him, and He will guide me. Dear Mary, to-day, has been quite insensible. It has indeed been a very painful day, but it is the condition of this world. Dear spirit! she has been so set on her Lord's coming of late, that it seemed quite to absorb her thought and heart. And now she will quickly join the holy assembly who are waiting to come with Him. Surely such times as these, when the Lord is taking a ripe shock of corn from your field, are seasons to rejoice that your prayer for the speedy accomplishment of the number of God's elect has been heard, and yet how hard it is for nature not to feel deep sorrow that a message has come for one of yours.

'Poor dear Kitto and the little boys are now become the sole nurses of the dear baby by night and by day. O, may the Lord watch over them and bless them. My last night's attendance on my dear wife leaves me little hope of escaping the plague, unless it be our Father's special will to preserve me, for in her delirium she required so many times to be lifted from place to place, and to have all her clothes changed, that I can now only cry to the Lord to preserve me, if it may be, a little while, for the dear children's sake.

'The Lord has graciously provided us with a servant of Mrs T.'s to come and attend my dear Mary. Oh may my soul bless Him for this timely help, just when our own servant was taken ill. This woman has been in the midst of all the contagion, and has never taken it; so it may be the Lord's will to show how He can work even in the midst of the darkest trials. She sits down beside the dear sufferer, keeps the flies from her face, and does everything for her the fondest heart could desire. She came out with us from England, having gone there with Mrs T.; is a native of these countries, knows all that is required in sickness, and how to perform the duties of a nurse, with the most unwearied patience, tenderness, and watchfulness. She also knows something of English, and having been with dear Mrs T. in England, is acquainted with English customs. Surely the Lord heard my cry in the day of my deep distress, for such a person perhaps could not be got again within a thousand miles. That she should have been left too when all the rest went away. She has made dear Mary look so comfortable; she washes her and changes her, and though insensible, she lies so quiet, and looks so composed. She said she knew the Lord would be very gracious, and He has been so indeed; He sees it right to take His sheep home to His fold; but He has so overwhelmed me by this proof of His loving-kindness, this ray of light arising in the midst of my darkness, that it seems to have led my heart yet more and more to love Him and to confide in Him, that He may yet stay His rough wind in the day of His east wind. This kind friend, Mrs T's servant, proposes to remain with us until all our family are either well or dead . . .

'Dearest Mary is gradually sinking into the bosom of the Lord, and to join in the society her soul has so long and so truly loved, of the lovers of the Lamb of God.

'The dear little baby also is but poorly. Her dear little cry of "mamma, mamma," cuts my poor heart like a knife; – to think, that from to-day, or probably to-morrow, she must cease to know that endearing name, and such a mother too! However, the Lord tells His children to leave their fatherless, and doubtless their motherless, ones to Him.

'*May* 13*th*. — My dearest wife has reached the light of another day, still quietly sinking without a sigh and without a groan. This my prayer for her in the night of my darkness the Lord has mercifully heard. At present all the remaining ones of the family are well. I have separated the dear little boys and Kitto, and allow them to hold intercourse with none. The dear baby, and myself, and the maid, and the little boy of our sick servant, are also much separated, and this nurse whom the Lord sent us, alone attends the sick; but yet so contagious is this fearful disease, that when it has once entered your dwelling, you can know no other safety than in your Lord's preserving care. These are indeed days of trial, but doubtless they will have their precious fruit in all God's children; for the eyes of the Lord are upon the righteous, and His ears are open unto their cry – for the Lord redeemeth the soul of His servants, therefore none of them that trust in Him shall be desolate – no, not even I, poor and worthless as I am, I shall yet praise Him who is the Lord of my life, and my God.

'The dear boys also keep up their spirits much better than the first two or three days after their dear mamma was taken ill. The magnitude of present danger to themselves, and to all, in some measure divides their thoughts, and prevents them from resting alone on the deeply affecting prospect before them, for they loved her most truly, and, O how much reason had they to love her!

'I have just heard that the streets begin again to be crowded, shops here and there to be opened, and the gardeners are bringing things from without into the city. To think that so near the end we should have been thus visited, how mysterious! Yet my soul says, What thou seest not, thou shalt see. If it does but lead to my Lord's glory, I am sure it will lead to my dear sufferer's; then why should I repine?

'Water is also reduced to 1s.3d. the skin, the price it was at before. For these proofs of mercy to the people, we will bless God in the midst of our own personal sorrows.

'*May* 14*th*. — This day dearest Mary's ransomed spirit took its seat among those dressed in white, and her body was consigned to the earth that gave it birth – a dark heavy day to poor nature, but still the Lord was the light and stay of it.

'I cannot help exceedingly blessing my heavenly Father, however these calamities (for to nature they are such, though not to the heirs of glory) may end, that He has allowed me to continue in health so long as to see everything done I could have desired and infinitely more than I could have expected for her whom I have so much reason to love.'

Anthony Groves survived, though his wife and children died. He went to India and returned to England in 1835. There he married for the second time; he went back to India with his new wife, Harriet, and an adopted child, to carry on his missionary work. His wife edited the memoir from which the diary extracts are taken.

'Leaning his head on his hand, he sweetly fell asleep on Friday, May 20th ,1853' and, according to a friend who was at his bedside, his last words were 'Precious Jesus'.

THE BRIDE OF ABYDOS

George Gordon, Lord Byron
(1788 – 1844)

———◆———

Unlike many other writers at this time who used accounts by travellers in the East for their background material, Byron had gone in person to Turkey, including the Greek parts of it, and spent two years there on an extended grand tour.

The book came out in 1813, with a dedication to a friend, Lord Holland. By the time it was published, a year after *Childe Harold,* which had gone through seven editions, Byron had become the darling of London society. He himself called *The Bride of Abydos* 'a Turkish story', when he wrote to Mr Gifford, who had looked at it in MSS and was now asked to 'do the same favour in the probationary state of printing'. It was written, he said in his letter to Gifford, quoted by Tom Moore, '*I cannot say for amusement, nor obliged by hunger and request of friends, but in a state of mind from circumstances which occasionally occurs to 'us youth' that rendered it necessary for me to apply my mind to something, anything but reality, and under this not very brilliant inspiration it was composed.*

Send it either to the flames or a hundred hawkers' load, on wings of wind to fly or fall abroad.'

———◆———

FROM
THE BRIDE OF ABYDOS

CANTO THE FIRST

I

Know ye the land where the cypress and myrtle
Are emblems of deeds that are done in their clime,
Where the rage of the vulture, the love of the turtle,
Now melt into sorrow, now madden to crime?
Know ye the land of the cedar and vine,

Where the flowers ever blossom, the beams ever shine
Where the light wings of Zephyr, oppressed with perfume,
Wax faint o'er the gardens of Gul in her bloom;

Where the citron and olive are fairest of fruit,
And the voice of the nightingale never is mute:
Where the tints of the earth, and the hues of the sky,
In colour though varied, in beauty may vie,
And the purple of Ocean is deepest in dye;
Where the virgins are soft as the roses they twine,
And all, save the spirit of man, is divine?
'Tis the clime of the East; 'tis the land of the Sun –
Can he smile on such deeds as his children have done?
Oh! wild as the accents of lovers' farewell
Are the hearts which they bear, and the tales which
they tell.

II

Begirt with many a gallant slave,
Apparell'd as becomes the brave,
Awaiting each his lord's behest
To guide his steps, or guard his rest,
Old Giaffir sate in his Divan:
Deep thought was in his aged eye;
And though the face of Mussulman
Not oft betrays to standers by
The mind within, well skill'd to hide.
All but unconquerable pride,
His pensive cheek and pondering brow
Did more than he was wont avow.

III

'Let the chamber be clear'd' – The train disappear'd –
'Now call me the chief of the Haram guard.'
With Giaffir is none but his only son,
And the Nubian awaiting the sire's award.
'Haroun – when all the crowd that wait
Are pass'd beyond the outer gate,
(Woe to the head whose eye beheld
My child Zuleika's face unveil'd!)
Hence, lead my daughter from her tower;

Her fate is fix'd this very hour:
Yet not to her repeat my thought;
By me alone be duty taught!'
'Pacha! to hear is to obey.'
No more must slave to despot say –
Then to the tower had ta'en his way,
But here young Selim silence brake,
First lowly rendering reverence meet;
And downcast look'd, and gently spake,
Still standing at the Pacha's feet:
For son of Moslem must expire,
Ere dare to sit before his sire!

'Father! for fear that thou shouldst chide
My sister, on her sable guide,
Know – for the fault, if fault there be,
Was mine, then fall thy frowns on me –
So lovelily the morning shone,
That – let the old and weary sleep –
I could not; and to view alone
The fairest scenes of land and deep.
With none to listen and reply
To thoughts with which my heart beat high
Were irksome – for whate'er my mood,
In sooth I love not solitude;
I on Zuleika's slumber broke,
And, as thou knowest that for me
Soon turns the Haram's grating key,
Before the guardian slaves awoke
We to the cypress groves had flown,
And made earth, main, and heaven our own!
There linger'd we, beguiled too long
With Mejnoun's tale, or Sadi's song;
Till I, who heard the deep tambour
Beat the Divan's approaching hour,
To thee, and to my duty true,
Warn'd by the sound, to greet thee flew:
But there Zuleika wanders yet –
Nay, Father, rage not – nor forget
That none can pierce that secret bower

But those who watch the women's tower.'

IV

'Son of a slave' – the Pacha said –
'From unbelieving mother bred,
Vain were a father's hope to see
Aught that beseems a man in thee.
Thou, when thine arm should bend the bow,
And hurl the dart, and curb the steed,
Thou, Greek in soul if not in creed,
Must pore where babbling waters flow,
And watch unfolding roses blow.
Would that yon orb, whose matin glow
Thy listless eyes so much admire,
Would lend thee something of his fire!
Thou, who would'st see this battlement
By Christian cannon piecemeal rent;
Nay, tamely view old Stambol's wall
Before the dogs of Moscow fall,
Nor strike one stroke for life and death
Aginst the curs of Nazareth!
Go – let thy less than woman's hand
Assume the distaff – not the brand.
But, Haroun! – to my daughter speed:
And hark – of thine own head take heed –
If thus Zuleika oft takes wing –
Thou see'st yon bow – it hath a string!'

V

No sound from Selim's lip was heard,
At least that met old Giaffir's ear,
But every frown and every word
Pierced keener than a Christian's sword.
'Son of a slave! – reproach'd with fear!
Those gibes had cost another dear.
Son of a slave! – and *who* my sire?'
Thus held his thoughts their dark career;
And glances ev'n of more than ire
Flash forth, then faintly disappear.
Old Giaffir gazed upon his son

And started; for within his eye
He read how much his wrath had done;
He saw rebellion there begun:
'Come hither, boy – what, no reply?
I mark thee – and I know thee too;
But there be deeds thou dar'st not do:
But if thy beard had manlier length,
And if thy hand had skill and strength,
I'd joy to see thee break a lance,
Albeit against my own perchance.'

As sneeringly these accents fell,
On Selim's eye he fiercely gazed:
That eye return'd him glance for glance,
And proudly to his sire's was raised,
Till Giaffir's quail'd and shrunk askance –
And why – he felt, but durst not tell.
'Much I misdoubt this wayward boy
Will one day work me more annoy:
I never loved him from his birth,
And – but his arm is little worth,
And scarcely in the chase could cope
With timid fawn or antelope,
Far less would venture into strife
Where man contends for fame and life –
I would not trust that look or tone:
No – nor the blood so near my own.
That blood – he hath not heard – no more –
I'll watch him closer than before.
He is an Arab to my sight,
Or Christian crouching in the fight –
But hark! – I hear Zuleika's voice;
Like Houris' hymn it meets mine ear:
She is the offspring of my choice;
Oh! more than ev'n her mother dear,
With all to hope, and nought to fear –
My Peri! ever welcome here!
Sweet as the desert fountain's wave
To lips just cool'd in time to save –
Such to my longing sight art thou;
Nor can they waft to Mecca's shrine

More thanks for life, than I for thine.
Who blest thy birth, and bless thee now.'

VI

Fair, as the first that fell of womankind,
When on that dread yet lovely serpent smiling,
Whose image then was stamp'd upon her mind –
But once beguiled – and ever more beguiling;
Dazzling, as that, oh! too transcendent vision
To Sorrow's phantom-peopled slumber given,
When heart meets heart again in dreams Elysian,
And paints the lost on Earth revived in Heaven;
Soft, as the memory of buried love;
Pure, as the prayer which Childhood wafts above;
Was she – the daughter of that rude old Chief,
Who met the maid with tears – but not of grief.

Who hath not proved how feebly words essay
To fix one spark of Beauty's heavenly ray?

CANTO THE SECOND

I

The winds are high on Helle's wave,
As on that night of stormy water
When Love, who sent, forgot to save
The young, the beautiful, the brave,
The lonely hope of Sestos' daughter.
Oh! when alone along the sky
Her turret-torch was blazing high,
Though rising gale, and breaking foam,
And shrieking sea-birds warn'd him home;
And clouds aloft and tides below,
With signs and sounds, forbade to go,
He could not see, he would not hear,
Or sound or sign foreboding fear;
His eye but saw that light of love,
The only star it hail'd above;
His ear but rang with Hero's song,
'Ye waves, divide not lovers long!' –
That tale is old, but love anew
May nerve young hearts to prove as true.

II

The winds are high, and Helle's tide
 Rolls darkly heaving to the main;
And Night's descending shadows hide
 That field with blood bedew'd in vain,
 The desert of old Priam's pride:
 The tombs, sole relics of his reign,
All – save immortal dreams that could beguile
 The blind old man of Scio's rocky isle!

VI

Wrapt in the darkest sable vest,
 Which none save noblest Moslem wear,
To guard from winds of heaven the breast
 As heaven itself to Selim dear,
With cautious steps the thicket threading,
 And starting oft, as through the glade
 The gust its hollow moanings made,
Till on the smoother pathway treading,
 More free her timid bosom beat,
 The maid pursued her silent guide;
And though her terror urged retreat,
 How could she quit her Selim's side?
 How teach her tender lips to chide?

VII

They reach'd at length a grotto, hewn
 By nature, but enlarged by art,
Where oft her lute she wont to tune,
 And oft her Koran conn'd apart;
 And oft in youthful reverie
She dream'd what Paradise might be:
 Where woman's parted soul shall go
 Her Prophet had disdain'd to show;
 But Selim's mansion was secure,
Nor deem'd she, could he long endure
 His bower in other worlds of bliss,
 Without *her*, most beloved in this!
Oh! who so dear with him could dwell?
What Houri soothe him half so well?

XXVIII

Within the place of thousand tombs
That shine beneath, while dark above
The sad but living cypress glooms,
And withers not, though branch and leaf
Are stamp'd with an eternal grief,
Like early unrequited Love,
One spot exists, which ever blooms,
Ev'n in that deadly grove –
A single rose is shedding there
Its lonely lustre, meek and pale:
It looks as planted by Despair –
So white – so faint – the slightest gale
Might whirl the leaves on high;
And yet, though storms and blight assail,
And hands more rude than wintry sky
May wring it from the stem – in vain –
To-morrow sees it bloom again!

The stalk some spirit gently rears,
And waters with celestial tears;
For well may maids of Helle deem
That this can be no earthly flower.
Which mocks the tempest's withering hour,
And buds unshelter'd by a bower;
Nor droops, though spring refuse her shower,
Nor woos the summer beam:
To it the livelong night there sings
A bird unseen – but not remote:
Invisible his airy wings,
But soft as harp that Houri strings
His long entrancing note!
It were the Bulbul; but his throat,
Though mournful, pours not such a strain;
For they who listen cannot leave
The spot, but linger there and grieve,
As if they loved in vain!

OZYMANDIAS

Percy Bysshe Shelley

(1792–1822)

Published by Leigh Hunt in *The Examiner*, January 1818. Reprinted with *Rosalind and Helen,* 1819. There is a copy amongst the Shelley MSS at the Bodleian Library.

I met a traveller from an antique land
Who said: Two vast and trunkless legs of stone
Stand in the desert . . . Near them, on the sand,
Half sunk, a shattered visage lies, whose frown,
And wrinkled lip, and sneer of cold command,
Tell that its sculptor well those passions read
Which yet survive, stamped on these lifeless things,
The hand that mocked them, and the heart that fed:
And on the pedestal these words appear:
'My name is Ozymandias, king of kings:
Look on my works, ye Mighty, and despair!'
Nothing beside remains. Round the decay
Of that colossal wreck, boundless and bare
The lone and level sands stretch far away.

The upper part of a Statue of Ofymanduas at Thebes.
To Sr. Bourchier Wrey Baronet.

Ozymandius, from Dr Richard Pococke's *Description of the East*,
London, 1743

LION CUB LIONIZING

From Home Letters by Benjamin Disraeli, Earl of Beaconsfield

(1804 – 1881)

———◆———

A young Jew, born in 1804, and only baptized in July 1817, was pondering in London soon afterwards how he might fulfil his desire to see the lands of his ancestors and ease the state of his local indebtedness; he found that by pandering to the current craze for travel books and novels about the East he was able to induce a publisher to make him an advance.

The result was a proposition for a novel called *Alroy* (1837) by Benjamin Disraeli who made his journey in 1830 to Spain, Albania, Athens, Constantinople and Egypt. Naturally he wrote letters home during his journey, though they were not published until 1885 as *Home Letters written by the late Earl of Beaconsfield, 1830–31*.

———◆———

PREVESA: October 25, 1830

My Dearest Father,

I wrote to Ralph from Malta, and to you from Corfu, and left the letters to be forwarded by the October packet, when it arrived, if it ever did, of which to-day there is a report here. It was so late after its time that it was quite despaired of. Doubtless, however, you have received my letters by some source or other. I mentioned in my letter to you, that there was a possibility of our paying the Grand Vizier a visit at his quarters at Yanina, the capital of Albania. What was then probable has since become certain. We sailed from Corfu to this place, where we arrived on the eleventh instant, and found a most hospitable and agreeable friend in the Consul General, Mr Meyer, to whom Sir Frederick had given me a very warm letter. He is a gentleman of the old school, who has moved in a good sphere, and has great diplomatic experience of the East. He insists upon our dining with him every day, and what is even still more remarkable, produces a cuisine which would not be despicable in London, but in this savage land of anarchy is indeed as surprising as it is agreeable.

As the movements of his Highness were very uncertain, we lost no time in commencing our journey to Yanina. We sailed up to Salora (I mention these places, because you will be always able to trace my route in your new maps), and on the morning of the 14th, a company of six horsemen, all armed, we set off for Arta, where we found accommodation ready for us, in a house belonging to the consulate. Arta, once a town as beautiful as its situation, is in ruins, whole streets razed to the ground, and, with the exception of the consulate house, rebuilt since, scarcely a tenement which was not a shell. Here for the first time I reposed upon a divan, and for the first time heard the muezzin from the minaret, a ceremony which is highly affecting when performed, as it usually is, by a rich and powerful voice. Next morning we paid a visit to Kalio Bey, the Governor, once the wealthiest, and now one of the most powerful, Albanian nobles. He has ever been faithful to the Porte, even during the recent insurrection, which was an affair of the great body of the aristocracy. We found him keeping his state, which, in spite of the surrounding desolation, was not contemptible, in something not much better than a large shed. I cannot describe to you the awe with which I first entered the divan of a great Turk, or the curious feelings with which, for the first time in my life, I found myself squatting on the right hand of a Bey, smoking an amber-mouthed chibouque, drinking coffee, and paying him compliments through an interpreter. He was a very handsome, stately man, grave but not dull, and remarkably mild and bland in his manner, which may perhaps be ascribed to a recent imprisonment in Russia, where, however, he was treated with great consideration, which he mentioned to us. He was exceedingly courteous, and would not let us depart, insisting upon our repeating our pipes, an unusual honour. At length we set off from Arta, with an Albanian of his bodyguard for an escort, ourselves and guides, six in number, and two Albanians, who took advantage of our company. All these Albanians are armed to the teeth, with daggers, pistols, and guns, invariably richly ornamented, and sometimes entirely inlaid with silver, even the tassel. This was our procession:

An Albanian of the Bey's guard, completely armed.
Turkish guides, with the baggage.

Three Beyasdeers Inglases, or sons of English Beys, armed after their fashion.
Giovanni, covered with mustachios and pistols.
Boy carrying a gazel.
An Albanian completely armed.

The gazel made a capital object, but gave us a great deal of trouble. In this fashion we journeyed over a wild mountain pass – a range of the ancient Pindus – and two hours before sunset, having completed only half our course in spite of all our exertions, we found ourselves at a vast but dilapidated khan as big as a Gothic castle, situated on a high range, and built as a sort of half-way house for travellers by Ali Pasha when his long, gracious, and unmolested reign had permitted him to turn this unrivalled country, which combines all the excellences of Southern Europe and Western Asia, to some of the purposes for which it is fitted. This khan had now been turned into a military post; and here we found a young bey, to whom Kalio had given us a letter in case of our stopping for an hour. He was a man of very pleasing exterior, but unluckily could not understand Giovanni's Greek, and had no interpreter. What was to be done? We could not go on, as there was not an inhabited place before Yanina; and here were we sitting before sunset on the same divan with our host, who had entered the place to receive us, and would not leave the room while we were there without the power of communicating an idea. We were in despair, and we were also very hungry, and could not therefore in the course of an hour or two plead fatigue as an excuse for sleep, for we were ravenous and anxious to know what prospect of good existed in this wild and desolate mansion. So we smoked. It is a great resource, but this wore out, and it was so ludicrous smoking, and looking at each other, and dying to talk, and then exchanging pipes by way of compliment, and then pressing our hand to our heart by way of thanks. The Bey sat in a corner, I unfortunately next, so I had the onus of mute attention; and Clay next to me, so he and M. could at least have an occasional joke, though of course we were too well-bred to exceed an occasional and irresistible observation. Clay wanted to play écarté, and with a grave face, as if we were at our devotions; but just as we were about commencing, it occurred to us that we had some brandy, and that we would offer our host a glass, as it might be a hint for what should follow to so vehement a schnaps. Mash-Allah! Had the effect only taken place 1830 years ago, instead of in the present age

of scepticism, it would have been instantly voted a first-rate miracle.
Our mild friend smacked his lips and instantly asked for another cup;
we drank it in coffee cups. By the time that Meredith had returned,
who had left the house on pretence of shooting, Clay, our host, and
myself had despatched a bottle of brandy in quicker time and fairer
proportions than I ever did a bottle of Burgundy, and were extremely
gay. Then he would drink again with Meredith and ordered some
figs, talking I must tell you all the time, indulging in the most graceful
pantomime, examining our pistols, offering us his own golden ones
for our inspection, and finally making out Giovanni's Greek enough
to misunderstand most ludicrously every observation we communicated. But all was taken in good part, and I never met such a jolly
fellow in the course of my life. In the meantime we were ravenous, for
the dry, round, unsugary fig is a great whetter. At last we insisted upon
Giovanni's communicating our wants and asking for bread. The Bey
gravely bowed and said, 'Leave it to me; take no thought,' and nothing
more occurred. We prepared ourselves for hungry dreams, when to
our great delight a most capital supper was brought in, accompanied,
to our great horror, by – wine. We ate, we drank, we ate with our
fingers, we drank in a manner I never recollect. The wine was
not bad, but if it had been poison we must drink; it was such a compliment for a Moslemin; we quaffed it in rivers. The Bey called for the
brandy; he drank it all. The room turned round; the wild attendants
who sat at our feet seemed dancing in strange and fantastic whirls;
the Bey shook hands with me; he shouted English – I Greek. 'Very
good' he had caught up from us. 'Kalo, kalo' was my rejoinder. He
roared; I smacked him on the back. I remember no more. In the
middle of the night I woke. I found myself sleeping on the divan,
rolled up in its sacred carpet; the Bey had wisely reeled to the fire. The
thirst I felt was like that of Dives. All were sleeping except two, who
kept up during the night the great wood fire. I rose lightly, stepping
over my sleeping companions, and the shining arms that here and
there informed me that the dark mass wrapped up in a capote was a
human being. I found Abraham's bosom in a flagon of water. I think
I must have drunk a gallon at the draught. I looked at the wood fire
and thought of the blazing blocks in the hall at Bradenham, asked
myself whether I was indeed in the mountain fastness of an Albanian
chief, and, shrugging my shoulders, went to bed and woke without a
headache.

We left our jolly host with regret. I gave him my pipe as a memorial of having got tipsy together.

Next day, having crossed one more steep mountain pass, we descended into a vast plain, over which we journeyed for some hours, the country presenting the same mournful aspect, which I had too long observed: villages in ruins, and *perfectly* uninhabited, caravanseras deserted, fortresses razed to the ground, olive woods burnt up. So complete had been the work of destruction, that you often find your horse's course on the foundation of a village without being aware of it, and what at first appears the dry bed of a torrent, turns out to be the backbone of the skeleton of a ravaged town. At the end of the plain, immediately backed by very lofty mountains, and jutting into the beautiful lake that bears its name, we suddenly came upon the city of Yanina – suddenly, for a long tract of gradually rising ground had hitherto concealed it from our sight. At the distance we first beheld it, this city, once, if not the largest, one of the most prosperous and brilliant in the Turkish dominions, still looked imposing; but when we entered, I soon found that all preceding desolation had only been preparative to the vast scene of destruction now before me. We proceeded through a street, winding in its course, but of very great length, to our quarters. Ruined houses, mosques, with their tower only standing, streets utterly razed – these are nothing. We met great patches of ruin a mile square, as if a swarm of locusts had had the power of desolating the works of man as well as those of God. The great heart of the city was a sea of ruin. Arches and pillars, isolated and shattered, still here and there jutting forth, breaking the uniformity of the desolation, and turning the horrible into the picturesque. The great bazaar, itself a little town, was burnt down only a few months since when an infuriate band of Albanian soldiers heard of the destruction of their chiefs by the Grand Vizier.

But while the city itself presented this mournful appearance, its other characteristics were anything but sad. At this moment a swarming population, arrayed in every possible and fanciful costume, buzzed and bustled in all directions. As we passed on – and you can easily believe not unobserved where no 'Mylorts Ingles' (as regular a word among the Turks as the French and Italians) had been seen for more than nine years – a thousand objects attracted my restless attention and roving eye. Everything was so strange and splendid, that for a moment I forgot that this was an extraordinary scene, even for the East, and gave up my fancy to a full credulity in the now obsolete magnificence of Oriental life. Military chieftains clothed in the most brilliant colours and most showy furs, and attended by a cortège of officers equally splendid, continually passed us; now for the first time a dervish saluted me, and now a Delhi with his high cap reined in his desperate steed, as the suite of some pacha blocked up the turning of the street. The Albanian costume, too, is inexhaustible in its combinations, and Jews and Greek priests must not be forgotten. It seemed to me that my first day in Turkey brought before me all the popular characteristics of which I had read, and which I expected I occasionally might see during a prolonged residence. I remember this very day I observed a Turkish sheik in his entirely green vestments; a scribe with his writing materials in his girdle; and a little old Greek physician, who afterwards claimed my acquaintance on the plea of being able to speak English, that is to say, he could count nine on his fingers, no further (literally a fact). I gazed with a strange mingled feeling of delight and wonder. Suddenly a strange, wild, unearthly drum is heard, and at the end of the street a huge camel (to me it seemed as large as an elephant) with a slave sitting cross-legged on neck and playing an immense kettle-drum, appears, and is the first of an apparently interminable procession of his Arabian brethren. The camels were very large, they moved slowly, and were many in number; I should think there might have been between sixty and a hundred. It was an imposing sight. All immediately hustled out of the way of the caravan, and seemed to shrink under the sound of the wild drum. This procession bore corn for the Vizier's troops encamped without the wall.

It is in vain that I attempt to convey to you all that I saw and felt this wondrous week. To lionize and be a lion at the same time is a hard fate. When I walked out I was followed by a crowd; when I stopped to buy anything I was encompassed by a circle. How shall I convey to you an idea of all the Pachas, and all the Aghas, and all the Selictars, whom I have visited, and who have visited me; all the coffee I sipped, all the pipes I smoked, all the sweetmeats I devoured? But our grand presentation must not be omitted. An hour having been fixed for the audience, we repaired to the celebrated fortress-palace of Ali, which, though greatly battered in successive sieges, is still inhabitable, and yet affords a very fair idea of its old magnificence. Having passed the gates of the fortress, we found ourselves in a number of small streets, like those in the liberties of the Tower, or any other old castle, all full of life, stirring and excited; then we came to a grand place, in which on an ascent stands the Palace. We hurried through courts and corridors, all full of guards, and pages, and attendant chiefs, and in fact every species of Turkish population, for in these countries one head does everything, and we with our subdivision of labour and intelligent and responsible deputies have no idea of the labour of a Turkish Premier. At length we came to a vast, irregular apartment, serving as the immediate ante-chamber to the Hall of Audience. This was the finest thing I have ever yet seen. In the whole course of my life I never met anything so picturesque, and cannot expect to do so again. I do not attempt to describe it; but figure to yourself the largest chamber that you ever were perhaps in, full of the choicest groups of an Oriental population, each individual waiting by appointment for an audience, and probably about to wait for ever. In this room we remained, attended by the Austrian Consul who presented us, about ten minutes – too short a time. I never thought that I could have lived to have wished to kick my heels in a minister's ante-chamber. Suddenly we are summoned to the awful presence of the pillar of the Turkish Empire, the man who has the reputation of being the mainspring of the new system of regeneration, the renowned Redschid, an approved warrior, a consummate politician, unrivalled as a dissembler in a country where dissimulation is the principal portion of their moral culture.

The Hall was vast, built by Ali Pacha purposely to receive the largest Gobelins carpet that was ever made, which belonged to the chief chamber in Versailles, and was sold to him in the Revolution. It is entirely covered with gilding and arabesques. Here, squatted up on a corner of the large divan, I bowed with all the nonchalance of St James's Street to a little ferocious-looking, shrivelled, care-worn man, plainly dressed, with a brow covered with wrinkles, and a countenance clouded with anxiety and thought. I entered the shed-like divan of the kind and comparatively insignificant Kalio Bey with a feeling of awe; I seated myself on the divan of the Grand Vizier ('who,' the Austrian Consul observed, 'has destroyed in the course of the last three months,' not in war, 'upwards of four thousand of my acquaintance') with the self-possession of a morning call. At a distance from us, in a group on his left hand, were his secretary and his immediate suite; the end of the saloon was lined by lacqueys in waiting, with an odd name which I now forget, and which you will find in the glossary of Anastasius. Some compliments now passed between us, and pipes and coffee were then brought by four of these lacqueys; then his Highness waved his hand, and in an instant the chamber was cleared. Our conversation I need not repeat. We congratulated him on the pacification of Albania. He rejoined, that the peace of the world was his only object, and the happiness of mankind his only wish; this went on for the usual time. He asked us no questions about ourselves or our country, as the other Turks did, but seemed quite overwhelmed with business, moody and anxious. While we were with him, three separate Tartars arrived with despatches. What a life! and what a slight chance for the gentleman in the ante-chamber!

After the usual time we took our leave, and paid a visit to his son Amin Pacha, a youth of eighteen, but who looks ten years older, and who is Pacha of Yanina. He is the very reverse of his father, incapable in affairs, refined in his manners, plunged in debauchery and magnificent in his dress. Covered with gold and diamonds, he bowed to us with the ease of a Duke of Devonshire, said the English were the most polished of nations, etc. But all these visits must really be reserved till we meet. We found some Turks extremely intelligent, who really talk about Peter the Great, and all that, with considerable *goût*. With one of these, Mehemet Aga, Selictar to the Pacha of Lepanto, and an approved warrior, we became great friends. He showed us his new book of military tactics, and as he took a fancy to my costume insisted upon my calling to see his uniforms, which he gets made in Italy, and which really would not disgrace the 10th.

I forgot to tell you that with the united assistance of my English, Spanish, and fancy wardrobe, I sported a costume in Yanina which produced a most extraordinary effect on that costume-loving people. A great many Turks called on purpose to see it, but the little Greek physician who had passed a year at Pisa in his youth, nearly smoked me. 'Questo vestito Inglese o di fantasia?' he aptly asked. I oracularly replied, 'Inglese e fantastico.'

I write you this from that Ambracian Gulf where the soft Triumvir gained more glory by defeat than attends the victory of harsher warriors. The site is not unworthy of the beauty of Cleopatra. From the summit of the land this gulf appears like a vast lake walled in on all sides by mountains more or less distant. The dying glory of a Grecian eve bathes with warm light a thousand promontories and gentle bays, and infinite modulations of purple outline. Before me is Olympus, whose austere peak glitters yet in the sun; a bend of the land alone hides from me the islands of Ulysses and of Sappho. When I gaze upon this scene I remember the barbaric splendour and turbulent existence which I have just quitted with disgust. I recur to the feelings in the indulgence of which I can alone find happiness, and from which an inexorable destiny seems resolved to shut me out. Pray write regularly, as sooner or later I shall receive all your letters; and write fully.

As I have no immediate mode of conveying this safely to England, I shall probably keep it in my portfolio till I get to Napoli, and send it through Mr Dawkins.

A thousand loves to you all.

Your most affectionate,

B.D.

JOURNEY
THROUGH ROUMELI

From The Spirit of the East
by David Urquhart
(1805 – 1877)

———◆———

Urquhart fought in the Greek Navy during the War for Greek Independence
and was severely wounded. He was for a time an Attaché to Stratford Canning,
Ambassador to Turkey. He was founder of the *Portfolio* and the *Diplomatic
Review,* to which Karl Marx contributed. As M.P. for Stafford he vigorously
opposed Palmerston's foreign policy. His wife Harriet Fortescue, also a
writer, helped him in his work, contributing articles to the *Diplomatic
Review.* He figures briefly in the D.N.B. and the Encyclopaedia Britannica,
but is given perhaps rather less attention than he should receive in works
about the East. He was responsible for introducing the Turkish Bath to
England.

———◆———

Our baggage hastily packed, was constantly falling off; our wild
ghegue of a postilion, in the absence of any civilized means of intercourse, exhibited the state of his mind by an almost uninterrupted
flow of imprecation, now directed against the baggage, now against
the horses, and sometimes against ourselves.

An hour after sunset, we arrived, however, at a khan called Bal-
douna, four miles from Yanina, at the Eastern extremity of the
Lake . . . Our single *ghegue* had devoured the whole of our provisions.
Supperless, exhausted and not venturing to even ask for water for
fear of betraying our helplessness . . . we retired to rising ground, and
being unable to keep watch, we set up a figure with a turban, having
the end of a gun resting on its shoulder. Thus gaining confidence,
and satisfied with our device we laid ourselves down, and fell
asleep . . .

That evening, what were the contrasts we drew between the
scenes we had witnessed on the Makronoros and that now around

us; between the enthusiastic greeting and splendid hospitality of the Greek bands and the contemptuous scowl and the savage air of Skipetar hordes

Troops had been arriving and departing continually during the night. Between two and three thousand men might have passed. There was no order of any kind; they were grouped around chiefs of great or little repute, and the minor chiefs again clustering round the greater.

We managed to start by ourselves, and a little before a Bey with a large retinue, so as to appear to belong to his party . . .

We reached by a rapid descent the vale of the river Arta which seemed to penetrate to the very roots of Pindus, the magnificent peaks of which towered up before and about us . . .

At midday we arrived at the Khan of Roses where to our infinite joy and relief we were told Veli Bey really was. Miserable as the hovel was the group was a picture . . .

They dined with Veli Bey – his midday meal – before continuing with his army on the march. The next halt, that night, was to be on a summit of the Pindus, the range separating Thessaly from Epirus.

Veli Bey stood up on their entering which immediately relieved them of all doubt about his disposition. It established their position, not only in the camp and among his retainers but in Albania, where, in the 1820s, feeling against Britain's pro-Russian policy ran high.

Veli Bey wore the white Arab *benish* over the golden Albanian *fermeli*, which with the fustanel and leggings, embroidered in gold, to represent metal grieves, gave him the air of a Roman statue and was the most magnificent costume ever beheld. It was made for masters of the world. In Titian's woodcuts to the work on costumes, published at Venice in 1598, the Ambassador and the General of Venice are represented as wearing that magnificent cloak. It may be recognised by three tufts on one shoulder – that is when the arm is drawn through the hood . . .

When we resumed our march, the whole mountain above us was suddenly covered with men. This had been the place of rendezvous and refreshment; and in taking their siesta, the troops had composed themselves to sleep with a Skipetar's instinct of concealment. Soldiers now started up from under every bush and tree, and from behind every rock – the road ascended by divers zigzags over five or six successive summits. It was thronged with Spahis and lance-bearing Chaldupes; Beys on gallant chargers, and long lines of the kirtled Skipetars, in all the gorgeousness as of glancing armour and of shining colours, and in every variety of picturesque martial costume. These files set quickly in motion produced an effect which no words can convey; . . . now lost in the foliage, now in bold relief on the rocks – now drawn out in strait and lengthened line on the face of the dark mountain, now suddenly breaking from the regular path, and clambering like goats to the path above, thus diminishing and ascending heights till we could trace them only by the white line of their snowy capotes and fustanels and by the glittering of silver and steel . . . During twenty minutes mountains of snow white clouds rose into the deep blue sky, with during twenty minutes a thousand changes of light and shade. Then the storm approached, darkened, descended . . . pealed among the halls of Pindus. The road became a torrent; the rain was succeeded by hail driven by tremendous gusts of wind . . . thunder from cliff to cliff . . . stunning peals like explosions from the earth. These summer storms are rare and scarcely ever fall on the plains that could be seen through a gap in the clouds below the reflected rays of the setting sun gliding through meadows of velvet green. Where these storms do fall their fury is uncontrolled. Cattle and sheep are blown over precipices.

After the storm was over it was indeed a sight to view the gay Palicars, wringing their drenched fustanels, and with their dripping embroidery draggling in the mud. A sensation most delicious was produced by the fragrance of the atmosphere after storm; and standing on the edge of a cliff at the height of between four and five thousand feet we inhaled the air rising up warm and soft, and charged with odours of the blossoms and plants it had caressed as it rose from lowly plains to myrtle groves and mountain heather. Our companions revelled in the balmy air and bared their arms and breasts and stood like seagulls on rocks, stretching their necks to catch the breezes, expressing their delight by short cries and by the flutter of their extended wings.

About sunset we reached the Khan of Placa and a fresh body which we understood numbered five thousand muskets. The Khan was old and spacious with a court in the middle surrounded by galleries, corridors and deal separated apartments. The crowds of soldiers rendered weightier still by their wet capotes made the whole edifice shake and rock. Just in the busiest moment of unloading, a

new burst of hail and thunder rendered the animals quite ungovern-
able, a scene of indescribable confusion. For fires the timbers of the
old Khan were found to burn well. Half a dozen sheep were soon
cooking for our dinner with Veli Bey. After it he said it was in-
comprehensible and unbearable that England should have treated
them so badly. England, he repeated with measured pathos, raising
his hands as if to give effect to his faltering words; but at that moment
the strength of his feelings quite overcame him, he fell on his cushion,
and his pipe dropped from his mouth; we started up for cold water
and burnt feathers, but a loud snore apprised us that a temporary
relief in sleep from a sense of political degradation had come to him.

TRAVELLING GENT

From Eothen by
Alexander William Kinglake
(1809 – 1891)

Alexander William Kinglake wrote in the Preface to his book *Eothen*, published in 1844, that the studiously unpromising title, meaning in ancient Greek 'from the early dawn – from the East', was a forewarning that his account was quite superficial in character. He had, he said, discarded from it all valuable material derived from the works of others, he believed that from it *'all details of geographical discovery or antiquarian research – from all display of "sound learning and religious knowledge", from all historical and scientific illustrations – and from all useful statistics – from all political disquisitions – and from all good moral reflexions, the volume is thoroughly free.'* His journey was undertaken some ten years before publication and he had in fact taken much care in writing and rewriting his account of it.

From this beginning it might be thought that the book would be a great success. It was so. Until recently it was still listed as suitable holiday reading for English schoolboys, their masters doubtless including it as a light-hearted, yet most carefully written, English account of an adventurous journey through the nearer East. Kinglake, indeed, was so proud and shy about his style in English that he left orders that his letters and drafts were all to be destroyed after his death; this left little material for a biography, until his great-niece, Miss Beata Harford, helped in the making of one published in London (Travelling Gent, a Life of Alexander William Kinglake, by Gerald de Gaury, Routledge and Kegan Paul Limited, 1972).

JOURNEY FROM
BELGRADE TO CONSTANTINOPLE

In two or three hours our party was ready; the servants, the Tatars, the mounted Suridgees, and the baggage-horses altogether made up a strong cavalcade. The accomplished Mysseri, of whom you have heard me speak so often, and who served me so faithfully throughout my oriental journeys, acted as our interpreter, and was in fact the brain of our corps. The Tatar, you know, is a government courier properly employed in carrying despatches, but also sent with travellers to speed them on their way, and answer with his head for their safety. The man whose head was thus pledged for our precious lives was a glorious looking fellow, with the regular, and handsome cast of countenance, which is now characteristic of the Ottoman race. The continual marriages of these people, with the chosen beauties of Georgia and Circassia, have overpowered the original ugliness of their Tatar ancestors. His features displayed a good deal of serene pride, self-respect, fortitude, a kind of ingenuous sensuality and something of instinctive wisdom, without any sharpness of intellect. He had been a Janissary (as I afterwards found out), and kept up the odd strut of his old corps, which used to affright the Christians in former times – that rolling gait is so comically pompous, that a close imitation of it, even in the broadest farce, would be looked upon as a very rough over-acting of the character. It is occasioned in part by the dress and accoutrements. The heavy bundle of weapons carried upon the chest throws back the body so as to give it a wonderful portliness, while the immense masses of clothes that swathe his limbs, force the wearer in walking, to swing himself heavily round from left to right, and from right to left – in truth, this great edifice of woollen, and cotton, and silk, and silver, and brass, and steel, is not at all fitted for moving on foot; it cannot even walk without ludicrously deranging its architectural proportions, and as to running, I once saw our Tatar make an attempt at that laborious exercise, in order to pick up a partridge which Methley had winged with a pistol shot, and really the attempt was one of the funniest misdirections of human energy that I ever beheld . . . But put him in his stirrups, and then is the Tatar himself again: there you see him at his ease, reposing in the tranquillity of that true home (the home of his ancestors), which the saddle seems to afford him, and drawing from his pipe the calm pleasures of his 'own fireside', or else dashing sudden over the earth, as though for a moment he were borne by the steed of a Turkman chief, with the plains of central Asia before him. It was not till his subordinates had nearly completed their preparations for their march that our Tatar, 'commanding the forces', arrived; he came sleek, and fresh from the bath (for so is the custom of the Ottomans when they start upon a journey), and was carefully accoutred at every point. From his thigh to his throat he was loaded with arms and other implements of a campaigning life. There is no scarcity of water along the whole road from Belgrade to Stamboul, but the habits of our Tatar were formed by his ancestors, and not by himself, so he took good care that his leather water-flask was amply charged and properly strapped to the saddle, along with his blessed tchibouque. And now at last, he has cursed the Surridgees, in all proper figures of speech, and is ready for a ride of a thousand miles, but before he comforts his soul in the marble baths of Stamboul, he will be another and a smaller man – his sense of responsibility, his too strict abstemiousness and his restless energy, disdainful of sleep, will have worn him down to a fraction of the sleek Moostapha, that now leads our party from the gates of Belgrade.

The Surridgees are the fellows employed to lead the baggage-horses. They are most of them Gipsies. Poor devils! Their lot is an unhappy one – they are the last of the human race, and all the sins of their superiors (including the horses) can safely be visited upon them. But the wretched look often more picturesque than their betters, and though all the world look down upon these poor Surridgees, their tawny skins, and their grisly beards, will gain them honourable standing in the foreground of a landscape. We had a couple of these fellows with us, each leading a baggage-horse, to the tail of which last, another baggage-horse was attached. There was a world of trouble in persuading the stiff angular portmanteaus of Europe to adapt themselves to their new condition, and sit quietly on pack-saddles, but all was right at last, and it gladdened my eyes to see our little troop file off through the winding lanes of the city, and shew down brightly in the plain beneath; the one of our party that seemed to be most out of keeping with the rest of the scene, was Methley's Yorkshire servant, who rode doggedly on in his pantry jacket, looking out for 'gentlemen's seats'.

Methley and I had English saddles, but I think we should have done just as well (I should have certainly seen more of the country), if we had adopted saddles like that of our Tatar, who towered so loftily over the scraggy little beast that carried him. In taking thought for the East, whilst in England, I had made one capital hit which you must not forget – I had brought with me a pair of common spurs, which were a great comfort to me throughout my travels by keeping up the cheerfulness of the many unhappy nags which I had to bestride; the angle of the oriental stirrup is a very poor substitute for spurs.

The Ottoman horseman, raised by his saddle to a great height above the humble level of the back which he bestrides, and using an awfully sharp bit, is able to lift the crest of his nag, and force him into a strangely fast amble, which is the orthodox pace for the journey; my comrade and I thought it a bore to be *followed* by our attendants for a thousand miles, and we generally, therefore, did duty as the rear-guard of our 'grand army'; we used to walk our horses till the part in front had got into the distance, and then retrieve the lost ground by a gallop.

We had ridden for some two or three hours – the stir and bustle of our commencing journey had ceased – the liveliness of our little troop had worn off with the declining day, and the night closed in as we entered the great Servian forest, through which our road was to last for more than a hundred miles. Endless, and endless now on either side, the tall oaks closed in their ranks, and stood gloomily lowering over us, as grim as an army of giants with a thousand years' pay in arrear. One strived with listening ear, to catch some tidings of that Forest World within, – some stirring of beasts, some night bird's scream, but all was quite hushed, except the voice of the cicadas that peopled every bough, and filled the depths of the forest through, and through, with one same hum everlasting – more stilling than very silence.

At first our way was in darkness, but after a while the moon got up, and touched the glittering arms and tawny faces of our men with light so pale and mystic, that the watchful Tatar felt bound to look out for Demons, and take proper steps for keeping them off; he immediately determined that the duty of frightening away our ghostly enemies, (like every other troublesome work) should fall upon the poor Surridgees, who accordingly lifted up their voices, and burst upon the dreadful stillness of the forest with shrieks and dismal howls. These precautions were kept up incessantly, and were followed by the most complete success, for not one demon came near.

Long before midnight, we reached the hamlet in which we were to rest for the night; it was made up of about a dozen clay huts, standing upon a small tract of ground which had been conquered from the forest. The peasants that lived there spoke a Slavonic dialect, and Mysseri's knowledge of the Russian tongue, enabled him to talk with them freely. We soon took up our quarters in a square room, with white walls, and an earthen floor, quite bare of furniture and utterly void of women. They told us, however, that these Servian villagers were very well off, but they were careful to conceal their wealth, as well as their wives.

The burthens unstrapped from the packsaddles very quickly furnished our den; a couple of quilts spread upon the floor, with a carpet bag at the head of each became capital sofas – portmanteaus, and hat boxes, and writing cases, and books, and maps and gleaming arms, were soon strewed around us in pleasant confusion. Mysseri's canteen too, began to yield up its treasures, but we relied upon finding some provisions in the village. At first the natives declared that their hens were mere old maids, and all their cows unmarried, but our Tatar swore such a grand, sonorous oath and fingered the hilt of his yataghan with such persuasive touch that the land soon flowed with milk, and mountains of eggs arose.

And soon there was tea before us, with all its unspeakable fragrance, and as we reclined on the floor, we found that a portmanteau was just the right height for a table; the duty of candlesticks was ably performed by a couple of intelligent natives; the rest of them stood by the open door-way at the lower end of the room, and watched our banqueting with deep and serious attention . . .

I am bound to confess, however, that with all its charms, a mud floor, (like a mercenary match) does certainly promote early rising. Long before daybreak we were up, and had breakfasted; after this there was nearly a whole tedious hour to endure, whilst the horses were laden by torch-light; but this had an end, and at last we went on once more. Cloaked, and sombre, at first we made our sullen way through the darkness, with scarcely one barter of words, but soon the genial morning burst over us, and stirred the blood so gladly through our veins, that the very Surridgees, with all their troubles, could now look up for an instant, and almost believe in the temporary goodness of God.

The actual movement from one place to another, in Europeanized countries, is a process so temporary – it occupies, I mean, so small a proportion of the traveller's entire time, that his mind remains un-settled, so long as the wheels are going; he is alive enough to the external objects of interest, which the route may afford, and to the crowding ideas which are often invited by the excitement of a chang-ing scene, but he is still conscious of being in a provisional state, and his mind is constantly recurring to the expected end of his journey; his ordinary ways of thought have been interrupted, and before any new mental habits can be formed he is quietly fixed in his hotel. It will be otherwise with you when you journey in the East.

Day after day, perhaps week after week, and month after month, your foot is in the stirrup. To taste the cold breath of the earliest morn, and to lead or follow your bright cavalcade till sunset through forests and mountain passes, through valleys and desolate plains, all this becomes your Mode of Life, and you ride, eat, drink, and curse the mosquitoes, as systematically as your friends in England eat, drink and sleep. If you are wise, you will not look upon the long period of time thus occupied by your journeys as the mere gulfs which divide you from the place to which you are going, but rather as most rare and beautiful portions of your life, from which may come temper and strength. Once feel this, and you will soon grow happy, and contented in your saddle home . . . Our pace was commonly very slow, for the baggage horses served us for a drag, and kept us to a rate of little more than five miles in the hour, but now and then, and chiefly at night, a spirit of movement would suddenly animate the whole party; the baggage horses would be teazed into a gallop, and when once this was done, there would be such a banging of port-manteaus, and such convulsions of carpet bags upon their panting sides, and the Surridgees would follow them up with such a hurricane of blows, and screams, and curses, that stopping or relaxing was scarcely possible; then the rest of us would put our horses into a gallop, and so all shouting cheerfully, would hunt and drive the sumpter beasts like a flock of goats, up hill, and down dale, right on to the end of their journey.

The distances at which we got relays of horses varied greatly; some were not more than fifteen or twenty miles, but twice, I think, we performed a whole day's journey of more than sixty miles with the same beasts . . .

One day it seemed to me that our path was a little more rugged, and less level than usual, and I found that I was deserving for myself the title of Sabalkansky, or 'Transcender of the Balcan'. The truth is that as military barrier, the Balcan is a fabulous mountain; such seems to be the view of Major Keppell, who looked on it towards the East with the eye of a soldier, and certainly in the Sophia pass, which I followed, there is no narrow defile, and no ascent sufficiently difficult to stop, or delay, for a long time, a train of siege artillery.

Before we reached Adrianople, Methley had been seized with we knew not what ailment, and when we had taken up our quarters in the city, he was cast to the very earth by sickness. Adrianople enjoyed an English Consul, and I felt sure that, in Eastern phrase, his house would cease to be his house, and would become the house of my sick comrade; I should have judged rightly under ordinary circumstance, but the levelling plague was abroad, and the dread of it had dominion over the consular mind. So now, (whether dying or not, one could hardly tell) upon a quilt stretched out along the floor, there lay the best hope of an ancient line [Methley was the name of the family's estate and used by Kinglake for that of his companion, who later succeeded to the Earldom of Mexborough] without the material aids to comfort of even the humblest sort, and (sad to say) without the consolation of a friend or even a comrade worth having . . .

We called to aid a solemn Armenian (I think he was) half soothsayer, half hakim, or doctor, who all the while counting his beads, fixed his eyes steadily upon the patient, and then suddenly dealt him a violent blow on the chest. Methley bravely dissembled his pain, for he fancied that the blow was meant to try whether or not the plague were on him.

Here was really a sad embarrassment – no bed – nothing to offer the invalid in the shape of food, save a piece of thin, tough, flexible, drab-coloured cloth, made of flower and mill-stones in equal proportions, and called by the name of 'bread'; then the patient of course, had 'no confidence in his medical man', and on the whole, the best chance of saving my comrade seemed to be by taking him out of the reach of his doctor, and bearing him away to the neighbourhood of some more genial consul. But how was this to be done? Methley was much too ill to be kept in the saddle; and wheel-carriages as a means of travelling were unknown. There is, however, such a thing as an 'Araba', a vehicle drawn by oxen, in which the wives of a rich man are sometimes dragged four or five miles over the grass by way of recreation . . .

It was a sore thing for me to see my poor comrade brought to this, for young though he was, he was a veteran in travel; when scarcely yet of age, he had invaded India from the frontiers of Russia, and that so swiftly, that measuring by the time of his flight, the broad dominions of the King of Kings were shrivelled up to a Dukedom, and now poor fellow, he was to be poked into an Araba, like a Georgian girl. He suffered greatly, for there were no springs for the carriage, and no road for the wheels, and so the concern jolted on over the open country, with such twists, and jerks, and jumps, as might almost dislocate the supple tongue of Satan.

All day the patient kept himself shut up within the lattice-work of the Araba, and I could hardly know how he was faring until the end of the day's journey, when I found that he was not worse, and was buoyed up with the hope of some day reaching Constantinople.

I was always conning over my maps, and fancied that I knew pretty well my line, but after Adrianople I had made more southing than I knew for, and it was with unbelieving wonder, and delight, that I came suddenly upon the shore of the sea; a little while, and its gentle billows were flowing beneath the hoofs of my beast, but the hearing of the ripple was not enough communion – and the seeing of the blue Propontis was not to know, and possess it – I must needs plunge into its depths and quench my longing love in the palpable waves; and so when old Mostapha (defender against demons) looked round for his charge, he saw with horror and dismay, that he for whose life his own life stood pledged, was possessed of some devil who had driven him down into the sea – that the rider and the steed had vanished from earth, and that out among the waves was the gasping crest of a post horse, and the pale head of the Englishman moving upon the face of the waters.

We started very early indeed, on the last day of our journey, and from the moment of being off, until we gained the shelter of the imperial walls, we were struggling face to face with an icy storm that swept right down from the steppes of Tartary; keen, fierce, and steady as a northern conqueror. Methley's servant, who was the greatest sufferer, kept his saddle until we reached Stamboul, but was then found to be quite benumbed in limbs, and his brain was so much affected, that when he was lifted from his horse, he fell away in a state of unconsciousness, the first stage of a dangerous fever.

Methley, in his Araba, had been sheltered from the storm, but he was sadly ill. I bore myself up capitally for a delicate person, but I was so well watered, and the blood of my veins had shrunk away so utterly from the chilling touch of the blast, that I must have looked more fit for a watery grave, than for the city of the Prince, whom men call 'Brother of the Sun'.

Our Tatar, worn down by care, and toil, and carrying seven heavens full of water, in his manifold jackets, and shawls, was a mere weak, and vapid dilution of the sleek Moostapha, who scarce more than one fortnight before came out like a bridegroom from his chamber, to take command of our party.

Mysseri seemed somewhat over-wearied, but he had lost none of his strangely quiet energy; he wore a grave look, however, for he had now learnt that the plague was prevailing at Constantinople, and he was fearing that our two sick men, and the miserable looks of our whole party, might make us unwelcome at Pera.

Our poor, dear portmanteaus, whose sharp forms had rebelled so rudely against the pack saddles were now reduced to soft, pulpy substances, and the things which were in them could plainly be of no immediate use to anybody but a merman or a river-god; the carpet bags seemed to contain nothing but mere solutions of coats and boots, escaping drop by drop.

We crossed the Golden Horn in a caique; as soon as we had landed, some woebegone looking fellows were got together, and laden with our baggage. Then, on we went, dripping and sloshing, looking very like men that had been turned back by the Royal Humane Society, as being incurably drowned. Supporting our sick, we climbed up shelving steps, and threaded many windings, and at last came up into the main street of Pera, humbly hoping that we might not be judged guilty of plague, and so be cast back with horror from the doors of the shuddering Christians.

Such was the condition of our party, which fifteen days before had filed away so gaily from the gates of Belgrade. A couple of fevers, and a north-easterly storm had thoroughly spoiled our looks.

LEGEND OF BEHISTAN
Sir Henry Creswicke Rawlinson
(1810 – 1895)

———◆———

Rich was succeeded at Baghdad by his assistant Colonel Taylor, a man of such learning that Muslim scholars and divines were said to have consulted him regularly on matters of interpretation of both holy scripture and ancient lay documents. Of great modesty he committed none, or almost none, of his work to paper though he made important investigations of the mounds of Babylon and the other places of antiquity which surrounded him. He was a worthy replacement for the remarkable Claudius Rich.

It was Taylor's own successor, however, who brought even greater glory to the office of the British Residency in Baghdad. Major Henry Creswicke Rawlinson arrived to the welcome of a thirteen-gun salute in the year 1843. In the interval between the incumbancies of these men, Baghdad had suffered the almost unimaginable calamity described by Anthony Groves – an epidemic of the plague accompanied by the flooding of the Tigris which had decimated its population, killing over a hundred thousand people from a total of about one hundred and fifty thousand.

Rawlinson, the new Resident, was already familiar with great monuments of neighbouring Persia erected to the memory of the legendary kings Cyrus and Darius. He had stopped to examine briefly the inscription of Persepolis when he led a military detachment to Bushire in 1833. While serving there he made a routine journey to Tehran to warn the British ambassador of a Russian incursion at Herât, travelling 750 miles by horse in 150 hours.

His duties at the Residency were no less arduous than they had been for those who came before him. Turks and Baghdadis, Kurds and Yezidis and Chaldaeans were never easy people to govern or control. Yet such was Rawlinson's stature that all who came into contact with him, even the Turkish pashas, bowed unquestioningly to his will. Indeed, it was said that when he appeared in the city even the most fanatical adherents of the Shia and Sunni factions of Islam stopped fighting. He built himself a house of shrubbery overhanging the river Tigris and rigged a water-wheel to kick and splash water over his strange abode as he worked for years on end through the unbearably hot Iraq summers, deciphering the clay tablets which he and others found among the ruins of Babylon and Assyria, rendering from their wedge-shaped words the first known legends, the first recorded history, of man. When he was at the Residency he was usually to be seen with his favourite pets, a leopard, a lion cub and a mongoose. The larger animals often put a paw out of the Residency window to give a friendly pat on the head to a passer-by, though the gesture was seldom appreciated. He went back to Behistan time after time, hanging like a mountaineer from ropes pegged to the sheer face of the rock, as he swung across the great sculptured slab taking rubbings of the inscriptions, using a ladder attachment as a seat. In 1847 he enlisted the help of a young Kurdish lad, and between them they completed the task of making paper rubbings of the message of *Darius, King of Kings*, words which, by comparison with likely Greek and Persian equivalents, provided the rudiments of the alphabet which Rawlinson constructed for the Elamite and Babylonian tongues. Rawlinson gave credit to the boy: '*fixed upon this seat* [the ladder] *he took under my direction the paper cast of the Babylonian translation of the records of Darius'*, he noted in 1847. Fifty years later, those original copies, made with such care and at so much peril, were found in the British Museum, which was then receiving government aid to finance the archaeological exploration of Babylonia and Assyria. They were partly eaten away by mice, but fortunately Rawlinson had recorded them along with the hundreds of tablet-inscriptions at which he worked patiently in his river-house over many years, until his health gave way. He did not, however, record his adventures, but, fortunately, on one of his journeys in 1844 he was accompanied by Commander J. F. Jones of the Indian Navy, whose account of their passage along the Tigris and Diyala rivers to Kirmanshah was published in 1849.

They set out from Baghdad on 19 August 1844 and reached the plain of Kirmanshah on the 31st of the same month.

FROM NARRATIVE OF A JOURNEY
THROUGH PARTS OF PERSIA
AND KURDISTAN
BY COMMANDER J. F. JONES, I.N.

Though the town of Kirmanshah possesses in itself scarcely a single feature of interest, the neighbourhood must be viewed as a locality abounding in antiquarian riches. The extensive plain on which it is situated, joining that of Mahidasht to the west, extends also some distance to the east beyond the storied rock of Behistan. To the north, the bold and serrated crags of a spur from the great Shahu range, surmounted by the Peak of Parrow, confine its breadth to a distance of about six miles, while its length may be reckoned as exceeding thirty. The waters of the Kara-su, flowing from the N.W., are met by those of the Gamasab, derived from a N.E'ly. source, a few miles S.E. of the town. These form the main source of the Kerha (Choaspes). Over this vast plain is scattered the remnants of antique edifices, whose very names are lost in obscurity. Headless columns and baseless capitals, of an unknown and unique order, border the main road, which passes through the plain. These serve to attract and excite the attention of the traveller, who is soon rewarded for his past toils by the sight of monuments of a more absorbing interest. I allude to the Taki-Bostan sculptures, and the engraved tablets of Darius at Behistan. The latter, the most elaborate and extensive in Persia, in connection with the cuneiform inscriptions of Persepolis, of Hamadan, and of Van, have already awakened the intellectual repose of enlightened orientalists, and will shortly incite, through the talents and acumen of my fellow traveller, an additional interest over the whole of the European world. This locality, indeed, though comprising but a comparatively small proportion of the large expanse now open to research, offers in itself many powerful stimuli to engage the active mind of the antiquarian and geographer . . .

Sept. 4th. — The ladders for the ascent of the Behistan cliffs, being ready, we left Kirmanshah at 5.5 A.M., on a delightfully cool morning. Proceeded due east, or 90°, until 6.5, when the Kara-Su was crossed by a substantial bridge called Puli Shah. Continued in the same direction over a fine plain having the Parrow range of hills at a distance of four miles to the left of the road. Passed by several villages of cultivators, and exchanged greetings with some caravans of pilgrims en route from the capital to Baghdad and Kerbela. At 9h. A.M. the road inclined a little more northerly towards the hills over the site of some ancient buildings whose alignments can now scarcely be traced; but the numerous fragments of columns, cut stones, pedestals, and capitals of a Sassanian design, attest it as a ruin of that age.

From 9.45 to 10.15, the road turned to the north in a gradual curve as we rounded the termination of the Parrow range, known by the appellation of the 'Rock of Behistan'. At the latter time the Caravanserai, or Khan of the same name, received us as its tenants for some days to come. Its murky vaults, redolent of every effluvium, smoke-begrimed and covered with pendant bats, afford a striking contrast to the marble hall and fountained apartment of our abode of yesterday: and yet, after all, this is the life that charms. The real traveller, indeed, knows neither inconvenience nor discomfort; he sits down to his scanty fare of an onion, cheese, and pure water, with more zest than awaits the epicure at a sumptuous repast. So long as he keeps his health – which is certain unless in a very noxious climate – he suffers neither indigestion nor ennui, and enjoys that quiet sleep which is only experienced after a day of active exercise both of the mind and body.

The afternoon of this day was devoted to cleaning the sculptures and inscriptions preparatory to Major Rawlinson's revising his former labors. The ladders had been carefully fixed, and the requisite ropes for assisting the ascent up the steep face of the lower portion of the scarp properly adjusted, beforehand. In about a quarter of an hour, not without sundry scratches and bruises, the platform at the base of the tablet was gained, and operations commenced accordingly. From this time until the 11th of the month we remained in this vicinity. The Major constantly and indefatigably employed himself, from daylight to dark, revising, restoring, and adding to, his former materials, This was a work of great irksomeness and labor in the confined space he was compelled to stand in, with his body in close proximity to the heated rock and under a broiling September sun . . .

For the observation of all, a more appropriate spot could scarcely have been selected than the Rock of Behistan, where this petral record now exists, in the same state, and in almost the same degree of perfection, as when first executed. About 300 feet above the debris, at the foot of the mountains, and overlooking the plain, the face of the rock has been chiselled so as to expose a smooth surface for the reception of the work. This surface may be divided into four tablets. The main one, devoted to the sculpture illustrative of the writing beneath them, is the largest, and is thirty feet in length and twenty-six feet high. Of this the sculptured slab, with a pedestal of eleven inches, occupies fourteen feet; the remaining portion being dedicated to the reception of the archaic legend, written on four columns in the Persepolitan cuneiform character. Each of these columns, containing ninety-six lines, are six feet and four inches in breadth; and a supplementary half column, now much defaced, appears to have been subsequently appended. Immediately to the left of these, as they are viewed, a projecting slab, twenty-one feet in length, exhibits in three columns a transcript in the more elaborate Median tongue. Their height is the same, but in breadth they exceed by six inches the dimensions of the Persepolitan columns. Immediately above the Median tablet, – with its base, indeed, resting on and slightly projecting over it, – is a semi-isolated rock, inclining inwards towards the hill. This has been scraped on its face and sides, and bears a legend in the still more complicated Babylonian cuneiform, – in all probability a translation in that language of the original text. To the right of the main tablet the hill has also been smoothened for a further space of six feet, and is covered with characters, but so much destroyed, either by time or the action of water, that it is even difficult to distinguish the nature of the character. I am induced to believe, however, that this portion of the work may be either a record of a subsequent age, or that the same pains had not been taken for the preservation of it as was bestowed on Persepolitan and Median designs. In the latter the rock bears evidence of a careful preparation, and has undergone the process of varnishing before the engraver commenced his labors. This varnish is composed of a hard, flinty, and very durable, substance, and, where not destroyed by the constant trituration of rainwater finding its way down from the heights above, is as perfect and smooth as the day it was laid on. The natural rock, indeed, is not difficult to cut, but the prepared portion resisted a steel chisel that we brought with us, with which we could only succeed in chipping the surface. The great depth, and well-defined outline, of the letters, exhibit considerable skill on the part of the engraver. They are one and a quarter inch in length.

The sculptures comprise a group of fourteen figures, and are no doubt intended to elucidate the text below them. If we except the central and more elevated figure, which may represent the supreme Ormazd, and those of Darius and his two attendants, to the left of the design, we may pronounce the rest of the group as deficient in artistical beauty, and, indeed, show but a hieratic style. Their forms are diminutive, stiff, and ill-defined; and their habiliments, though well marked, betray no elegance of drapery whatever: the limbs are coarse and misshapen, and their countenances devoid either of animation or expression. Nine of these figures are standing, and are attached to each other by a long cord passing around their necks. Their hands are bound behind them. The badness of design, and dwarflike forms, in this portion of the sculptures, I presume, is intentional, to denote the inferior and degrading position of the captives, – the metamorphosis serving to convey to the minds of the ignorant and uninitiated the more exalted position and greater virtues of the conqueror, who is represented by a commanding stature, in the attitude of a victor, with his left foot on the body of a prostrate foe, the tenth of the captive group. The form of the Great

Darius is portrayed by a superior execution. His features are well developed, and exhibit that energy and determination of character for which he was celebrated. A degree of finish and study pervade the figure of the monarch, who is singularly enough represented with bare feet, while his captives and followers are either sandal-clad or wear a coarse species of shoes. His head, surmounted by the diadem, displays, after the fashion of the day, a carefully-curled mop of bushy hair, extending nearly to the shoulders. The upper lip, too, is adorned with an elegant moustache, and the beard, fantastically disposed in stiff and separately curved tresses, adds much to the dignity of his appearance. The left hand grasps the bow, the symbol of regal power; while the right is elevated and extended towards the prisoners, in the attitude of angry expostulation. The wrists are adorned with bracelets, and a girdle or zone, terminating in two tassels, encircles the waist of the monarch, and serves to bind the flowing tunic that he is habited in. A loose vest or jacket, with large open sleeves, completes his attire. The attendant guards, in their dress, differ but little from the monarch. They have sandals on their feet, and the head is covered with a circular cap only. The one nearest to majesty also bears the regal bow, and a well-stocked quiver hangs pendant at his back. The farthest removed from the king differs from the last only in being armed with a spear, which is held upright by both hands in front, the shaft resting on the ground.

The aerial figure which hovers over the centre of the group would seem to represent the Supreme Being; and this idea is in a measure confirmed by its also presiding over the sculptured monuments of antiquity met with at Persepolis. As the old Persian records always contained an invocation to the deity, so it would appear that their statuary tablets likewise required to be hallowed by the introduction of the Omniscient Creator. Some writers have imagined that the figure merely denoted the spirit of a departed monarch, and was symbolical of the immaterial substance of man. Others have denominated it the 'Ferooher' of the Zend-Avesta: the soul or spirit that presided over all the royal acts – a constant guardian over the regal head: an emblem of the favouritism of Ormazd – a type of the anointed of the Lord.

From its elevated and exact central position on the slab at Behistan, I think, however, we may conclude it to be the effigy of the Creator himself.

It is a half-length figure, clothed with the short vest similar to that of the king, from which depends a long flowing and plaited robe, spread out fan-wise at its skirts; a zone or girdle, terminating in snake-like ends on either side, confines this at the waist . . .

At the base of the mountain, on the projecting angle before alluded to, and close to a copious spring which issues from the hill, and irrigates a part of the neighbouring plain, once stood a colossal group of figures executed in alto-relievo. They are, however, so much mutilated by the despoiler Time, or by the desecrating Arab, that nothing but a faint outline is now distinguishable. The centre of the tablet has even been barbarously cut away, to expose a smooth surface for the reception of an Arabic inscription celebrating the virtues and liberality of one Sheikh Ali Khan, the founder of the caravanserai of Behistan. The tablet bears, too, a Greek record, of which but a few unconnected words are now traceable . . .

On the debris of the mountain, about 300 yards farther to the north, a singular isolated stone, of a triangular shape, was discovered; this I believe has before been noticed. It bears, carved on its sides, in basso-relievo, a rough but well defined design of three figures a little under the natural size. The principal bas-relief exposes a front view of a clumsy human form, with the right arm extended, the hand grasping a globe or ball, resting on the summit of an 'incus' shaped block. The left arm is supported close to the body, and bears in the hand a cup-shaped utensil, probably representing the 'Patera' of the sacrifices, or the 'Havan' of the Zend-Avesta, and the first named may, therefore, denote the 'Ara' of the Zoroastrian doctrines; a second figure on the face of the stone nearest the mountain, represents a foot-soldier, in the act of advancing with a bow in his hand, executed in the same clumsy style; the third is so much worn by time that no peculiarity is distinguishable.

This stone, on the whole, is a venerable vestige of a former age: any attempt to assign a date to it would, however, be but an idle speculation . . .

Our labors having been brought to a close on the 10th September, the ladders were cast headlong from the rock into the plain below, to prevent mutilation of the tablets. They were shivered into a thousand pieces, and caused a shudder at the thought of a false footstep consigning one to the same fate.

September 11th. – A raw chilly morning saw us on horseback at 3.30 A.M., on our return to Kirmanshah. The beautiful star Canopus, the forerunner of winter in these parts, first shewed itself above our horizon on this day. As we intended to visit the celebrated Arch of the 'Tak-i-Bostan', our road now lay more to the north than the route we had formerly traversed on our way to Behistan. Skirting the bold chain of Parrow, we arrived at the Tak-i-Bostan at 8.40 A.M., glad enough to shelter ourselves in the shade of the arch from the rays of the sun, which by this time had become somewhat oppressive.

PUNCH
IN THE EAST

William Makepeace Thackeray
(1811 – 1863)

———

The 19th day of October, 1844 (the seventh day of the month
Hudjmudj, and the 1229th year of the Mohammedan Hejira, corresponding with the 16,769th anniversary of the 48th incarnation of
Veeshnoo), is a day that ought hereafter to be considered eternally
famous in the climes of the East and West. I forget what was the day
of GENERAL BONAPARTE's battle of the Pyramids; I think it
was in the month Quintidi of the year Nivrose of the French Republic,
and he told his soldiers that forty centuries looked down upon them
from the summit of those buildings – a statement which I very much
doubt. But I say THE 19TH DAY OF OCTOBER, 1844, is the most
important era in the modern world's history. It unites the modern
with the ancient civilisation; it couples the brethren of WATT and
COBDEN with the dusky family of PHARAOH and SESOSTRIS:
it fuses HERODOTUS with THOMAS BABINGTON
MACAULAY; it intertwines the piston of the blond Anglo-Saxon
steam-engine with the Needle of the Abysinnian CLEOPATRA: it
weds the tunnel of the subaqueous BRUNEL with the mystic edifice
of CHEOPS. Strange play of wayward fancy! Ascending the Pyramid,
I could not but think of Waterloo Bridge in my dear native London –
a building as vast and as magnificent, as beautiful, as useless, and
lonely. Forty centuries have not as yet passed over the latter structure,
'tis true; scarcely an equal number of hackney-coaches have crossed it.
But I doubt whether the individuals who contributed to raise it are
likely to receive a better dividend for their capital than the swarthy
shareholders in the Pyramid's speculation, whose dust has long since
been trampled over by countless generations of their sons.

If I use in the above sentence the longest words I can find, it is
because the occasion is great and demands the finest phrases the
dictionary can supply; it is because I have not read TOM MACAULAY
in vain; it is because I wish to show I am a dab in history, as the above

dates will testify; it is because I have seen the Reverend Mr Milman preach in a black gown at Saint Margaret's, whereas at the Coronation he wore a gold cope. The 19th of October was *Punch*'s Coronation: I officiated at the august ceremony. To be brief – as illiterate readers may not understand a syllable of the above piece of ornamental eloquence – ON THE 19TH OF OCTOBER, 1844 I PASTED THE GREAT PLACARD OF PUNCH ON THE PYRAMID OF CHEOPS. I did it. The Fat Contributor did it. If I die, it could not be undone. If I perish, I have not lived in vain.

If the forty centuries are on the summit of the Pyramids, as BONAPARTE remarks, all I can say is, I did not see them. But *Punch* has really been there; this I swear. One placard I pasted on the first landing-place (who knows how long Arab rapacity will respect the sacred hieroglyphic!). One I placed under a great stone on the summit; one I waved in the air, as my Arabs raised a mighty cheer round the peaceful victorious banner; and I flung it towards the sky, which the Pyramid almost touches, and left it to its fate, to mount into the azure vault and take its place among the constellations; to light on the eternal Desert, and mingle with its golden sands . . .

I wonder were there any signs or omens in London when that event occurred! Did an earthquake take place? Did Stocks or the Barometer preternaturally rise or fall? It matters little. Let it suffice that the thing has been done, and forms an event in History by the side of those other facts to which these prodigious monuments bear testimony. Now to narrate briefly the circumstances of the day.

On Thursday, October 17, I caused my dragoman to purchase in the Frank bazaar at Grand Cairo the following articles, which will be placed in the Museum on my return.

A is a tin pot holding about a pint, and to contain B, a packet of flour (which of course is not visible, as it is tied up in brown paper), and C, a pig-skin brush of the sort commonly used in Europe – the whole costing about 5 piastres, or one shilling sterling. They were all the implements needful for this tremendous undertaking.

Horses of the Mosaic Arab breed, I mean those animals called Jerusalem ponies by some in England, by others denominated donkeys, are the common means of transport employed by the subjects of MEHEMET ALI. My excellent friend BUCKSHEESH PASHA would have mounted me either on his favourite horse, or his best dromedary. But I declined those proffers – if I fall, I like better to fall from a short distance than a high one. –

I have tried tumbling in both ways, and recommend the latter as by far the pleasantest and safest. I chose the Mosaic Arab then – one for the dragoman, one for the requisites of refreshment, and two for myself – not that I proposed to ride two at once, but a person of a certain dimension had best have a couple of animals in case of accident.

I left Cairo on the afternoon of October 18, never hinting to a single person the mighty purpose of my journey. The waters were out, and we had to cross them thrice – twice in track-boats, once on the shoulders of abominable Arabs, who take a pleasure in slipping and in making believe to plunge you in the stream. When in the midst of it, the brutes stop and demand money of you – you are alarmed, the savages may drop you if you do not give – you promise that you will do so. The half-naked ruffians who conduct you up the Pyramid, when they have got you panting to the most steep, dangerous, and lonely stone, make the same demand, pointing downwards while they beg, as if they would fling you in that direction on refusal. As soon as you have breath, you promise more money – it is the best way – you are a fool if you give it when you come down.

The journey I find briefly set down in my pocket-book as thus: Cairo-Gardens – Mosquitoes – Women dressed in blue – Children dressed in nothing – Old Cairo – Nile, dirty water, ferry-boat – Town – Palm trees, ferry-boat, canal, palm-trees, town – Rice fields – Maize fields – Fellows on dromedaries – Donkey down – Over his head – Pick up pieces – More palm-trees – More rice-fields – Water-courses – Howling Arabs – Donkey tumble down again – Inundations – Herons or cranes – Broken bridges – Sands – Pyramids. – If a man cannot make a landscape out of that he has no imagination.

Let him paint the skies very blue – the sands very yellow – the plains very flat and green – the dromedaries and palm-trees very tall – the women very brown, some with veils, some with nose-rings, some tattooed, and none with stays – and the picture is complete. You may shut your eyes and fancy yourself there. It is the pleasantest way, *entre nous*.

It is all very well to talk of sleeping in the tombs; that question has been settled in a former paper, where I have stated my belief that people do not sleep at all in Egypt. I thought to have had some tremendous visions under the shadow of those enormous Pyramids reposing under the stars. PHARAOH, or CLEOPATRA, I thought,

Thackeray assisted up a pyramid, from *Punch*, 1844

might appear to me in a dream. But how could they, as I didn't go to sleep! I hoped for high thoughts, and secret communings with the Spirit of Poesy – I hoped to have let off a sonnet at least, as gentlemen do on visiting the spot – but how could I hunt for rhymes, being occupied all night in hunting for something else! If this remonstrance will deter a single person from going to the Pyramids, my purpose is fully answered.

But my case was different. I had a duty to perform – I had to introduce *Punch* to CHEOPS and had vowed to leave his card at the gates of History – I had a mission, in a word. I roused at sunrise the snoring dragoman from his lair. I summoned the four Arabs who had engaged to assist me in the ascent, and in the undertaking. We lighted a fire of camel's dung at the North-East corner of the Pyramid, just as the god of day rose over Cairo! The embers began to glow, water was put into the tin pot before mentioned, – the pot was put on the fire – 'twas a glorious – a thrilling moment!

At 46 minutes past 6, A.M., (by one of DOLLOND's Chronometers) the water began to boil.

At 47 minutes the flour was put gradually into the water – it was stirred with the butt-end of the brush brought for the purpose, and SCHMAKLEK BEG, an Arab, peeping over the pot too curiously, I poked the brush into his mouth at 11 minutes before 7, A.M.

At 7, THE PASTE WAS MADE – doubting whether it was thick enough, SCHEMAKLEK tried it with his finger. It was pronounced to be satisfactory.

At 11 minutes past 7, I turned round in a majestic attitude to the four Arabs, and said, 'Let us mount.'

Having given the signal – the Sheikh of the Arabs seized my right arm, and his brother the left. Two volunteer Arabs pushed me (quite unnecessarily) behind. The other two preceded – one with a water-bottle for refreshment; the other with the posters – the pot – the paintbrush and the paste. Away we went – away!

I was blown at the third step. They are exceedingly lofty; about 5 feet high each, I should think – but the ardent spirit will break his heart to win the goal – besides I could not go back if I would. The two Arabs dragged me forward by the arms – the volunteers pushed me up from behind. It was in vain I remonstrated with the latter, kicking violently as occasion offered – they still went on pushing. We arrived at the first landing-place.

I drew out the poster – how it fluttered in the breeze! – With a trembling hand I popped the brush into the paste pot, and smeared the back of the placard, then I pasted up the Standard of our glorious leader – at 19 minutes past 7, by the clock of the great minaret at Cairo, which was clearly visible through my refracting telescope. My heart throbbed when the deed was done. My eyes filled with tears – I am not at liberty to state here all the emotions of triumph and joy which rose in my bosom – so exquisitely overpowering were they. There was *Punch* – familiar old *Punch* – his back to the desert, his beaming face turned towards the Nile.

'Bless him!' I exclaimed, embracing him; and almost choking, gave the signal to the Arabs to move on.

These savage creatures are only too ready to obey an order of this nature. They spin a man along, be his size never so considerable. They rattled up to the second landing so swiftly that I thought I should be broken-winded for ever. But they gave us little time to halt. Yallah! Again we mount! – 'tis the last and most arduous ascent – the limbs quiver, the pulses beat, the eyes shoot out of the head, the brain reels, the knees tremble and totter, and you are on the summit. I don't know how many hundred thousand feet it is above the level of the sea, but I wonder after that tremendous exercise that I am not a roarer to my dying hour.

When consciousness and lungs regained their play, another copy of the placard was placed under a stone – a third was launched into air in the manner before described, and we gave three immense cheers for *Punch,* which astonished the undiscovered mummies that lie darkling in tomb-chambers, and must have disturbed the broken-nosed old Sphinx who has been couched for thousands of years in the desert hard by. This done, we made our descent from the Pyramids.

And if, my dear sir, you ask me whether it is worth a man's while to mount up those enormous stones, I will say in confidence that thousands of people went to see the Bottle Conjuror, and that we hear of gentlemen becoming Free-Masons every day.

THE DISCOVERY OF NINEVEH

From Nineveh and its Remains by Sir Austen Henry Layard

(1817 – 1894)

———————

Rawlinson had not yet arrived in Baghdad to embellish the achievements of Rich when, in 1839, Henry Layard made his first visit to Asia Minor, '*scarcely leaving untrod one spot hallowed by tradition, or unvisited one ruin consecrated by history*'. Colonel Taylor still worked with infinite patience and energy at the Residency, ever studying and recording in his chosen isolation, cared for by his Armenian wife and two daughters, visited by a never-ending procession of learned men.

Layard was so intrigued by the signs of antiquity which surrounded him on his first journey that he abandoned a plan to go to India. Instead he went to Constantinople where he met the patron and first sponsor of his intended work, the British ambassador Stratford Canning. Layard was to return to the Ottoman capital in later years, famous and wealthy despite a chequered intervening career in politics, as emissary to the Porte. For the moment, however, he entertained a single ambition: to return to the mounds which had incited his curiosity in the region of Mosul, mounds which Claudius Rich had instinctively identified with ancient Nineveh and which the Frenchman Paul Emile Botta was by then investigating. He wrote of his '*longing to cross the great river, and to explore those lands which are separated on the map from the confines of Syria by a vast blank stretching from Aleppo to the banks of the Tigris.*'

Layard reached Mosul on 10 April 1840. After visiting the mounds of Kouyunjik and Nebbi Yunus, he journeyed down the Tigris to the vast ruin of Kalat Sherghat at a point 50 miles from the junction of the river with its tributary, the Zab. '*This was the pyramid Xenophon had described, and near which the ten thousand had camped*', twenty-two centuries before. Even then the mound marked the spot of an ancient city. Xenophon called it Larissa. Layard left the site as he found it, returning in the summer of 1842. On the way he met the French Consul Paul Botta who was digging at Kouyunjik, though he was shortly to move north to Khorsabad where he made his most important finds. The Englishman was the first to call the world's attention to his French companion's work. But not for another four years did he begin to dig seriously at the mound which he believed to mark the city of Nimrud, Calah of the Bible (Genesis 10-11). He was accompanied by his close friend Hormuzd Rassam, brother of the British vice-consul at Mosul, who was his right hand during the years of patient digging and momentous discovery among the ruins of ancient Assyria. He also took a party of Chaldaean Christians to help with the work, while he contended with the Qadhi and Mufti who stirred up trouble around him. Layard later returned to Kouyunjik, the real site of ancient Nineveh, where the palace of Ashurbanipal was discovered with its royal library, containing more than 20,000 cuneiform-inscribed tablets.

———◆———

The Abou Salman Arabs, who encamp around Nimroud, are known for their thieving propensities, and might have caused me some annoyance. Thinking it prudent, therefore, to conciliate their chief, I rode over one morning to their principal encampment. Sheikh Abd-ur-rahman received me at the entrance of his capacious tent of black goat-hair, which was crowded with his relations, followers, and strangers, who were enjoying his hospitality. He was one of the handsomest Arabs I ever saw; tall, robust, and well-made, with a countenance in which intelligence was no less marked than courage and resolution. On his head he wore a turban of dark linen, from under which a many-coloured handkerchief fell over his shoulders; his dress was a simple white shirt, descending to the ankles, and an Arab cloak thrown loosely over it. Unlike Arabs in general, he had shaved his beard; and, although he could scarcely be much beyond forty, I observed that the little hair which could be distinguished from under his turban was grey. He received me with every demonstration of hospitality, and led me to the upper palace, divided by a goat-hair curtain from the harem. The tent was capacious; half was appropriated for the women, the rest formed the place of reception, and was at the same time occupied by two favourite mares and a colt. A few camels were kneeling on the grass around, and the horses of the strangers were tied by the halter to the tent-pins. From the carpets and cushions, which were spread for me, stretched on both sides a long line of men of the most motley appearance, seated on the bare ground. The Sheikh himself, as is the custom in some of the tribes, to show his respect for his guest, placed himself at the furthest end; and could only be prevailed upon, after many excuses and protestations, to share the carpet with me. In the centre of the group, near a small fire of camel's dung, crouched a half-naked Arab, engaged alternately in blowing up the expiring embers, and in pounding the roasted coffee in a copper mortar, ready to replenish the huge pots which stood near him.

After the customary compliments had been exchanged with all around, one of my attendants beckoned to the Sheikh, who left the tent to receive the presents I had brought to him – a silk gown and a supply of coffee and sugar. He dressed himself in his new attire and returned to the assembly. 'Inshallah,' said I, 'we are now friends, although scarcely a month ago you came over the Zab on purpose to appropriate the little property I am accustomed to carry about me.' 'Wallah, Bey,' he replied, 'you say true, we are friends; but listen: the Arabs either sit down and serve his Majesty the Sultan, or they eat from others, as others would eat from them. Now my tribe are of the Zobeide, and were brought here many years ago by the Pashas of the Abd-el-Jelleel. These lands were given us in return for the services we rendered the Turks in keeping back the Tai and the Shammar, who crossed the rivers to plunder the villages. All the great men of the Abou Salman perished in encounters with the Bedouin, and Injeh Bairakdar, Mohammed Pasha, upon whom God has had mercy, acknowledged our fidelity and treated us with honour. When that blind dog, the son of the Cretan, may curses fall upon him! came to Mosul, I waited upon him, as it is usual for the Sheikh; what did he do? Did he give me the cloak of honour? No; he put me, an Arab of the tribe of Zobeide, a tribe which had fought with the Prophet, into the public stocks. For forty days my heart melted away in a damp cell, and I was exposed to every variety of torture. Look at these hairs,' continued he, lifting up his turban, 'they turned white in that time, and I must now shave my beard, a shame amongst the Arabs. I was released at last; but how did I return to the tribe? – a beggar, unable to kill a sheep for my guests. He took my mares, my flocks, and my camels, as the price of my liberty. Now tell me, O Bey, in the name of God, if the Osmanlis have eaten from me and my guests, shall I not eat from them and theirs?'

The fate of Abd-ur-rahman had been such as he described it; and so had fared several chiefs of the desert and of the mountains. It was not surprising that these men, proud of their origin and accustomed to the independence of a wandering life, had revenged themselves upon the unfortunate inhabitants of the villages, who had no less cause to complain than themselves. However, the Sheikh promised to

Discovery of the Gigantic Head at Nineveh, from Layard's
Nineveh and its Remains, London, 1849

abstain from plunder for the future, and to present himself to Ismail Pasha, of whose conciliatory conduct he had already heard.

It was nearly the middle of February before I thought it prudent to make fresh experiments among the ruins. To avoid notice I only employed a few men, and confined myself to the examination of such parts of the mound as appeared to contain buildings ...

The corner-stone led me to a figure of singular form. A human body, clothed in robes similar to those of the winged men already described, was surmounted by the head of an eagle or of a vulture. The curved beak, of considerable length, was half open, and displayed a narrow pointed tongue, which was still coloured with red paint. On the shoulders fell the usual curled and bushy hair of the Assyrian images, and a comb of feathers rose on the top of the head. Two wings sprang from the back, and in either hand was the square vessel and fir-cone.

On all these figures paint could be faintly distinguished, particularly on the hair, beard, eyes, and sandals. The slabs on which they were sculptured had sustained no injury, and could be without difficulty packed and moved to any distance. There could no longer be any doubt that they formed part of a chamber, and that, to explore it completely, I had only to continue along the wall, now partly uncovered.

On the morning following these discoveries I rode to the encampment of Sheikh Abd-ur-rahman, and was returning to the mound when I saw two Arabs of his tribe urging their mares to the top of their speed. On approaching me they stopped. 'Hasten, O Bey,' exclaimed one of them – 'hasten to the diggers, for they have found Nimrod himself. Wallah, it is wonderful, but it is true! We have seen him with our eyes. There is no God but God;' and both joining in this pious exclamation, they galloped off, without further words, in the direction of their tents.

On reaching the ruins I descended into the new trench and found the workmen, who had already seen me, as I approached, standing near a heap of baskets and cloaks. Whilst Awad advanced, and asked for a present to celebrate the occasion, the Arabs withdrew the screen they had hastily constructed, and disclosed an enormous human head sculptured in full out of the alabaster of the country. They had uncovered the upper part of a figure, the remainder of which was still buried in the earth. I saw at once that the head must belong to a winged lion or bull, similar to those of Khorsabad and Persepolis. It was in admirable preservation. The expression was calm, yet majestic, and the outline of the features showed a freedom and knowledge of art, scarcely to be looked for in the works of so remote a period. The cap had three horns, and, unlike that of the human-headed bulls hitherto found in Assyria, was rounded and without ornament at the top.

I was not surprised that the Arabs had been amazed and terrified at this apparition. It required no stretch of imagination to conjure up the most strange fancies. This gigantic head, blanched with age, thus rising from the bowels of the earth, might well have belonged to one of those fearful beings which are pictured in the traditions of the country, as appearing to mortals, slowly ascending from the regions below. One of the workmen, on catching the first glimpse of the monster, had thrown down his basket and had run off towards Mosul as fast as his legs could carry him. I learnt this with regret as I anticipated the consequences.

Whilst I was superintending the removal of the earth, which still clung to the sculpture, and giving directions for the continuation of the work, a noise of horsemen was heard, and presently Abd-ur-rahman, followed by half his tribe, appeared on the edge of the trench. As soon as the two Arabs had reached the tents, and published the wonders they had seen, every one mounted his mare and rode to the mound to satisfy himself of the truth of these conceivable reports. When they beheld the head they all cried together, 'There is no God but God, and Mohammed is his Prophet!' It was some time before the Sheikh could be prevailed upon to descend into the pit, and convince himself that the image he saw was of stone. 'This is not the work of men's hands,' exclaimed he, 'but of those infidel giants of whom the Prophet – peace be with him! – has said that they were higher than the tallest date tree; this is one of the idols which Noah – peace be with him! – cursed before the flood.' In this opinion, the result of a careful examination, all the bystanders concurred.

I now ordered a trench to be dug due south from the head, in the expectation of finding a corresponding figure, and before night-fall reached the object of my search about twelve feet distant. Engaging two or three men to sleep near the sculptures, I returned to the village, and celebrated the day's discovery by a slaughter of sheep, of which all the Arabs near partook. As some wandering musicians chanced to be at Selamiyah, I sent for them, and dances were kept up during the greater part of the night. On the following morning

Arabs from the other side of the Tigris, and the inhabitants of the surrounding villages, congregated on the mound. Even the women could not repress their curiosity, and came in crowds, with their children, from afar. My Cawass was stationed during the day in the trench, into which I would not allow the multitude to descend.

As I had expected, the report of the discovery of the gigantic head, carried by the terrified Arab to Mosul, had thrown the town into commotion. He had scarcely checked his speed before reaching the bridge. Entering breathless into the bazaars, he announced to every one he met that Nimrod had appeared. The news soon got to the ears of the Cadi, who, anxious for a fresh opportunity to annoy me, called the Mufti and the Ulema together, to consult upon this unexpected occurrence. Their deliberations ended in a procession to the Governor, and a formal protest, on the part of the Mussulmans of the town, against proceedings so directly contrary to the laws of the Koran. The Cadi had no distinct idea whether the bones of the mighty hunter had been uncovered, or only his image; nor did Ismail Pasha very clearly remember whether Nimrod was a true-believing prophet, or an infidel. I consequently received a somewhat unintelligible message from his Excellency, to the effect that the remains should be treated with respect, and be by no means further disturbed; that he wished the excavations to be stopped at once, and desired to confer with me on the subject.

I called upon him accordingly, and had some difficulty in making him understand the nature of my discovery. As he requested me to discontinue my operations until the sensation in the town had some-what subsided, I returned to Nimroud and dismissed the workmen, retaining only two men to dig leisurely along the walls without giving cause for further interference. I ascertained by the end of March the existence of a second pair of winged human-headed Lions, differing from those previously discovered in form, the human shape being continued to the waist, and furnished with arms. In one hand each figure carried a goat or stag, and in the other, which hung down by the side, a branch with three flowers. They formed a northern en-trance into the chamber of which the lions previously described were the western portal. I completely uncovered the latter, and found them to be entire. They were about twelve feet in height, and the same number in length. The body and limbs were admirably portrayed; the muscles and bones, although strongly developed to display the strength of the animal, showed at the same time a correct knowledge

Eagle-headed figure from N. W. Palace of Nimrud by Sir Henry
Layard, *Nineveh and its Remains*

of its anatomy and form. Expanded wings sprang from the shoulder and spread over the back; a knotted girdle, ending in tassels, encircled the lions. These sculptures, forming an entrance, were partly in full and partly in relief. The head and fore-part, facing the chamber, were in full; but only one side of the rest of the slab was sculptured, the back being placed against the wall of sun-dried bricks. That the spectator might have both a perfect front and side view of the figures, they were furnished with five legs; two were carved on the end of the slab to face the chamber, and three on the side. The relief of the body and three limbs was high and bold, and the slab was covered, in all parts not occupied by the image, with inscriptions in the cuneiform character. These magnificent specimens of Assyrian art were in perfect preservation; the most minute lines in the details of the wings and in the ornaments had been retained with their original freshness. Not a character was wanting in the inscriptions.

I used to contemplate for hours these mysterious emblems, and muse over their intent and history. What more noble forms could have ushered the people into the temple of their gods? What more sublime images could have been borrowed from nature by men who sought, unaided by the light of revealed religion, to embody their conception of the wisdom, power, and ubiquity of a Supreme Being? They could find no better type of intellect and knowledge than the head of the man; of strength, than the body of the lion, of ubiquity, than the wings of the bird. These winged human-headed lions were not idle creations, the offspring of mere fancy; their meaning was written upon them. They had awed and instructed races which flourished 3000 years ago. Through the portals which they guarded, kings, priests, and warriors had borne sacrifices to their altars, long before the wisdom of the East had penetrated to Greece, and had furnished its mythology with symbols long recognised by the Assyrian votaries. They may have been buried, and their existence may have been unknown, before the foundation of the eternal city. For twenty-five centuries they had been hidden from the eye of man, and they now stood forth once more in their ancient majesty. But how changed was the scene around them. The luxury and civilisation of a mighty nation had given place to the wretchedness and ignorance of a few half-barbarous tribes. The wealth of temples, and the riches of great cities, had been succeeded by ruins and shapeless heaps of earth. Above the spacious hall in which they stood, the plough had passed and the corn now waved. Egypt has monuments no less ancient and no less wonderful; but they have stood forth for ages to testify her early powers and renown; whilst those before me had now appeared to bear witness, in the words of the prophet, that once 'the Assyrian was a cedar in Lebanon with fair branches and with a shadowing shroud of an high stature; and his top was among the thick boughs . . . his height was exalted above all the trees of the field, and his boughs were multiplied, and his branches became long, because of the multitude of waters when he shot forth. All the fowls of heaven made their nests in his boughs, and under his branches did all the beasts of the fields bring forth their young, and under his shadow dwelt all great nations; 'for now is Nineveh a desolation and dry like a wilderness, and flocks lie down in the midst of her: all the beasts of the nations, both the cormorant and bittern, lodge in the upper lintels of it; their voice sings in the windows; and desolation is in the thresholds.'

As Layard's team excavated the interior chambers of the mound it became apparent that the palace which once belonged to King Shalmaneser III of Assyria had been partially destroyed by fire, as indeed had most of the palaces of that distant empire. And so he changed the direction of digging towards the centre of the vast chamber he had been investigating. In a few days workmen had unearthed the top of a slab which was well preserved and apparently still in its original position. Two massive figures of humans were uncovered, sculptured in low relief. Ornaments delicately graven on the robes, tassels, fringes, bracelets and armlets, elaborate hair styles, beards; all were entire. The figures, furnished with wings, stood back to back. One carried a fallow deer and his right hand a branch bearing flowers, representing, it seemed, divinities presiding over the seasons. For the first time since he had started to dig on the still uncertain sites of Nineveh, Layard had begun to find the undamaged remains of Assyrian civilization. The winged bulls, lions and humans; great relief-decorated panels and cuneiform-inscribed tablets were destined to excite the interest and the envy of the western world and bring archaeological teams from several countries to compete with Britain and France for the spoils. Even as Layard dug at Nimroud and Botta at Khorsabad, the dangers became obvious. The careful methods of scientific archaeology so well used in later years by the Deutsche Orient Gesellshaft, the British Museum and University of Pennsylvania expeditions at Babylon on the Euphrates were unknown in the mid-nineteenth century. Though Layard and Botta worked with immense patience and skill at Khorsabad, Kouyunjik and Nimroud, their workmen were unskilled, and the task of removing vast sculptures, weighing as much as twenty tons by pulley ropes which crackled with static electricity and sometimes burst into flame, was hazardous. Then came the problems of loading them on to the native rafts of the Tigris, *kelleks*, kept afloat by inflated goatskins, and sending them down river to Baghdad and Basra for despatch to Bombay and then Europe. The losses were slight in view of the risks; but losses, some tragically irrecoverable, were sustained. The moment Layard turned his back, Arab fanatics were liable to descend on the mounds to destroy the devilish works he had begun to reveal; or to steal them in the growing realization that there were ready markets for such things. In the evening after the labour of day Layard would sit at the door of his tent and gaze out at the calm, reposed scene, at the plain glittering with innumerable fires. '*As the night advanced they vanished one by one, until the landscape was wrapped in darkness and in silence.*'

'RUFFIAN DICK' IN THE HIJAZ

From Personal Narrative of a Pilgrimage to Al-Madinah and Meccah by Sir Richard F. Burton

(1821–1890)

———◆———

Dark and the Desert and Destriers me ken,
And the Claive and the Joust, and Paper and Pen.
Al-Mutanabbi: trans. Sir Richard Burton.

No reputation in the entire history of exploration exceeds that of Richard Francis Burton. Fame and notoriety accompanied him in his lifetime and pursued him beyond the grave. His accomplishments have been listed too often to bear repetition. He is at once the hero of scholar and schoolboy, the bane of officialdom and the inspiration of the officer; an academic who despised formal education, the man of learning who specialised in sword play and the 'cross-buttock' throw. As he said of himself, '*an Elizabethan born out of his time*'. His books and other writings, like his journeys and accomplishments, are too numerous to list. He threw them off, almost contemptuously, between his travels, usually multi-volume works containing in text and footnotes ample evidence of his command of many languages, ancient and modern, eastern and western; of his knowledge of classics, contemporary writing, anthropology, ethnology, geography, philosophy. Sometimes too there was evidence of a choleric temperament. Geographical notes made so assiduously on his travels in India, Africa, Arabia, South America and elsewhere, were often wildly inaccurate. But he was not a man to stop and check a position or an observation. Wherever he went he attracted the riff-raff of desert and jungle, dominating his unruly companions as he dominated, and scandalized, Victorian society on his return.

'Ruffian Dick', as his friends called him, joined the Indian Army as a
subaltern in 1842 following his rustication from Oxford (occasioned by
'eccentric behaviour' and a duel in which he caused some harm to a fellow
undergraduate). But the discipline of the army proved no more to his liking
than that of university. It was said that he left India after ten years' service
with an unparalleled knowledge of eastern life, in particular of the lower
classes, and a complete command of almost every Oriental language. On his
return home he wrote a string of works: *Scinde, or the Unhappy Valley* (1851);
Sindh and the Races that Inhabit the Valley of the Indus (1851); *Goa and the Blue
Mountains* (1851); *Falconry in the Valley of the Indus* (1852).

But it was his journey to the holy cities of Arabia, Mecca and Al Medina, in
1853, which brought him instant fame. He travelled first in the guise of a
Persian dervish but decided to change his identity to that of a Pathan by the
name of Abdullah. Such was his mastery of disguise and language that he
could play either part with conviction. He wanted to go to central Arabia,
but the East India Company refused him permission, perhaps knowing only
too well that his unruly disposition might cause more trouble than either
bargained for at that time of disturbance in the region of Najd. He went to
the Hijaz as a 'second-best' venture. His two-volume account of the journey
was published in 1855 and was an immediate success. Then came the
controversial journeys into Somalia and 'darkest' Africa, his visit to Brazil in
the service of the Foreign Office, to the Gold Coast, to Midian in search of
gold, Sind revisited, all leading to the issue of voluminous books. Finally,
his most widely known work, the translation of the *Arabian Nights* in
sixteen volumes (1885–1888). In between came *Vikram and the Vampire*
(1870), the unfinished *Book of the Sword,* the unpublished *Scented Garden,* his
translation of *Tales from the Gulistan of Sadi of Shiraz* and many other works.
He translated the *Lusidas of Camoens* and wrote a sketch of the poet's life.

On entering the Sinai desert we journeyed on till near sunset through
the wilderness without ennui. It is strange how the mind can be amused amid scenery that presents so few objects to occupy it. But in
such a country every slight modification of form or colour rivets
observation: the senses are sharpened, and perceptive faculties, prone
to sleep over a confused shifting of scenery, act vigorously when
excited by the capability of embracing each detail. Moreover desert
views are eminently suggestive; they appeal to the future, not to the
past; they arouse because they are by no means memorial. To the
solitary wayfarer there is an interest in the wilderness unknown to
Cape seas and Alpine glaciers, and even to the rolling prairie, – the

Meccan caravan entering fortress of Akaba, from *Journey through*
Arabia Petraea by Leon de Labarde, London, 1836

effect of continued excitement on the mind stimulating its powers to their pitch.

Above, through a sky terrible in its stainless beauty, and the splendours of a pitiless blinding glare, the Simoon caresses you like a lion with flaming breath. Around lie drifted sand heaps, upon which each puff of wind leaves its own trace in solid waves, flayed rocks, the very skeletons of mountains, and hard unbroken plains, over which he who rides is spurred by the idea that the bursting of a water skin, or the pricking of a camel's hoof would be a certain death of torture, – a haggard land infested with wild beasts, and wilder men, – a region whose very fountains murmur the warning words 'Drink and away!' What can be more exciting? what more sublime? Man's heart bounds in his breast at the thought of measuring his puny force with nature's might, and of emerging triumphant from the trial. This explains the Arab's proverb, 'Voyaging is a victory.' In the desert even more than upon the ocean, there is present death: hardship is there, and piracies, and shipwreck – solitary, not in crowds, where, as the Persians say, 'death is a festival', – and this sense of danger, never absent, invests the scene of travel with an interest not its own.

Let the traveller who suspects exaggeration leave the Suez road for an hour or two, and gallop northwards over the sands: in the drear silence, the solitude, and the fantastic desolation of the place, he will feel what the Desert may be.

And then the Oases,* and little lines of fertility – how soft and how beautiful! – even though the Wady El Ward (the Vale of Flowers) be the name of some stern flat upon which a handful of wild shrubs blossom while struggling through a cold season's ephemeral existence. In such circumstances the mind is influenced through the body. Though your mouth glows, and your skin is parched, yet you feel no langour, the effect of humid heat; your lungs are lightened, your sight brightens, your memory recovers its tone, and your spirits become exuberant; your fancy and imagination are powerfully aroused, and the wildness and sublimity of the scenes around you stir up all the energies of your soul – whether for exertion, danger, or strife. Your morale improves: you become frank and cordial, politeness and

*Nothing can be more incorrect than the vulgar idea of an Arabian Oasis, except it be the popular conception of an Arabian desert. One reads of 'isles of the sandy sea', but one never sees them. The real 'wady' is, generally speaking, a rocky valley bisected by the bed of a mountain torrent, dry during the hot season. In such places the Bedouins love to encamp, because they find food and drink, – water being always procurable by digging.

the slavery of civilisation are left behind you in the city. Your senses are quickened: they require no stimulants but air and exercise, – in the Desert spirituous liquors excite only disgust. There is a keen enjoyment in a mere animal existence. The sharp appetite disposes of the most indigestible food, the sand is softer than a bed of down, and the purity of the air suddenly puts to flight a dire cohort of diseases. Hence it is that both sexes, and every age, the most material as well as the most imaginative of minds, the tamest citizen, the most peaceful student, the spoiled child of civilisation, all feel their hearts dilate, and their pulses beat strong as they look down from their dromedaries upon the 'glorious Desert'. Where do we hear of a 'traveller' being disappointed by it? It is another illustration of the ancient truth that nature returns to man, however unworthily he has treated her. And believe me, gentle reader, that when once your tastes have conformed to the tranquillity of such travel, you will suffer real pain in returning to the turmoil of civilisation. You will anticipate the bustle and the confusion of artificial life, its luxury and its false pleasures, with repugnance. Depressed in spirits, you will for a time after your return feel incapable of mental or bodily exertion. The air of cities will suffocate you, and the care-worn and cadaverous countenances of citizens will haunt you like a vision of judgment.

I turned off the road, and was suddenly saluted by a figure rising from a little hollow with an 'As' Salmo Alaykum' of truly Arab sound.

I looked at the speaker for a moment without recognising him. He then advanced with voluble expressions of joy, invited me to sup, seized my camel's halter without waiting for an answer, 'nakh'd' him, led me hurriedly to a carpet spread in a sandy hollow, pulled off my slippers, gave me cold water for ablution, told me that he had mistaken me at a distance for a 'Sherif' of the Arabs, but was delighted to find himself in error, and urged me to hurry over ablution, otherwise that night would come on before we could say our prayers. It was Mohammed El Bayuni, the Meccan boy of whom I had bought my pilgrim-garb at Cairo. There I had refused his companionship, but here for reasons of his own – one of them was an utter want of money, – he would take no excuse. When he prayed he stood behind me, thereby proving pliancy of conscience, for he suspected me from the first of being at least a heretic.

After prayer he lighted a pipe, and immediately placed the snake-like tube in my hand; this is an argument which the tired traveller can rarely resist.

On his first visit to the House of Allah when the camels were unloaded, appeared a dish of fine vermicelli, browned and powdered with loaf-sugar. The boy Mohammed, I, and Shaykh Nur, lost no time in exerting our right hands; and truly, after our hungry journey, we found the Kunafah delicious. After the meal we procured cots from a neighbouring coffee-house, and we lay down, weary, and anxious to snatch an hour or two of repose. At dawn we were expected to perform our Tawaf al-Kudum, or 'Circumambulation of Arrival', at the Harim.

Scarcely had the first smile of morning beamed upon the rugged head of the eastern hill, Abu Kubays, when we arose, bathed, and proceeded in our pilgrim-garb to the Sanctuary. We entered by the Bab al-Ziyadah, or principal northern door, descended two long flights of steps, traversed the cloister, and stood in sight of the Bayt Allah.

There at last it lay, the bourn of my long and weary Pilgrimage, realising the plans and hopes of many and many a year. The mirage medium of Fancy invested the huge catafalque and its gloomy pall with peculiar charms. There were no giant fragments of hoar antiquity as in Egypt, no remains of graceful and harmonious beauty as in Greece and Italy, no barbarous gorgeousness as in the buildings of India: yet the view was strange, unique – and how few have looked upon the celebrated shrine! I may truly say that, of all the worshippers who clung weeping to the curtain, or who pressed their beating hearts to the stone, none felt for the moment a deeper emotion than did the Haji from the far-north. It was as if the poetical legends of the Arab spoke truth, and that the waving wings of angels, not the sweet breeze of morning, were agitating and swelling the black covering of the shrine. But, to confess humbling truth, theirs was the high feeling of religious enthusiasm, mine was the ecstasy of gratified pride.

A JOURNEY FROM JERUSALEM TO ANAIZA IN QASIM

Carlo Claudio Guarmani

(1828–1884)

———◆———

Guarmani was born at Leghorn and went with his family to live in Beirut at the age of twenty-two. He became the agent of the Imperial French Postal Service in Jerusalem and made frequent journeys into the Syrian desert where he became acquainted with the Badawin tribes of the area. The chief of his interests, however, was not so much the Arab as his horse. His expert knowledge was sought by European horse breeders and in 1863 he was called to Paris to meet the director of Napoleon III's Imperial Stud. He was summoned also by King Victor Emmanuel II of Italy and returned to Syria with orders to buy horses for both France and Italy. His subsequent journeys took him to places as yet unexplored by Europeans; and his wanderings in the desert regions of Syria, the Great Nafud and al-Najd resulted in two books remarkable for their keenness of observation, their accuracy and understanding of Badawin life. The first, *El Kamsa*, 'The Five', was devoted to the Arab horse and the title was based on the five strains of noble pedigree – Kuhaylan, Ubayyan, Saqlawi, Hamdani and Hadban. It was published in 1864, dedicated to the Italian king. The story of his expedition to central Arabia, *Il Negd Settentrionale*, was published by the Franciscan Fathers in Jerusalem in 1866, though the Prussian Consul in Jerusalem brought out an abridged version in German a year earlier. The latter work was translated into English in 1916, when the British Intelligence Service in the Middle East needed access to Guarmani's expert knowledge of the territories and tribes of the northern Arabian deserts. By far the best translation from the Italian was that of Lady Capel-Cure.

———◆———

FROM *NORTHERN NAJD,* A JOURNEY FROM JERUSALEM TO ANAIZA IN QASIM BY CARLO GUARMANI, TRANSLATED FROM THE ITALIAN BY LADY CAPEL-CURE

A Note from the Introduction by Douglas Carruthers

The geographical interest attached to Guarmani's journey into Najd lies in the fact that he was our only authority to date for that wide region between the Pilgrim route to Mecca and the Syrian route to Middle Arabia, by way of the Wadi Sirhan, a region which was not visited again for forty years. He was only forestalled by two travellers, Wallin and Palgrave, at the oases of Hail and Jauf, and by Wallin alone at Taima, while he can claim priority over all Arabian travellers by visiting Khaibar,* and also by journeying on thence to Anaiza and Buraida, which oasis he was the second European to enter. Moreover, he was the first to see and to describe the numerous outlying oases and pastoral settlements of the Shammar dominion towards the south-west. He made a better general map than did either Wallin or Palgrave, while his descriptions of these districts deserve praise from all who know Arabia.

A BLOOD FEUD AND WAITING WOMEN

Feisal el-Sceilan was the sixth of the seven sons of Neif to die a violent death. The surviving son is the Sheikh Azzak. Feisal was buried where his body was left. Lord Cornwallis, Governor-General of British India, when he lay dying at Ghazipore, repeated unwittingly a Beduin maxim: 'Where the tree falls there let it rest.'

If a Beduin dies in an encampment, he is buried beside his tent; if he falls in war or on *gazzu* the wild beasts devour him. Arab ceremonies are as simple as their lives. A most curious and interesting manner of burial is practised in Bethlehem, of which I was again a spectator this year, the very day of my departure for Neged.

The principal street was thronged with people; a funeral procession was anxiously awaited. The relations, friends, and all those residing in the same district were required to be present at the obsequies. The meeting place was before the door of the house. The deceased was a Christian of the Orthodox Greek Church, which we Catholics call

*Not quite. Varthema went there more than three centuries before.

'Schismatic'; he was surrounded by his nearest relatives; the women had ceased weeping or were weeping quietly, his priest prayed and the men repeated the prayer after him. The greatest sadness reigned in the house and complete indifference outside; children played about joking noisily, and continually crawled between the legs of my poor horse.

The crowd, already a large one, was increasing; every dirty lane in the village contributed lookers-on; the men came in silence, the women screaming their noisy *tenanik*.

At last the funeral procession came out. Three boys carried the cross and candlesticks; behind them came the priest and then the bier, covered with an old black velvet pall and carried by all the men in succession. The procession went on towards the church, where prayers were to be said before taking the body to the cemetery. Only the male portion of the population followed; the women waited in the road for the relatives of the dead man, who did not keep them long. They rushed from the house like a horde of furies, screaming and gesticulating, with dry eyes, flowing hair and breasts uncovered. They ran to the cemetery, and in order to run quicker, held up their long skirts far above the knee. On reaching the grave, the mother and wife threw themselves on the ground, one on each side; the rest of the relations sat round and behind them, while all the women of the village pressed as close as possible. The mother, tearing her shirt open from the top to the bottom, displayed her bare bosom, and wrinkled stomach; she then began to sing in a hoarse, monotonous voice the praises of her son, accompanying the song with a rhythmical movement of the head from right to left, and raising her hands to her chest with the utmost regularity, the left hand on the right and the right on the left. From time to time, when singing of having borne and nursed her son, she hit her chest and stomach with her closed fist in anger. The relatives repeated her words after her, making the same movements with both their heads and hands. The wife constantly interrupted the mother; her voice was stronger, her song less slow, and less lugubrious. She accompanied it, swaying her body backwards and forwards.

The arrival of the funeral procession put an end to the women's lamentations over the grave, whence they were packed off very roughly. They then went and formed themselves into two circles in the market-place. In the principal ring were the relations; the second was composed of their female friends from their own quarter.

The songs began over again, but were no longer lugubrious, the verses being recited quickly. The women in the outer circle walked at a moderate pace; at intervals, indicated by a pause in the song, they let go their hands to wave their handkerchiefs. Those in the inner circle behaved like delirious witches and bacchantes; and when, as often happened, one of them cried out 'two jumps, three jumps for the dead man', it seemed as if one was witnessing a dance of wild beasts, they leapt and screamed so madly. The woman who jumped the highest was considered the best and most zealous.

While the women were behaving thus, the men, having rendered to the earth that which belonged to it, began to argue amongst themselves. Each one claimed the right of inviting the company to dinner, and of sending food for the day to the dead man's family. The good priest was informed of the female saturnalia taking place in the market-place although he had forbidden it a thousand times; he soon made the meeting accept the invitation of the loudest speaker, broke up the women's choruses by stoning them, and forced them to retire to their houses as quickly as they had left them an hour earlier. Their flight was so absurd that it was impossible not to laugh, and all joined in. Thus a mourning scene was turned into one of noisy hilarity.

In Bethlehem, as in all the towns, villages and encampments of Palestine, the *naddabat,* mentioned in Amos and Jeremiah, are often found; they are the women who weep as a profession, 'who understand making a funeral lament'. In the towns they are paid for it, but the villagers and tribesmen do not sell their tears. They are obliged to have a strong voice because the song of their lamentation must be very loud; they accompany the female relations of the dead to the burying-place on the day of the death, and return there twice, on the seventh and the fortieth days. In the villages and encampments they are practically useless, for there is no woman who cannot improvise some sort of lament; in the towns it is quite another thing, for without the *naddabat* a dead person could not be properly mourned.

THE CODE OF THE
EMIR ZAMEL OF ANEIZEH

'Oh Believers! there is no other divinity but God – the undivided, omnipotent, merciful Creator of the universe, by reason of His Will.

'Deny the existence of angel, "djin", "afrit", and devil; for the

Creator has no need of intermediary spirits between Himself and His children.

'Deny the divine origin of all writings, the Koran, Bible and the Gospels; for the Book of God is read in his works.

'Oh Believers! predestination is for all created, free arbitration is conceded to you, guided by your intelligence; yet all is in God's hands and none can evade the final Destiny.

'Believe that your body which is of the earth will return to the earth, whilst your souls which are of God will return to God who gave them.

'Believe that each one will receive reward or punishment according to his deserts; for evil evil, and for good, even better – the punishment in proportion to the crime, but the reward eternal, because you are frail and God is merciful.

'Oh Believers! Turn not a deaf ear to the warning voice of your heart if you stray from the paths of your God, the God of all peoples, the only God.'

IN ARABIA DESERTA

Charles M. Doughty

(1834–1926)

When the 1921 edition of Doughty's *Arabia Deserta* was issued, T. E.
Lawrence wrote in its Introduction: 'Those just men who begin at the
beginning of books are being delayed by me from reading Doughty, and so
I am making worse my presumption in putting my name near what I believe
to be one of the greatest prose works of our literature. It is a book which
begins powerfully, written in a style which has apparently neither father nor
son, so closely wrought, so tense, so just in its words and phrases, that it
demands a hard reader . . . The history of the march of the caravan down the
pilgrim road, the picture of Zeyd's tent, the description of Ibn Rashid's court
at Hail, the negroid village in Kheybar, the urbane life at Aneyza, the long
march across the desert of Western Nejd to Mecca, each seems better than
the one before till there comes the very climax of the book near Taif, and
after this excitement a gentle closing chapter of the road down to Jidda . . .
To have accomplished such a journey would have been achievement enough
for the ordinary man. Mr Doughty was not content till he had made the book
justify the journey as much as the journey justified the book, and in the
double power, to go and to write, he will not soon find his rival.'

Doughty himself wrote in the preface to the 1888 first edition of *Arabia
Deserta*: 'We set but a name upon the ship, that our hands have built (with
incessant labour) in a decennium, in what day she is launched forth to the
great waters; and few words are needful in this place. The book is not milk
for babes: it might be likened to a mirror, wherein is set forth faithfully some
parcel of the soil of Arabia smelling of samn and camels.'

The lingering day draws down to the sun setting; the herdsmen,
weary of the sun, come again with the cattle, to taste in their menzils
the first sweetness of mirth and repose. – The day is done, and there
rises the nightly freshness of this purest mountain air: and then to the
cheerful song and the cup at the common fire. The moon rises ruddy

from that solemn obscurity of jebel like a mighty beacon:– and the
morrow will be as this day, days deadly drowned in the sun of the
summer wilderness.

Pleasant, as the fiery heat of the desert daylight is done, is our homely
evening fire. The sun gone down upon a highland steppe of Arabia,
whose common altitude is above three thousand feet, the thin dry air
is presently refreshed, the sand is soon cold; wherein yet at three
fingers' depth is left a sunny warmth of the past day's heat until the
new sunrise. After a half hour it is the blue night, and clear hoary
starlight in which there shines the girdle of the milky way, with a
marvellous clarity. As the sun is setting, the nomad housewife brings
in a truss of sticks and dry bushes, which she has pulled or hoed with a
mattock (a tool they have seldom) in the wilderness; she casts down
this provision by our hearthside, for the sweet-smelling evening fire.
But to Hirfa, his sheykhly young wife, Zeyd had given a little Beduin
maid to help her. The housewife has upon her woman's side an hearth
apart, which is the cooking-fire. Commonly Hirfa baked then, under
the ashes, a bread-cake for the stranger: Zeyd her husband, who is
miserable, or for other cause, eats not yet, but only near midnight,
as he is come again from the mejlis and would go in to sleep . . .
    Here passing, in my former journeys, we saw Arab horsemen which
approached us; we being too many for them, they came but to beg
insolently a handful of tobacco. In their camps, such would be kind
hosts; but had we fallen into their hands in the desert we should have
found them fiends, they would have stripped us, and perchance in a
savage wantonness have cut some of our throats. These were three
long-haired Beduins that bid us *salaam* (peace); and a fourth shock-
haired cyclops of the desert, whom the fleetness of their mares had
outstripped, trotted in after them, uncouthly seated upon the rawbone
narrow withers of his dromedary, without saddle, without bridle, and
only as an herdsman driving her with his voice and the camel-stick.
His fellows rode with naked legs and unshod upon their beautiful
mares' bare backs, the halter in one hand, and the long balanced
lance, wavering upon the shoulder, in the other. We should think
them sprawling riders; for a boast or war-like exercise, in the presence
of our armed company, they let us view how fairly they could ride a
career and turn: striking back heels and seated low, with pressed
thighs, they parted at a hand-galop, made a tourney or two easily upon
the plain; and now wheeling wide, they betook themselves down in

the desert, every man bearing and handling his spear as at point to strike a foeman; so fetching a compass and we marching, they a little out of breath came gallantly again. Under the most ragged of these riders was a very perfect young and startling chestnut mare, – so shapely there are only few among them. Never combed by her rude master, but all shining beautiful and gentle of herself, she seemed a darling life upon that savage soil not worthy of her gracious pasterns: the strutting tail flowed down even to the ground, and the mane (*orfa*) was shed by the loving nurture of her mother Nature . . .

We moved on in silence: I said only that at the next menzil we would leave Merjan. He was cause, also, that we suffered thirst in the way; since we must divide with him a third of my small herdsman's girby. Worse than all was that the peevish lad continually corrupted the little good nature in Eyad, with his fanatical whisperings, and drew him from me. I repented of my misplaced humanity towards him, and of my yielding to such rafiks to take another way. Yet it had been as good to wink at the lad's offence, if in so doing I should not have seemed to be afraid of them. The Turkish argument of the rod might bring such spirits to better knowledge; but it is well to be at peace with the Arabs upon any reasonable conditions, that being of a feminine humour, they are kind friends and implacable enemies.

The Harra is here like a rolling tide of basalt: the long bilges often rise about pit-like lava bottoms, or *niggeras*, which lie full of blown sand. Soon after this we came to the edge of the lava-field; where upon our right hand, a path descended to Thurghrud, half a journey distant. 'Come, I said, we are to go thither.' But Eyad answered, 'The way lies now over difficult lavas! and, Khalil,* we ought to have held eastward from the morning: yet I will go thither for thy sake, although we cannot arrive this night, and we have nothing to eat.' Merjan cried to Eyad not to yield, that he himself would not go out of the way to Thurghrud. Eyad: 'If we go forward, we may be with Aarab to-night: so Salih said truly, they are encamped under yonder mountain.' This seemed the best rede for weary men: I gave Eyad the word to lead forward. We descended then from the Harra side into a plain country of granite grit, without blade or bush. 'Yet here in good years, said Eyad, they find pasture; but now the land is mahal, because no autumn rain had fallen in these parts.' – So we marched some miles, and passed by the (granitic) Thullan Buthra.

' – But where are we come! exclaimed the rafiks, gazing about them:

*Man of God — Doughty's title among the Arabs.

there can be no Aarab in this khala; could Salih have a mind to deceive us?' The sun set over our forlorn march; and we halted in the sandy bed of a seyl to sleep. They hobbled the thelul's forelegs, and loosed her out in the moonlight; but there was no pasture. We were fasting since yesterday, and had nothing to eat, and no water. They found a great waif root, and therewith we made a good fire; the deep ground covered us, under mountains which are named Ethmad (pl. of Thammad).

KHEYBAR
'THE APOSTLE'S COUNTRY'

We passed the gates made of rude palm boarding into the street of the Hejaz negro village, and alighted in the dusk before the house of an acquaintance of Ghroceyb. The host, hearing us busy at the door of his lower house, looked down from the casement and asked in the rasping negro voice what men we were? Ghroceyb called to him, and then he came down with his brother to receive the guests. They took my bags upon their shoulders, and led us by some clay stairs to their dwelling-house, which is, as at el-Ally, an upper chamber, here called suffa. The lower floor, in these damp cases, is a place where they leave the orchard tools, and a stable for their few goats which are driven in for the night. This householder was named Abd el-Hady, 'Servitor of Him who leadeth in the way of truth', a young man under the middle age, of fine negro lineaments. – These negro-like Arabians are not seldom comely.

Our host's upper room was open at the street side with long casements, taga, to the floor; his roof was but a loose strawing of palm stalks, and above is the house terrace of beaten clay, to which you ascend (they say erka!) by a ladder of two or three palm beams, with steps hacked in them. Abd el-Hady's was one of the better cottages, for he was a substantial man. Kheybar is as it were an African village in the Hejaz. Abd el-Hady spread his carpet and bade us welcome, and set before us Kheybar dates, which are yellow, small and stived to-gether; they are gathered ere fully ripe (their Beduin partners' impatience and distrust of each other!) and have a drug-like or fenny savour, but are 'cooler' than the most dates of the country and not unwholesome. After these days' efforts in the Harra we could not eat; we asked for water to quench our burning thirst. They hang their sweating girbies at the stair-head and under them is made a hole in the flooring, that the drip may fall through. The water, drawn, they said, from the spring head under the basalt, tasted of the ditch; it might be sulphurous. We had left our thelul kneebound in the street.

Many persons, when they heard say that strangers had arrived came up all this evening to visit us:– the villagers were black men. Ghroceyb told them his tale of the ghrazzu; and the negroes answered 'Wellah! except we sally in the morning to look for them –!' They feared for the outlying corn lands and lest any beast of theirs should be taken. There came with the rest a tall and swarthy white man of a soldierly countenance, bearing a lantern, and his yard-long tobacco-pipe. I saw he was of the mixed inhabitants of the cities. He sat silent with hollow eyes and smoked tobacco, often glancing at us; then he passed the chibuk to me and enquired the news. He was not friendly with Abd el-Hady, and waived our host's second cup. The white man sat on smoking mildly, with his lantern burning; after an hour he went forth (and this was to denounce us, to the ruffian lieutenant at Kheybar). My rafik told me in a whisper, 'That was Ahmed; he has been a soldier and is now a tradesman at Kheybar.' – His brother was Mohammed en-Nejumy, he who from the morrow became the generous defender of my adversity at Kheybar: they were citizens of Medina. It was near midnight when the last coffee drinkers departed; then I whispered to Ghroceyb: 'Will they serve supper, or is it not time to sleep?' 'My namesake, I think they have killed for thee; I saw them bring up a sheep to the terrace, long ago.' – 'Who is the sheykh of the village?' – 'This Abd el-Hady is their sheykh, and thou wilt find him a good man.' My rafik lied like a (guileful) nomad, to excuse his not carrying me to the W. Aly village.

Our host and his brother now at length descended from the house-top, bearing a vast metal tray of the seethed flesh upon a mess of thura (it may be a sort of millet): since the locusts had destroyed their spring corn, this was the only bread-stuff left to them at Kheybar.

The new day's light beginning to rise Ghroceyb went down to the street in haste; 'Farewell, he said, and was there any difference between us forgive it, Khalil'; and taking my right hand (and afraid perchance of the stranger's malediction) he stooped and kissed it. Hady, our host's brother, mounted also upon the croup of his thelid; this strong-bodied young negro with a long matchlock upon his shoulder rode forth in his bare tunic, girded only with the hazam or gunner's belt. Upon the baldric are little metal pipes, with their powder charges and upon the girdle leather pouches for shot, flint and

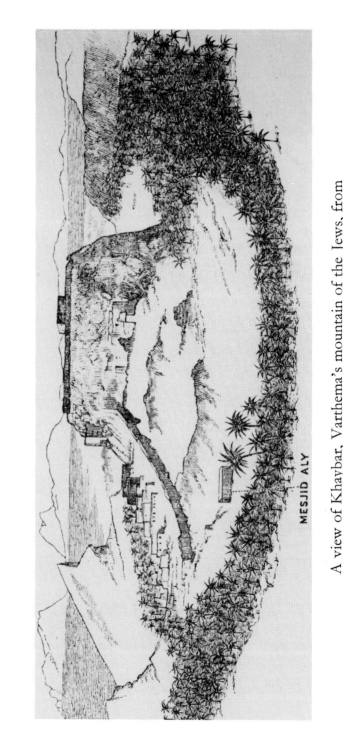

MESJID ALY

A view of Khaybar, Varthema's mountain of the Jews, from
Doughty's *Travels in Arabia Deserta*, London, 1888

steel, and a hook whereupon a man – they go commonly barefoot – will hang his sandals. The hazams are adorned with copper studs and beset with little rattling chains; there are some young men who may be seen continually muhazamin, girded and vain-glorious with these little tinkling ornaments of war. It is commonly said of tribes well provided with fire-arms 'They have many muhazamin.' – Hady rode to find the traces of the ghrazzu of yesterday.

Some of the villagers came up to me immediately to enquire for medicines: they were full of tedious words; and all was to beg of me and buy none. I left them sitting and went out to the place, for this was Kheybar.

Our host sent his son to guide me; the boy led down by a lane and called me to enter a doorway and see a spring. I went in – it was a mesjid! and I withdrew hastily. The father (who had instructed the child beforehand), hearing from him when we came again that I had left the place without praying, went down and shut his street door. He returned and took his pistol from the wall, saying, 'Let us go together and he would show me round the town.' When we were in the street he led me by an orchard path out of the place.

We came by a walled path through the palms into an open space of rush-grass and black vulcanic sand, es-Sefsafa: there he showed me the head of a stream which welled strongly from under the figgera. The water is tepid and sulphurous as at el-Ally, and I saw in it little green-back and silver-bellied fishes:– all fish are named hut by the Arabians. 'Here, he said, is the (summer) menzil of the Dowla, in this ground stand the askars' tents.' We sat down, and gazing into my face he asked me, 'Were I afraid of the Dowla?' 'Is the Dowla better or Ibn Rashid's goverment?' – 'The Dowla delivered us from the Beduw, – but is more burdenous.'

We passed through a burial ground of black vulcanic mould and salt-warp: the squalid grave-heaps are marked with headstones of wild basalt. That funeral earth is chapped and ghastly, bulging over her enwombed corpses, like a garden soil, in springtime, which is pushed by the new-aspiring plants. All is horror at Kheybar! –nothing there which does not fill a stranger's eye with discomfort . . .

A better order has been established at Kheybar; gates have been put to the village streets, and every housewife must daily sweep before her own doors, or be beaten by the Siruan:– and Abdullah told me he had beaten many. The ways were formerly foul with pestilent ordures, in the giddy heat of the summer sun; and the passing stranger or soldier who had drawn there his breath, was in danger to fall down anon, deadly sick. In the first year 'well nigh all the soldiers died' of cholera and the valley fever. Amm Mohammed thought that hardly a score of them lived to re-enter the walls of Medina! and the negro villagers now say this proverb with horrid laughter; 'Kheybar is the grave of the asaker.' 'Kheybar, said the melancholy Aman, in his Albanian-learned Arabic, is kabr ed-dunnia, the whole world's sepulchre.' There came a military doctor from Medina, with new remedies, to cure the sick; but he himself sickened in the morning, and he was laid a yard deep, in his shroud, ere midday in the subbakha earth – dead at Kheybar! 'I have cleansed the town quoth Abdullah, and now they see it done, even this people is grateful to me.'

Kheybar is but one long thelul journey from Medina, yet lying out of common ways even this name, as said, had been scarce known in the Holy City; or it sounded in their ears with a superstitious strangeness, – for who has not heard told in the Haj fables, of the Yahud Kheybar? At Medina is an iron plated door (it closes now the soldiers' quarters) which passes for the ancient castle-gate of Kheybar: 'Our lord Aly, they say, flung forth the leaves from his two hands when he won the place; and one of them fell down upon a hill at Medina, but the other fell at Baghdad.' It is said likewise of the mountain Ehad near to el-Medina, whereon is the sepulchre of Hamzy uncle of the Neby, that of old time this jebel was at Kheybar but it has since flitted to the Holy City; and some of their wise men contend that J. Hamzy was formerly at Baghdad. The rude Moslemin can persuade themselves in this sort: 'J. Hamzy stands at Medina; but was formerly in another part; therefore this mountain has removed hither!' Upon a time I laughed a little with Amm Mohammed, 'Your lord Aly threw stiffly! it is about a score of the longest cannon shots to Medina.' – 'But this is not all, Khalil, for they say that once our lord Aly stood and lifted the universal world.' – 'And where then was your lord Aly? must he not stand out of the world to remove it?' The Nejumy answered, 'Now I think upon it, sheykh Khalil, I am well-nigh of thy opinion, that these are but the sayings of vain superstition and not in the religion.' I made Amm Mohammed a globe of the clay we cast up in our digging, and portraied the seas and continents upon it. He was pleased, but could not easily follow my words, since the whole world is that in their estimation: he let his tools fall and cried, laughing, 'Said not the Kheyabara well of thee, well of thee, sheykh Khalil, that thou art a magician? – but hyak, let us homeward and eat tamr.'

It is certain that the Jews have at this day a fabulous opinion of Kheybar; some of them (in the East) have told me that the Yahud Kheybar are the Beny Rechab. – And even Orientalists in Europe have asked me 'Be there now no Jews at all at Kheybar?' I have known a missionary to the Jews in the Levant who at his first coming thither, if he had not fallen sick, would have set forth, riding on an ass, to pass the great deserts toward Kheybar; moved with a youthful zeal to convert those fabulous lost sheep to the religion of the Nasar! But let none any more jeopardy his life for Kheybar! – I would that these leaves might save the deaths of some: and God give me this reward of my labour! for who will, he may read in them all the tale of Kheybar. Merchants of Kasim have related to me that 'there are descendants of the Yahud Kheybar in Bagdad, who are accounted noble (asily) among the Jews; there are besides rich traders of them in India:' – but their words were, I found, as strange tales in the ears of the respectable (Bagdad) merchant Jews in Bombay.

In the third week of my being in this captivity at Kheybar, the slave-spirited Abdullah wrote to the Pasha of Medina. Since the village governor knew no letters, the black sheykh Salih was his scrivener and wrote after him: Upon such a day of the last month, when the gates of Kheybar were opened in the morning, we found a stranger without waiting to enter. He told us that a Beduwy with whom he arrived in the night, had left him there and departed. When we asked him what man he was? he answered 'an Engleysy'; and he acknowledged himself to be a Nasrany. And I not knowing what there might be in this matter have put the stranger in ward, and have seized his baggage, in which we have found some books and a paper from Ibn Rashid. So we remain in your Lordship's obedience, humbly awaiting the commandments of your good Lordship. – 'Now well,' said Abdullah; 'and seal it, Salih. Hast thou heard this that I have written, Khalil?' – 'Write only the truth. When was I found at your gates? I rode openly into Kheybar.' – 'Nay, but I must write thus, or the Pasha might lay a blame upon me and say, "Why – didst thou suffer him to enter?" – That Heteymy lodged in the place all night and he was a gomany! also his thelul lay in the street, and I did not apprehend him: Oh God! where was then my mind? I might (the thief murmured) have taken his dromedary! Listen, everyone of you here present! for the time to come ye are to warn me when any strangers arrive, that if there be anything against them, they may be arrested, immediately.'

Abdullah had in these days seized the cow of an orphan – for which all the people abhorred him – a poor minor without defence, that he might drink her milk himself: so he wrote another letter to the Pasha, 'I have sequestered a cow arrears of taxes, and will send her unto your lordship; the beast is worth fifteen reals at Kheybar, and might be sold for fifty at el-Medina.' In a third paper he gave up his account of the village tithing to the Dowla: all the government exactions at Kheybar were together 3600 reals. (For this a regiment of soldiers may march every year to (their deaths at) Kheybar!) Abdullah's being not fully a score were reckoned in his paysheet at forty. If any man died, he drew the deceased's salary himself to the end of his term of service. Once every year he will be called to muster his asakar; but then with some easy deceit, as by hiring or compelling certain of the village, and clothing them for a day or two, he may satisfy the easy passing over of his higher officers; who full of guilty bribes themselves lean lightly upon other men's criminal cases. Abdullah added a postscript. 'It may please your honour to have in remembrance the poor askars that are hungry and naked, and they are looking humbly unto your good Lordship for some relief.' In thirty and two months they had not been paid! – what wonder then such wretches, defrauded by the Ottoman government, become robbers! Now they lifted up their weary hearts to God and to Pasha, that a new khusna, or 'paymaster's' chest of treasure from Stambul might be speedily heard of at el-Medina. There were years of wasting warfare in Europe; of which the rumble was heard confusedly at this unprofitable distance. So Abdullah sealed his letters which had cost him and his empressed clerk three days' labour, until their black temples ached again.

These were days for me sooner of dying than of life; and the felonous Abdullah made no speed to deliver me . . .

PILGRIMAGE TO NAJD

From a Pilgrimage to Najd by Lady Anne Blunt

(1837–1917)

———◆———

Daughter of the Earl of Lovelace and granddaughter of Lord Byron, wife of the acerbic poet-politician Wilfrid Scawen Blunt, Lady Anne endured a miserable later life. Their daughter, Lady Wentworth, was to write with bitterness that Wilfrid played havoc with her mother's heart, '*wrecked her life and, jealous of her intellectual gifts, appropriated the credit of her brains to himself with shameless arrogance*'. Yet the early years of their marriage were idyllic, and never so much as when they went together to central Arabia, four years after their union, in 1879. A year before they had travelled along the Euphrates, polishing their Arabic, sharing a common interest in the Arab horse (on which subject she became the foremost English authority), imbued with a fascination for the desert. They set out for Jabal Shammar and its capital Hail by way of Damascus and Jauf, on 13 December 1879. She wrote with simple charm and transparent joy of their journey to the citadel of Ibn Rashid and of their experiences among the tribes.

———◆———

As we stayed some time at Hail, I will not give the detail of every day. It would be tedious, and would involve endless repetitions, and not a few corrections, for it was only by degrees that we learned to understand all we saw and all we heard.

Our reception was everything that we could have wished. As we rode into the courtyard of the kasr, we were met by some twenty well-dressed men, each one of whom made a handsomer appearance than any Arabs we had previously seen in our lives. 'The sons of Sheykhs,' whispered Mohammed, who was rather pale, and evidently much impressed by the solemnity of the occasion. In their midst stood a

Jabal Shammar by Lady Anne Blunt, *Pilgrimage to Najd*, London, 1881

magnificent old man, clothed in scarlet, whose tall figure and snow-white beard gave us a notion of what Solomon might have been in all his glory. He carried a long wand in his hand – it looked like a sceptre – and came solemnly forward to greet us. 'The Emir,' whispered Mohammed, as we all alighted. Wilfrid then gave the usual 'salam aleykum', to which every one replied 'aleykum salam', in a loud cheerful tone, with a cordiality of manner that was very reassuring. I thought I had never seen so many agreeable faces collected together, or people with so excellent a demeanour. The old man, smiling, motioned to us to enter, and others led the way. We were then informed that these were the servants of the Emir, and the old man his chamberlain. They showed us first through a dark tortuous entrance, constructed evidently for purposes of defence, and then down a dark corridor, one side of which was composed of pillars, reminding one a little of the entrance to some ancient Egyptian temple. Then one of the servants tapped at a low door, and exchanged signals with somebody else inside, and the door was opened, and we found ourselves in a large kahwah, or reception room. It was handsome from its size, seventy feet by thirty, and from the row of five pillars, which stood in the middle, supporting the roof. The columns were about four feet in diameter, and were quite plain, with square capitals, on which the ends of the rafters rested. The room was lighted by small square air-holes near the roof, and by the door, which was now left open. The whole of the inside was white, or rather, brown-washed, and there was no furniture of any sort, or fittings, except wooden pegs for hanging swords to, a raised platform opposite the door where the mortar stood for coffee-pounding, and a square hearth in one corner, where a fire was burning . . .

Coffee was soon served, and after this the conversation became general between our servants and the servants of the Emir, and then there was a stir, and a general rising, and the word was passed round, 'yiji el Emir,' the Emir is coming. We, too, got up, and this time it really was the Emir. He came in at the head of a group of still more smartly-dressed people than those we had seen before, and held out his hand to Wilfrid, to me, and to Mohammed, exchanging salutations with each of us in turn, and smiling graciously. Then we all sat down, and Wilfrid made a short speech of the sort we had already agreed upon, which the Emir answered very amiably, saying that he was much pleased to see us, and that he hoped we should make his house our house. He then asked Mohammed for news of the road;

of Johar and Meskakeh, and especially about the war going on between Sotamm and Ibn Smeyr. So far so good, and it was plain that
we had nothing now to fear; yet I could not help looking now and
then at those pegs on the wall, and thinking of the story of the young
Ibn Jabars and their slaves, who had been so treacherously murdered
in this very hall, and by this very man, our host.

The Emir's face is a strange one. It may be mere fancy, prompted by
our knowledge of Ibn Rashid's past life, but his countenance recalled
to us the portraits of Richard the Third, lean, sallow cheeks, much
sunken, thin lips, with an expression of pain, except when smiling, a
thin black beard, well defined black knitted eyebrows, and remarkable
eyes, – eyes deep sunk and piercing, like the eyes of a hawk, but ever
turning restlessly from one of our faces to the other, and then to those
beside him. It was the very type of a conscience-stricken face, or of one
which fears an assassin. His hands, too, were long and claw-like, and
never quiet for an instant, incessantly playing, while he talked, with
his beads, or with the hem of his abba. With all this, the Emir is very
distinguished in appearance, with a tall figure, and, clothed as he was
in purple and fine linen, he looked every inch a king. His dress was
magnificent; at first we fancied it put on only in our honour, but this
we found to be a mistake, and Ibn Rashid never wears anything less
gorgeous. His costume consisted of several jibbehs of brocaded
Indian silk, a black abba, interwoven with gold, and at least three
kefiyehs, one over the other, of the kind made at Baghdad. His aghal,
also, was of the Baghdad type, which I had hitherto supposed were
only worn by women, bound up with silk and gold thread, and set
high on the forehead, so as to look like a crown. In the way of arms he
wore several golden-hilted daggers and a handsome golden-hilted
sword, ornamented with turquoises and rubies. Hail work, as we
afterwards found. His immediate attendants, though less splendid,
were also magnificently clothed . . .

ARAB RECIPE
FOR REARING A COLT

To the present day in the north the Anazeh distinguish the descendants
of the mares brought with them from Nejd as 'Nejdi', while they call
the descendants of the mares captured from the tribes of the North,
'Shimali' or Northerners . . .

Of anything like racing we could learn nothing. Trials of speed are no longer in fashion, as they must have been once, and skill in turning and doubling is alone of any value. That some tradition, however, of training still exists among the Arabs, the following recipe for rearing a colt seems to prove. It was given us in answer to our description of English racing and racehorses, and probably represents a traditional practice of Arabia as old as the days of Mahomet.

'If,' said our informant, 'you would make a colt run faster than his fellows, remember the following rules:

'During the first month of his life let him be content with his mother's milk, it will be sufficient for him. Then during five months add to this natural supply goat's milk, as much as he will drink. For six months more give him the milk of camels, and besides a measure of wheat steeped in water for a quarter of an hour, and served in a nose-bag.

'At a year old the colt will have done with milk; he must be fed on wheat and grass, the wheat dry from a nose-bag, the grass green if there is any.

'At two years old he must work, or he will be worthless. Feed him now, like a full-grown horse, on barley; but in summer let him also have gruel daily at midday. Make the gruel thus: Take a double-handful of flour, and mix it in water well with your hands till the water seems like milk; then strain it, leaving the dregs of the flour, and give what is liquid to the colt to drink.

'Be careful from the hour he is born to let him stand in the sun; shade hurts horses, but let him have water in plenty when the day is hot.

'The colt must now be mounted, and taken by his owner everywhere with him, so that he shall see everything, and learn courage. He must be kept constantly in exercise, and never remain long at his manger. He should be taken on a journey, for work will fortify his limbs.

'At three years old he should be trained to gallop. Then, if he be of true blood, he will not be left behind. Yalla!'

THE DESERT AND THE SOWN

Gertrude Lowthian Bell

(1868–1926)

———◆———

Granddaughter of Sir Isaac Bell, ironmaster of the Tees, Gertrude Bell, already distinguished academically, when that was still rare for a woman, began to travel when she was still in her teens. A number of relatives and connections in the East led her in that direction and on to studies in history and archaeology.

In a letter to Lord Cromer in the foreword to her book *Amurath to Amurath* she wrote '*The banks of the Euphrates echo with ghostly alarums; the Mesopotamian deserts are full of the rumour of phantom armies; you will not blame me if I passed among them "trattando l'ombre come cose salde"*.'

In *The Desert and the Sown,* she describes, among other enjoyable passages, how she came upon one of the greatest and most famous of the Crusader Castles that is halfway between Homs and the Mediterranean, the Kalaat el-Husn or Kerak des Chevaliers, and how she passed an idle day in Seleucia.

By the beginning of the First World War she was well known for her eastern travels and her knowledge of the peoples, and so became employed in the British Government service and finally in the secretariat of the High Commissioner in Iraq, and attended after the war the important Cairo Conference. She held the post of Director of Antiquities in Iraq at the time of her death in 1926.

———◆———

Beyond the village a plain some three miles wide, the Bkei'a, stretched to the foot of the steep buttress of the Nosairayyeh hills, and from the very top of the mountain frowned the great crusader fortress towards which we were going. The sun shone on its turrets, but a black storm was creeping up behind it; we could hear the thunder rumbling in the hills, and jagged lightning shot through the clouds behind the castle. The direct road across the Bekei'a was impassable for horsemen, owing to the flooded swamps, which were deep enough, said the villagers, to engulf a mule and its load; we turned therefore reluctantly to the right, and edged round the foot of the hills. Before we had gone far we met two riders sent out to welcome us by the Kaimakam of Kala'at el Husn, and as they joined us the storm broke and enveloped us in sheets of rain. Splashing through the mud and drenched with rain we reached the foot of the hills at five o'clock, and here I left my caravan to follow the road and with one of the Kaimakam's horsemen climbed by a steep and narrow bridle-path straight up to the hill-top. And so at sunset we came to the Dark Tower and rode through a splendid Arab gateway into a vaulted corridor, built over a winding stair. It was almost night within; a few loopholes let in the grey dusk from outside and provided the veriest apology for daylight. At intervals we passed doorways leading into cavernous blackness. The stone steps were shallow and wide but much broken; the horses stumbled and clanked over them as we rode up and up, turned corner after corner and passed under gateway after gateway until the last brought us out into the courtyard in the centre of the keep. I felt as though I were riding with some knight of the Fairy Queen, and half expected to see written over the arches: 'Be bold!' 'Be bold!' But there was no magician in the heart of the castle – nothing but a crowd of villagers craning their necks to see us, and the Kaimakam, smiling and friendly, announcing that he could not think of letting me pitch a camp on such a wet and stormy night, and had prepared a lodging for me in the tower.

The Kaimakam of Kala'at el Husn is a distinguished man of letters. His name is 'Abd ul Hamid Beg Rafi'a Zadeh, and his family comes from Egypt, where many of his cousins are still to be found. He lives in the topmost tower of the keep, where he had made ready a guest chamber commodiously fitted with carpets and a divan, a four-post bedstead and a mahogany wardrobe with looking-glass doors of which the glass had been so splintered in the journey a-camel back from Tripoli that it was impossible to see the smallest corner of one's face in it. I was wet through, but the obligations of good society had to be fulfilled, and they demanded that we should sit down on the divan and exchange polite phrases while I drank glasses of weak tea. My host was preoccupied and evidently disinclined for animated conversation – for a good reason, as I subsequently found – but on my replying to his first greeting he heaved a sigh of relief, and exclaimed: 'Praise be to God! your Excellency speaks Arabic. We had feared that we should not be able to talk with you, and I had already invited a

Syrian lady who knows the English tongue to spend the evening for the purpose of interpreting.'

We kept up a disjointed chat for an hour while the damp soaked more and more completely through my coat and skirt, and it was not until long after the mules had arrived and their packs had been unloaded that the Kaimakam rose and took his departure, saying that he would leave me to rest. We had, in fact, made a long day's march; it had taken the muleteers eleven hours to reach Kala'at el Husn. I had barely had time to change my wet clothes before a discreet knocking at the inner door announced the presence of the womenfolk. I opened at once and admitted a maid servant, and the wife of the Kaimakam, and a genteel lady who greeted me in English of the most florid kind. This last was the Sitt Ferideh, the Christian wife of the Government land surveyor, who is also a Christian. She had been educated at a missionary school in Tripoli, and I was not long left in ignorance of the fact that she was an authoress, and that her greatest work was the translation of the *Last Days of Pompeii* into Arabic. The Kaimakam's wife was a young woman with apple cheeks who would have been pretty if she had not been inordinately fat. She was his second wife; he had married her only a month or two before, on the death of his first, the mother of his children. She was so shy that it was some time before she ventured to open her lips in my presence, but the Sitt Ferideh carried off the situation with a gushing volubility, both in English and in Arabic, and a cheerful air of emphasising by her correct demeanour the fervour of her Christianity. She was a pleasant and intelligent woman, and I enjoyed her company considerably more than that of my hostess. The first word that the Khanum ventured to utter was, however, a welcome one, for she asked when I would please to dine. I replied with enthusiasm that no hour could be too early for me, and we crossed a muddy courtyard and entered a room in which a bountiful meal had been spread out. Here we were joined by an ancient dame who was presented to me as 'a friend who has come to gaze upon your Excellency'. And we all sat down to the best of dinners eaten by one at least of the party with the best of sauces. A thick soup and four enormous dishes of meat and vegetables, topped by a rice pudding, composed the repast. When dinner was over we returned to my room, a brazier full of charcoal was brought in, together with hubble-bubbles for the ladies, and we settled ourselves to an evening's talk. The old woman refused to sit on the divan, saying that she was more accustomed to the floor, and disposed herself neatly as close as possible to the brazier, holding out her wrinkled hands over the glowing coals. She was clad in black, and her head was covered by a thick white linen cloth, which was bound closely above her brow and enveloped her chin, giving her the air of some aged prioress of a religious order. Outside the turret room the wind howled; the rain beat against the single window, and the talk turned naturally to deeds of horror and such whispered tales of murder and death as must have startled the shadows in that dim room for many and many a century. A terrible domestic tragedy had fallen upon the Kaimakam ten days before: his son had been shot by a school-fellow at Tripoli in some childish quarrel – the women seemed to think it not unusual that a boy's sudden anger should have such consequences. The Kaimakam had been summoned by telegraph; he had ridden down the long mountain road with fear clutching at his heart, only to find the boy dead, and his sorrow had been almost more than he could bear. So said the Sitt Ferideh.

The ancient crone rocked herself over the brazier and muttered:

'Murder is like the drinking of milk here! God! there is no other but Thou.'

A fresh gust of wind swept round the tower, and the Christian woman took up the tale.

'This Khanum,' said she, nodding her head towards the figure by the brazier, 'knows also what it is to weep. Her son was but now murdered in the mountains by a robber who slew him with his knife. They found his body lying stripped by the path.'

The mother bent anew over the charcoal and the glow flushed her worn old face.

'Murder is like the spilling of water!' she groaned. 'Oh Merciful!'

It was late when the women left me. One of them offered to pass the night in my room, but I refused politely and firmly . . .

It was with the determination not to waver in a decision that had contributed, largely, I make no doubt, to happy and prosperous journeyings, that I rode down to Chaulik, the port of ancient Seluecia. I found my resolve the less difficult to observe because the Armenians talked little but Armenian and Turkish, at any rate the few words of Arabic that some of them possessed were not sufficient to enable them to enter into a detailed account of their wrongs. He who served me that afternoon as a guide was a man of so cheerful a disposition that he would certainly have selected by preference a different topic. His name was Ibrahim, he was bright-eyed and intelligent, and his cheerfulness was deserving of praise, since his yearly income amounted to no more than 400 piastres, under £2 of English money. From this he proposed to save enough to bribe the Turkish officials at the port that they might wink at his escape in an open boat to Cyprus: 'for,'said he, 'there is no industry here but the silkworms, and they give me work for two months in the year, and for the other ten I have nothing to do and no way of earning money.' He also informed me that the Nosairis who inhabited the adjoining villages were unpleasant neighbours.

'There is feud between you?' said I.

'Ey wallah!' said he with emphatic assent, and related in illustration the long story of a recent conflict which, as far as it was comprehensible, seemed to have been due entirely to the aggressions of the Armenians.

'But you began the stealing,' said I when he had concluded.

'Yes' said he. 'The Nosairis are dogs.' And he added with a smile: 'I was imprisoned in Aleppo for two years afterwards.'

'By God! you deserved it,' said I.

'Yes,' said he, as cheerfully as ever.

And this, I rejoice to say, was all that Ibrahim contributed to the store of evidence on the Armenian question.

The Bay of Seleucia is not unlike the Bay of Naples and scarcely less beautiful. A precipitous ridge of the hills, honeycombed with rock-hewn tombs and chambers, forms a background to the mulberry-gardens, and, sweeping round, encloses the bay to the north. Below it lie the walls and water-gates of the port, silted up with earth and separated from the sea by a sandy beach. The Orontes flows through sand and silt farther to the south, and the view is closed by a steep range of hills culminating at the southern point in the lovely peak of Mount Cassius, which takes the place of Vesuvius in the landscape. I pitched my camp near the northern barrier in a little cove divided from the rest of the bay by a low spur which ran out into a ruin-covered headland that commanded the whole sweep of the coast, and I pleased myself with the fancy that it was on this point that the temple and tomb of Seleucus Nicator had stood, though I do not know whether its exact situation has ever been determined. Below it on the beach lay an isolated rock in which a columned hall had been excavated. This hall was fragrant of the sea and fresh with the salt winds that blew through it: a very temple of nymphs and tritons. Ibrahim took me up and down the face of the precipitous cliffs by little paths and by an old chariot-road that led to the city on the summit of the plateau. He said that to walk round the enclosing wall of the upper city took six hours, but it was too hot to put his statement to the test. We climbed into an immense number of the artificial caves, in many of which there were no loculi. They may have been intended for dwellings or storehouses rather than for tombs. At this time of the year they were all occupied by the silkworm breeders, who were now at their busiest moment, the larvae having just issued from the egg. The entrance of each cave was blocked by a screen of green boughs to keep out of the sun, and the afternoon light filtered pleasantly through the budding leaves. At the southern end of the cliff there was a large necropolis, consisting of small caves set round with loculi, and of rock-hewn sarcophagi decorated, when they were decorated at all, with the garland motive that adorns the sarcophagi at Antioch. The most important group of tombs was at the northern end of the cliff. The entrance to it was by a pillared portico that led into a double cave. The larger chamber contained some thirty to forty loculi and a couple of canopied tombs, the canopies cut out of the living rock; the smaller held about half the number of loculi, the roof of it was supported by pillars and pilasters, and I noticed above the tombs a roughly cut design consisting of a scroll of ivy-shaped and of indented leaves . . .

To one more spectacle Ibrahim tempted me. He declared that if I would follow him through the mulberry-gardens below the cliffs he would show me 'a person made of stone'. My curiosity was somewhat jaded by the heat and the long walk but I toiled back wearily over stones and other obstacles to find a god, bearded and robed, sitting under the mulberry trees. He was not a very magnificent god; his attitude was stiff, his robe roughly fashioned, and the top of his head was gone, but the low sun gilded his marble shoulder and the mulberry boughs whispered his ancient titles. We sat down beside him, and Ibrahim remarked:

'There is another buried in this field, a woman, but she is deep deep under the earth.'

'Have you seen her?' said I.

'Yes,' said he. 'The owner of the field buried her, for he thought she might bring him ill luck. Perhaps if you gave him money he might dig her up.'

I did not rise to the suggestion; she was probably better left to the imagination.

Close to the statue I saw a long moulded cornice which was apparently *in situ*, though the wall it crowned was buried in a cornfield: so thickly does the earth cover the ruins of Seleucia. Some day there will be much to disclose here, but excavation will be exceedingly costly owing to the deep silt and to the demands of the proprietors of mulberry grove and cornfield. The site of the town is enormous, and will require years of digging if it is to be properly explored.

Near my tents a sluggish stream flowed through clumps of yellow iris and formed a pool in the sand. It provided water for our animals and for the flocks of goats that Armenian shepherd boys herded morning and evening along the margin of the sea. The spot was so attractive and the weather so delightful that I spent an idle day there, the first really idle day since I had left Jerusalem, and as I could not hope to examine Seleucia exhaustively, I resolved to see no more of it than was visible from my tent door. This excellent decision gave me twenty-four hours, to which I look back with the keenest satisfaction, though there is nothing to be recorded of them except that I was not to escape so lightly from Armenian difficulties as I had hoped. I received in the morning a long visit from a woman who had walked down from Kabuseh, a village at the top of the gorge above the Gariz. She spoke English, a tongue she had acquired at the missionary schools of 'Aintab, her home in the Kurdish mountains. Her name was Kymet. She had left 'Aintab upon her marriage, a step she had never ceased to regret, for though her husband was a good man and an honest, he was so poor that she did not see how she was to bring up her two children. Besides, said she, the people round Kabuseh, Nosairis and Armenians alike, were all robbers, and she begged me to help her to escape to Cyprus. She told me a curious piece of family history, which showed how painful the position of the sect must be in the heart of a Mohammadan country, if it cannot be cited as an instance of official oppression. Her father had turned Muslim when she was a child, chiefly because he wished to take a second wife. Kymet's mother had left him and supported her children as best she might, rather than submit to the indignity that he had thrust upon her, and the bitter quarrel had darkened, said Kymet, all her own youth. She sent her husband down next morning with a hen and a copy of verses written by herself in English. I paid for the hen, but the verses were beyond price. They ran thus:

Welcome, welcome, my dearest dear, we are happy by your coming!
    For your coming welcome! Your arrival welcome!
Let us sing joyfully, joyfully,
    Joyfully, my boys, joyfully!

The sun shines now with moon clearly, sweet light so bright, my dear
boys;
  For your reaching welcome! By her smiling welcome!
The trees send us, my dear boys, with happiness the birds rejoice;
  Its nice smelling welcome! In their singing welcome!

I remain,
Yours truly,
GEORGE ABRAHAM.

I hasten to add, lest the poem should be considered compromising,
that its author was not George Abraham, who as I found in the
negotiations over the hen had no word of English; Kymet had
merely used her husband's name as forming a more impressive
signature than her own. Moreover the boys she alludes to were a
rhetorical figure. I can offer no suggestion as to what it was that the
trees sent us; the text appears to be corrupt at this point. Perhaps 'us'
should be taken as the accusative.

It was with real regret that I left Seleucia. Before dawn, when I
went down to the sea to bathe, delicate bands of cloud were lying
along the face of the hills, and as I swam out into the warm still water
the first ray of the sun struck the snowy peak of Mount Cassius that
closed so enchantingly the curve of the bay. We journeyed back to
Antioch as we had come, and pitched tents outside the city by the
high road. Two days later we set off at 6.30 for a long ride into
Alexandretta. The road was abominable for the first few miles, broken
by deep gulfs of mud, with here and there a scrap of pavement that
afforded little better going than the mud itself. After three hours we
reached the village of Karamurt, and three quarters of an hour further
we left the road and struck straight up the hills by a ruined khan that
showed traces of fine Arab work. The path led up and down steep
banks of earth between thickets of flowering shrubs, gorse and Judas
trees, and an undergrowth of cistus. We saw to the left the picturesque
castle of Baghras, the ancient Pagrae, crowning a pointed hill: I do not
believe that the complex of mountains north of Antioch has ever
been explored systematically, and it may yet yield fragments of
Seleucid or Roman fortifications that guarded the approach to the city.
Presently we hit upon the old paved road that follows a steeper course
than the present carriage road; it led us at one o'clock (we had stopped
for three quarters of an hour to lunch under the shady bank of a

stream) to the summit of the Pass of Bailan, where we joined the main road from Aleppo to Alexandretta. There was no trace of fortification, as far as I observed, at the Syrian Gates where Alexander turned and marched back to the Plain of Issus to meet Darius, but the pass is very narrow and must have been easy to defend against northern invaders. It is the only pass practicable for an army through the rugged Mount Amanus. The village of Bailan lay an hour further in a beautiful situation on the northern side of the mountains looking over the Bay of Alexandretta to the bold Cilician coast and the white chain of Taurus. From Bailan it is about four hours' ride to Alexandretta.

As we jogged down towards the shining sea by green and flowery slopes that were the last of Syria, Mikhail and I fell into conversation. We reviewed, as fellow travellers will, the incidents of the way, and remembered the adventures that had befallen us by flood and field, and at the end I said:

'Oh Mikhail, this is a pleasant world, though some have spoken ill of it, and for the most part the children of Adam are good not evil.'

I CEASE NOT FROM DESIRE
From the Divan of Hafiz,
translated by Gertrude Bell

I cease not from desire till my desire
Is satisfied; or let my mouth attain
My love's red mouth, or let my soul expire,
Sighed from those lips that sought her lips in vain.
Others may find another love as fair;
Upon her threshold I have laid my head,
The dust shall cover me, still lying there,
When from my body life and love have fled.

TO KURDISTAN IN DISGUISE

From To Mesopotamia and Kurdistan in Disguise by Ely Bannister Soane

(1881–1923)

———◆———

Soane first went to Persia as an assistant in the Imperial Bank of Persia in 1905. He embraced Islam, as a Shiah, and became manager of the branch of the bank in Shiraz. After resigning in 1907 he studied Kurdish and made the journey described in his book *To Mesopotamia and Kurdistan in Disguise*, 1912.

Later he joined the Anglo-Persian Oil Company and was in charge of drilling at Chaya Surkh near Khanizin. He was arrested by the Turks who sent him to Baghdad where he was released, and was later made an assistant political officer with the troops at Dizful by the British. In March 1917, after the fall of Baghdad, he was sent to Sulaimania, though soon obliged to take sick leave, until 1920. Ordered home to England, again a sick man, he died at sea in February 1923.

———◆———

From Diarbekr I purposed to travel as far as Mosul down the Tigris on a kalak, or raft of skins and poles. The few Europeans who have adopted this pleasant method of travelling, usually hired half the raft, erected a booth or tent and carried a cook and servants, travelling tranquilly, with no more to do than admire the scenery and take snapshot photographs. In my assumed character I could not go in for this style of luxury, and had to look out for a passage by a kalak carrying cargo, upon the top of which I might be allowed to sit, for a consideration.

However, I was to have a tent after all, and it came about thus :–

I was eating my frugal lunch of dry bread and lettuces one day in the caravanserai, when an aged man in the long garments and felt waistcoat of a southern Kurd came up to my room, and entering with a salutation, sat down, and accepted my invitation to share the meal. He introduced himself as Haji Vali, a native of Erbil, on the western marches of Kurdistan, a Bab Kurd, returning from his seventeenth journey to Mecca. He, like me, sought a passage to Mosul, and came with the news that a kalak was ready; and, moreover, possessed a shelter of sticks and calico which had been made for an effendi now unable to travel, and which could be bought for a mejidie or so. The old man knew a little Persian, and spoke, besides his native Kurdish in which we conversed, Turkish and Arabic. The assurance with which he had joined me at my meal, and the certainty he seemed to feel that I should become a partner with him in our passage to Mosul, I found a feature of all his doings.

He had an abrupt, dictatorial manner, which he tempered with bluff heartiness, and, used to the respect which his seventeen journeys to Mecca had earned for him, was not accustomed to receiving a refusal to any of his propositions. So when he proposed to me – whom he called Musa – addressing me as 'his beloved son', that we should share all expenses, I agreed. No sooner was this settled than he departed, to return later with his goods and chattels, some being saddle-bags, and little sacks of charcoal, a tin samovar, and a packet of letters and papers which he entrusted to me, as being more secure in the pocket of my overcoat; for in the fashion of the long tunic of the East he possessed no pockets, but two wallets hanging at his sides, and must needs thrust any valuables in his breast. The kalak owner now appeared with the Armenian doorkeeper as witness and intermediary in the negotiations. This kalak owner was a gaunt Kurd, pretty well seven feet tall, a cadaverous-looking giant who, squatting on the ground, seemed an ordinary man's height. An impediment in his speech and a single fierce-looking eye made him a fearsome-looking fellow. He was very easy to haggle with, though, and started by demanding six mejidies for transporting us to Mosul, we to be allowed to use the tent, which should become his property at the journey's end. We held out for five mejidies, and half the proceeds of the sale of the tent at Mosul. Eventually, after the consumption of many cigarettes, and after he had three several times risen and got half-way down the stairs in apparent indignation at our inflexibility, with the Armenian as disinterested go-between, we arranged on the price of two mejidies each, the tent being the Kurd's property. The kalak was to start next morning, and we must transport ourselves and our belongings outside the town to a spot where a stone bridge crosses the river some mile below Diarbekr.

In the meantime we must purchase food for some days; the journey, if we received no checks, would occupy five days, but if high winds arose or much rain fell we must be resigned to twelve days or even longer. So we visited the bazaar. First to a baker's, where we ordered a sack full of thick flaps of bread, that he would cook by noon, and half toast besides, making them as it is called, 'firni', which prevents the bread going mouldy. Then to buy sugar, at which operation my knowledge of 'European' – as Haji Vali called an ability to read Latin characters – was needed, for the Armenian shopkeeper tried to pass off upon us as 'English sugar' some inferior produce of Austria, and his surprise and Haji Vali's delight were about equal when I exposed the fraud by reading the label.

To buy anything was a great nuisance. When I was alone I never had the patience to beat the seller down to the last farthing, and would pay an eighth of a penny more for an article than its proper price; but old Haji Vali would have none of this. He knew the price of every-thing in every city from Medina to Bagdad, and woe betide the Christian who swore to a false price. At last, however, we actually did finish our purchases, which, if I remember, were as follows: a sack each of charcoal and bread, ten pounds of rice, one pound of tea, three sugar loaves, six pewter teaspoons, seven pounds of clarified butter, odd quantities of lentils and pease, three long strings of dried 'lady's fingers', a little vegetable; pepper and rock salt; some dried fruits. These we carried to the caravanserai, bent double under the sacks and bags we shouldered. The purchase of these things took us from nine in the morning till nearly sunset, and involved as much talking and argument as a session of parliament.

Having locked up our purchases and tied up our goods, ready to be taken away next morning, we went out for a last look at Diarbekr; but the old man, sick of bazaars, surprised me by a request, unlike what one would expect from one of a people that usually expresses so little regard for the aspect of things natural, and the beauties of the world we live in.

Taking my arm, he said:

'Musa, my son, after the day's toil, let us go outside the gate to a quiet spot among the trees upon the cliff, where we can sit and look upon the view.'

So, very gratefully, I consented, and we took our way by the gate, turned to the right, and passing the hideous military school, came to the cliff that overhangs the Tigris. We descended a little by a footpath, and found a clump of trees on a narrow ledge, whence, sheltered from the view of passers above, we could look out northwards,

across the plain, and to the ever dark hills of Kurdistan. The old man
sat silent for a long time, but at last expressed his sentiments in one
long 'Allahu akbar!' ('God is great').

And then he pointed out to me the beauties of the great rushing
stream, the vivid colouring of its yellow banks, and the light green of
the groves of trees that sprang with a new year's life far below us.

Again he sat silent, and gazed with narrowed eyes at the far
mountains, and when he spoke again, it was the soul of the Kurd
and of the mountaineer that threw the harsh words of his dialect from
his tongue:

'God! and God! and God! He, the Indivisible, His glories are
manifest to our eyes, and His mercies to our hearts and minds. Yet
my son, think not that these mountains – upon which the body
roams, while the soul, soaring above, meets the Unknown in a medium
pure as the snow-field that stretches above – are His masterpiece. For
verily, as these mighty hills are the greatest of His works here, yet
they are but as the pebble upon their flanks compared to His works in
Heaven.

'See this work, how it exists. Who are we to boast of the power
He gave us, Who takes it away after our four days of transition?
See these city walls, the great among us made them, and they shall
fall in a space of time incalculably small in His sight, yet the stones of
them are His handiwork, and long enduring, have endured, even as
those hills. And when the walls shall sink, one, building the sign of his
ambition with the ruin of another's, shall use these same stones,
remembering the former builder of walls.

'Ah! that he forget not the Maker of the stones that last, and the
hills that endure.'

The old man spoke quietly, yet as he spoke, the blue eyes dimmed
and the voice shook – indeed there are anomalies in this world, dual
personalities, among the sons of the East that one never suspects.

This old man, who had spent his life in an occupation we should
deride as hypocritical – for he was a guide to Mecca, and while over-
charging the uninitiated, achieved spurious merit – had yet in his old
heart a spot where the poetry that lives in the Aryan breast yet lurked,
and emanated, ascribing everything to that fearful Omnipotence that
the Muhammadan worships.

In the Persian I have often met this dual personality – the hard,
cautious man, who descends to any trickery and deception, even crime,
for the meanest ends, and in a revulsion of feeling reviles himself,

sees himself as others see him, in the purest poetry of language and thought expresses the most beautiful sentiment, and falls to earth again.

The mountains, always the mountains, held the old man's gaze. There is a fascination about them that it is not necessary to be a Kurd or a Persian to be able to acquire. The impassive monuments of old-time glacier and volcanic upheaval, relics of convulsions that rent continents, that rise straight up from the flat, broad plains, may well seize upon all that is impressionable in anyone, and inspire the dullest with that craving to penetrate the mysteries of their deep valleys, and view the world from their blanched heads.

Truly, Diarbekr, that looks out from its fine bluff upon the lands of four old empires – Assyria to the south, Armenia to the north, Media to the east, and Rome to the west, might have much to meditate upon, were it allowed time for meditation between the continual rebellion and persecution that tear it.

Sunset, that meant gates closed, forced us to return, and once within the gates, Haji forgot his mood, and recommenced his talk of the journey, of the prices of our various purchases, of the unscrupulousness of Armenians, and the exaction of the Turks, who sent up the price of everything.

Next morning early we roused up, and while I went out into the streets to find a porter, Haji busied himself arranging the goods for carrying. A sturdy Kurd, whom I found in a mosque yard, arranged to carry our things for five piastres (10*d*.) and we loaded him up with a box and the saddle-bags, upon which we cast our bedding. The rest we must carry ourselves, for Haji, who would spend as little as possible himself, would not allow me to waste a coin where it could be saved.

It took us a little while to convince the Armenian shop-keeper that a couple of shillings was enough for five days' occupation of his room; but this once done, he helped to load us up, and at length we departed. Haji's load was the sack of charcoal, and a bag containing the rice and some sundries, while I shouldered the bread and suspended from myself bags containing tea and sugar loaves, odds and ends of all descriptions, and a charcoal brazier that picked pieces out of me wherever it struck its many sharp corners. The whole length of Diarbekr we struggled, for the south gate was our first objective, and not till then did I realise the size of the place. The straight street ran on as it seemed to infinity, but the gate (so like the gate from

Princess, Prince and Ordinary Class, from Sir John Chardin's
'Travels into Persia' in Pinkerton's *Voyages and Travels*, London, 1811

Winchelsea to the Romney marshes) did appear at last, and by some extraordinary providence the police did not worry. The sun was getting up at the pace he always does in the East, which I am sure is greater than anywhere else, and we sweated and panted as we waddled along, bent double under our loads. The porter, with the strength of his kind, outdistanced us, and with his steady march was soon lost among the trees that border the winding road. Haji's breath gave out here, and we had to rest, but at last we did get to the bank of the river, and threw our loads down upon some bags of apricots that were to go to Mosul.

And now, since we are arrived at the kalak, a description of the ingenious craft is necessary. Briefly, two hundred inflated goatskins arranged in the form ten by twenty, are bound to a few thin transverse poplar trunks above them. Over these again seven or eight more tree-trunks not more than 7 inches thick, are placed crosswise, and upon these, to form a deck, is placed a layer of bales. Between two pairs of these bales a basket-work affair is fixed, which, with a stake, forms a rough thole-pin. A pair of enormous sweeps swings on these, and the oarsmen, standing upon one bale, build a bridge of twigs across to the next row, and wield the sweeps standing. Under the sweeps an empty space is always left across the raft, where the skins are visible between the rafters.

The raft, from its shape and construction, cannot be propelled, and the *raison d'être* of the oars is for turning, by which the kalak is directed into the right currents, and to pull the craft out of the danger that rocks standing in the stream often threaten. In the upper river, between Diarbekr and Mosul, particularly during the springtime, progress at night is impossible, for the side-currents which sweep round the rocky banks at the velocity of a galloping horse would hopelessly smash the raft. Wind, too, naturally exerts a great driving force upon a craft that draws but three inches of water, and its strength, too much for oars to fight against, often compels a halt.

When we arrived, Kurdish porters were loading up the last of the cargo, dried apricots and rice mostly, from round about Urfa. The crew were busy blowing up partially deflated skins with a tube which they inserted into a protruding leg of the skin. Our tent, or 'tenta' as the Arabs called it, was wedged between two walls of bales, and entering, we found it had a plank floor laid over the tree-trunks forming the raft.

We had two fellow-passengers – one an Arab merchant of Mosul, a man of tremendous piety, who spent his whole time smoking cigarettes and calling on the Lord. The other was as diametrically opposite to him in character as possible: a time-expired soldier, a youth of twenty-three, who was returning from the Hejaz Railway, where he had formed part of the military police guard, to Kirkuk, his native town. Foul-mouthed, blasphemous, a thief, possessing no money and expecting us to keep him, he was a type of what the Turk becomes when the army has moulded him to its standard of ruffianism.

The crew of the raft was composed of two Kurds, little men of the Zaza, a tribe that lives in the high mountains round the upper Tigris valley and headwaters. These people are different in appearance and manners from nearly all other Kurds. They are short men, of a shy, quick temperament, very sharp, and excellent workers, speaking a dialect which, while Kurdish, denotes by its form a very high antiquity. It is possible that these are lineal descendants of the hill-tribes that the Assyrians had so much trouble in controlling, and whom the Parthians and Romans of a later age never subdued. In the high, pointed felt cap and long-toed shoes they still preserve part of a dress familiar from the sculptures of the southern Armenian mountains.

The skipper of our craft was known as one of the most skilful of all the river men, and in the dreadful weather that followed he showed by his ability his claim to that reputation.

We cast off from the bank at ten o'clock this sunny morning, a light breeze from the north both assisting our progress and keeping the temperature at a degree of perfect comfort. Under such conditions, fine weather and a broad river that runs at a steady pace without too many shallows and rapids, there is probably no more pleasant method of travelling than by kalak. As it proceeds, the raft turns round and round slowly, giving a view of every side.

There is an ease and comfort about it all that only the traveller fresh from the road can appreciate. The abundance of cool, clean water is the chief delight of the journey, contrasting with the ever-present trouble of the road, with its water often enough scarce, and always obtained only at the expense of considerable manual labour. The dust and filth, the long, wearying stages, the trouble of loading and unloading and of seeking food in obscure bazaars when one is dead tired, the awakening from a sleep all too short in the dark before dawn, all these are past, and all there is to do is to lie at full length upon the bales and give oneself up to the luxury of pure laziness and enjoyment of the view.

For two days we floated down between flat banks, passing a few villages, all Kurdish. At night we tied up, gathered some sticks, made a fire, and cooked rice. Haji and myself were regarded as the first-class passengers, possessing, as we did, a tent, and living upon cooked food. The others had but dry bread and cheese, of which they had brought a sufficient supply to last. As the custom of Islam generally, and of the Kurd particularly, demands a fraternal fellowship among all travellers, we entertained the passengers and crew at our evening meal every night. The class distinction that asserts itself in every land on earth, whether it be the difference made by breeding, position, or hard cash, became apparent on the first evening. I had cleaned and washed the rice, boiled it, and produced a pilau, turning it out into our one dish, which was but a big copper saucepan-lid. We invited the company to partake, refusing to eat under any other conditions. The crew, however, were too shy, and asserting their own unworthiness, said they would eat afterwards. The Arab merchant, too, hung off with polite phrases, but was eventually forced to join. The soldier needed no encouragement, and would have sat down and begun without waiting for us to put out our hands to the dish, a terrible gaucherie; but for some reason both Arab and Kurd, who had conceived a strong dislike to him, fairly beat him off, saying that he was not of our class and rank, and might wait and eat afterwards. So, with very bad grace, he retired to sulkiness and cigarettes. A hearty appetite, helped by the pity-to-waste-it kind of sentiment, assures the total disappearance of a cooked meal among all the people of road and river in the East, so there were never any leavings, and the washing up of the one dish was always undertaken by the crew. Morning and afternoon, we made tea upon the raft, precedence in the dispensing of it being strictly observed. First myself, for all had given me the title of effendi, on the strength of a fez and overcoat, and regarded me as the aristocrat of the party, then Haji Vali my partner, then the Arab, and after we had each partaken of the regulation three glasses, the crew received their two, the soldier getting his share last of all.

The third day, great mountains began to rise high before us, stretching away across the course of the river, far to the east and west. The second night we tied up at a Kurdish village just before reaching some high cliffs that were the sentinels of the terrific gorges we were to pass later, and here our luck turned. First we learned that a section

An officer of the Pasha of Sulamaniyah from Claudius Rich's
A Residence in Koordistan, London, 1836

of the Kurdish tribe in the hills we could see ahead had rebelled, a quite usual occurrence, and to show their defiance of authority, were shooting at passers-by on the river. This was certainly disquieting, but a prospective danger is sometimes dwarfed by present discomfort. In the pouring rain that set in at sunset, we forgot all about robbers and rebels. A strong gale arose, with torrential rain, which wet our tent through, threatening to tear it away altogether. The Kurdish crew, who feared to leave their craft to the mercy of a wind and ever-strengthening current, that might carry it away and shatter it against rocks, were bound to sleep aboard, and in a piercing cold they lay sodden, rivulets running from their thin garments, and tried to sleep. We in the tent were not much better off. All our bedding got soaked, thick cotton quilts which take hours to dry; our rice and charcoal became pulp and mud respectively. Streams falling from pools in the calico roof spouted upon us, now on our faces, now in the nape of our necks. Pools formed upon our coverings, and soaked through. Our clothing could absorb no more, nor our bedding, and at last we, like the unfortunates outside, resigned ourselves to becoming shivering bodies wrapped in spongy swathings, our only advantage over them being a little shelter from the stinging wind. In the black darkness we had to crawl out over bales of apricots, slippery with the juice and wet that oozed from them, to secure our flimsy house: every few moments a new place had to be found for such valuables as matches, whose ever-changing refuge was invaded by the rain with a malignant persistency as regularly as we devised it.

Morning brought us no relief, and indeed made our case worse, for had we stayed at the village we could have taken shelter in its houses. By an irony of the elements, the wind held off at sunrise, and despite the rain we cast off. An hour downstream, where it narrowed among the hills and ever-rising cliffs, the wind swept down again, and we tied up by a strip of beach under a precipice, and so cut ourselves off from any chance of shelter. For three days and nights it rained and blew. Even our bread, the only thing we had to eat, became sodden. Haji developed rheumatism, and a temper so irritable that I migrated to the bales outside, and slept two nights upon the apricots, covered by soaked and clammy things that, while they kept the wind off, were so chill as to make their advantage problematical.

The fourth morning, however, broke fine, and in half an hour the clouds had torn to rags, the wind had gone overhead, driving the rack at a tremendous pace; but below the river ran blue between its yellow cliffs, now a good two hundred feet high, and we steamed in the welcome warmth; and now we saw how the three days' torrent had altered the conditions of affairs. Our mooring-stakes were a couple of feet under water, and the river, which from here runs in a gorge through the mountains – a gorge ever narrowing – was flying along at express speed. Our courageous skipper cast off, and we commenced to race along. The river pursues a remarkable course here. The reaches are straight and short, and owing to the similarity in colouring of the opposite banks it is impossible to see the turn – often less than a right angle – till right upon it. Huge hills rise up beyond their lower slopes covered with trees, and above all we could see snow-capped peaks. In these wild gorges, of a beauty of spring verdure, of a magnificence indescribable, we felt – as in all effect we were – but a chip swept along the great river. At every turn the current, setting towards the far bank, would sweep round, roaring against the vicious-looking rocks, and all hands were called to the oars to keep the raft from dashing upon them, and being torn to pieces. The river, narrowing between points sometimes, or running over submerged rocks at others, breaks up in high curling swell, and the current doubles its speed. Here we would experience the greatest excitement in guiding the raft to the exact centre of the converging ridges of waves and shooting through between them at a tremendous velocity, to rush upon the boiling commotion where they met. The raft would undulate, its non-rigid construction prevents its rocking, and waves would roll up, drenching us and our goods, and our half-dried garments, while the raft cracked ominously. At such points Haji and the Arab merchant, grasping the nearest firm object, would ejaculate fervently, 'Ya Rebbi! Sahl! Ya Rebbi!' ('Oh God, help! Oh God!'), and passing the danger spot, utter equally fervent thanksgiving. As we proceeded, the hills and cliffs got higher and steeper, great mountain sides rose at a slope apparently impossible to climb, to dizzy heights. Here and there would occur a narrow point of land, around which the stream curved, and upon every such was a little Kurdish village, the house of the head-man, well built of stone, with a loop-holed tower standing up on slightly higher ground. Once or twice shots were fired, but our pace took us far beyond the reach of the sportsmen, almost before they could reload. Seeing these great hills, these constant precipices, it was easy enough to understand why the armies of the old Powers of Mesopotamia in their marches northward always took the westerly plain roads, and left these hills to the tribes that have inhabited them ever since Central Asia poured out its hordes of Aryans far back in the years before history, to people the Western world.

One afternoon, when we were favoured with good weather, we turned into a long reach, and had before us one of the most remarkable sights the Tigris has to offer. The right bank of the river rose in a vertical cliff to a great height, and was faced across the broad stream by fellow cliffs not so high, but honeycombed with cave-dwellings. The right hand cliff (which was the result of a hill-side cut off by the river) was broken at one place and continued again, the ravine – but a few yards across – coming down to the water's edge. Upon the summit of this continued portion we could see a considerable town, so high up that human figures looked minute. Behind all, rose precipitous hill-sides, between whose gorges and valleys could be seen yet wilder crags and peaks. In the village or town two or three towers, narrow and tall, of the dimensions of a factory chimney, rose, looking more slender and high from the eminence upon which they stood. But most remarkable of all were the great piers of a once colossal bridge, that, springing from a lower point of the cliff, or rather from a spot upon its slope down to the foreshore, spans the space to the opposite cliff, bridging the Tigris further south than any existing stone bridge. Here the stream is broad and deep, and the mighty piers that tower above and shadow the passer-by in his humble kalak, speak volumes for the perseverance and talent of people past and gone, and, by comparison, the qualities of the Ottomans. And on both sides, on the left or east bank, where the cliff growing ever lower still hedges the river, and on the west, where receding it leaves a fertile foreshore, the faces are pierced with cave-dwellings, rock forts that communicate with one another. Curious chambers, open at the river-side, mere eyries, looked down upon the stream, and it is only a near approach that reveals the mode of access, a passage diving into the rock. From the village above a staircase has been cut, zigzagging down the cliff-face to where the river laps the solid rock wall ...

We cast off at the second hour of daylight, and floated out into a lake of swift-rushing eddies, crashing commotions of meeting streams. Here the Buhtan Su – the largest of the streams that go to make up the full Tigris – enters at a broad place, a bay among some abruptly rising hills. For a mile or so the reach of the combined rivers sweeps along broad and deep, then is forced to take the only possible outlet through a narrow gorge, between where the speed is positively giddy. As we approached the turn, a number of Kurds appeared, running down a valley to the river, and as they neared opened fire upon us, hitting nothing but a bale or two; but their attention was diverted most opportunely by another party, which, appearing on high, commenced a lively fusillade directed at our assailants. Very fortunately we were not in a position to stop and watch the developments, but as we were hustled round a bend we saw that a brisk fight was in progress. It interested me very much to note the behaviour of my fellow-travellers. The crew seemed to think the affair very ordinary, and never ceased rowing; in fact it would have been impossible to relinquish control of the raft in this corridor full of rocks. The Arab and Haji, too, while very careful to take shelter behind bales, knowing that we must soon be carried beyond reach of danger, were very little perturbed, only the Kurdish blood of the older man boiled to think that he had not a gun to respond. The Turkish soldier disappeared at the first shot, having wedged himself in among the apricot bags and the rafters, whence he at length emerged wet and muddy.

We were not to go far that day, for rain and storm came on again, and we had to tie up; but the morning came fine, and despite the precarious condition of the raft, which was now floating under water, we resolved to go on as far as Jazira, a small town at the foot of the mountains, and reached there completely water-logged, and sinking deeper every minute, a little after noon.

Here our crew were paid off and another couple taken over; the process of handing over being to count everything on board, passengers included, when the new man, entering into possession, looked around and was expected to carry out all necessary repairs, or re-arrange cargo and passengers as suited. He wasted no time, and plunged into the chilly water, pulling out deflated skins, blowing up others, replacing faulty ones, and tidying up generally till sunset . . .

'I am an old man,' he said, 'and by many cities have I wandered, from Salonica to Basrah, and Trebizonde to Mecca, but never have I missed the opportunity of cultivating the acquaintance of a Persian or Shi'a. Let us not forget one another. We are both strangers, both of that land that is the fairest of all the earth, where mercy and charity overspread the land, where Muslim treats Muslim as a brother and not a foe – like these Turks. Let it not, therefore, be said that I, Haji Rasul, though I am but a poor Kurd, have violated the tradition of Islam, Persia and the Kurds alike. Here I work by day, and in the verandah I sit at night, alone; help to relieve my loneliness by your constant company while you are here.'

IN RIYADH AND KUWAIT

From Through Wahhabiland on Camelback by Barclay Raunkiaer

(1888–1915)

Perhaps the most influential figure in the Arabian peninsula at the turn of the
nineteenth century was Shaikh Mubarak as-Sabah, the ruler of the small Gulf
state of Kuwait, which had maintained its independence from the Turk under
his implacable leadership and enjoyed the protection of Great Britain.
Mubarak became the protector of Abdurrahan ibn Faisal al Saud, pretender
to the throne of central Arabia, and his son Abdal Aziz, when the Sauds
were expelled from their capital by Ibn Rashid in 1885. (They returned to
Riyadh on the first day of 1902).

The most colourful portrait of the old ruler was provided by an
improbable visitor, the Dane Barclay Raunkiaer, who travelled through Iraq
and the central deserts of Arabia as the unofficial representative of the Danish
Royal Geographical Society in 1911. That Society had asked the permission
of the British government to send an expedition to the Peninsula by way of
Kuwait, in order to further the scientific work of Carsten Niebuhr and his
companions in the eighteenth century. Britain refused that permission, and
so Raunkiaer set out alone, with no Arabic, no contacts and the minimum of
provisions. He left Denmark on 12 November 1911, finding en route a single
companion, a Baghdadi Christian guide, though others accompanied him
between Najd and Kuwait.

He died within two years of his return to Denmark, in 1915.

Since leaving Baghdad, one week ago, the river steamer has been
following the intricate curves of the Tigris. Amid constant groundings
and other delays, the ship, with its motley swarm of tattered pilgrims
is sliding down a plum-coloured stream whose low clay banks are
overflowed by our wash. Villages of reed huts which could be swept
away by half a metre more of rise in the water have emerged, with

barking dogs and columns of blue smoke, to disappear again and become one with the endless, ochrous marsh.

The Arabs have not fired on us, a fact deserving notice because river steamers, and especially English ones, are at present subject to fierce ebullitions of a typically south Mesopotamian religious fanaticism mingled with political excitement and love of plundering all mankind. We have passed the luxuriant palm groves of Qurna and are now out in the broad stream of the Shatt el Arab where brownish yellow water of the Tigris joins the clearer green of Euphrates . . .

It is now settled that I am to go to Kuweit and there, relying upon Turkish recommendations, try to induce the present Sheikh, Mobarek el Sabah, to allow me to proceed southward, overland, to Hasa . . .

The distinctly chilly relations wont to subsist between Kuweit and Suk-el-Shiukh, with in consequence a zone of insecurity between the spheres of influence of their two Sheikhs, have somewhat improved. Accordingly, black tents of the Muntefik are scattered over the pale green plain to within a score of kilometres of Mobarek's fort at Jihara. As far as the eye can see, roam herds of black, long-haired goats and brown sheep, with here and there a grey donkey with white muzzle, for the most part in charge of the nomads' children. These wandering subjects of Saadun Pasha range in summer as far up as the Shatt el Gharaf (Shatt el Hai), between Nasaria and Kut el Amara.

After passing in mid-morning a depression called Zagla we saw no more nomads, vegetation became scantier, with rock outcrops in ground rising towards a low ridge at the south end of the plateau called el Motla. Through a notch in its crest, in which there twisted a dry water course, we descend to the plain and at midday reach Jihara, the first settlement in Mobarek's country. Jihara is a village in flat, open surroundings with about five hundred inhabitants. North of the houses are a few cornfields watered by *sherds* and a couple of date plantations, the number of palms not exceeding a hundred. We water our horses at a little pond of indifferent water, march through the village and take midday rest on its southern side by Mobarek's clay fort. The fort is of the usual Arabian type, a square court being enclosed by a crenellated wall with four corner towers freely loop-holed. Having enjoyed some *libn* bought in Jihara and the remains of the food brought with us from Zober, we march on over a very gently undulating plain, now near the sea, now some kilometres away from it. No nomads were to be seen, but we constantly pass Arabs, either singly or in groups driving loaded donkeys – a sign that there is more public security than usually obtains in Arabia.

Plagued by flies, the tired horses stumble on through deep, grey dust under an ever more burning sun. Late in the afternoon one of them falls lame, and its load has to be divided among the others. On we go, slowly and limpingly through the grey-green country. Not a breath of wind is astir. Eastwards stretches the Kuweit bay, glittering like a sheet of glass and on the far side of it lies Kuweit, a long low line of yellow dots. Hour after hour passes without our seeming to come any nearer to the town; a beautiful sunset left all the western sky aglow, but it was soon quenched by rapidly falling darkness and still we have not reached Kuweit. Already, at three o'clock in the afternoon, I had enquired of one of my Arabs how far it was to Kuweit. 'An hour's ride' he answered. Two hours later I repeated the question. 'An hour' was again the answer. When two hours on, I put the same question and got the same reply, I gave up further enquiry, profoundly distrusting the Arabs' estimate of time.

We reach the first houses of Kuweit between eight and nine at night. On the edge of the town not a human being is to be seen. To our left is the real town, with its houses of sun-dried clay. To our right is the movable town, that is to say, of caravaneers and bedouin, scattered over a part of the desert which penetrates like an arm of the sea into the real Kuweit. As we advance the tents become more numerous and closer together, the lights from small fires give passing glimpses of natives sipping coffee and of their resting beasts of burden.

In the innermost corner of the inlet of waste begins the bazaar, with numerous lanes and partly covered streets. We grope our way on through them in complete darkness, pass their fastened-up booths and after repeatedly changing direction arrive before a fortress-like building eight to ten metres high and of such great extent that its full bulk could not be made out in the night. Into this otherwise seemingly inaccessible mass of clay a very narrow lane penetrates and at its mouth we call a halt, because our pack-horses would have wholly blocked the passage. The lane is immediately filled by armed men of all shades of colour from Sudanese negroes to pale-skinned Arabs from the north, some of them bearing torches or lanterns. Very deliberately they take my letters of recommendation to be conveyed to Mobarek. Some time passes in impatient expectation before one of the Sheikh's trusted men, Mohammed, came and made a sign that we were to be admitted. We are led through a low door and down a dark passage between two rows of janitors, all armed to the teeth, and come out into a little irregular court surrounded by a medley of buildings. In one of these I was shown into a room, the baggage was piled in a corner, a carpet was spread over the straw mats which cover the floor and I myself take a place on the carpet, an object of great curiosity to the Sheikh's men.

An Abyssinian slave arrives with an enormous tinned copper tray on which are bowls of *libn*, bread and dates, and simultaneously Mohammed came on the Sheikh's behalf to pray me excuse the fact that we were not getting a proper meal; the evening meal had been eaten at six o'clock and there was nothing left from it.

While we were eating, Mohammed and another of the Sheikh's men began to put suspicious questions eagerly. Who am I ? Whence come ? Where going ? Am I partisan of the English or of the Germans ? Why am I guest of the Sheikh and not of the English political agent ? and so on, for ever and ever, without regard to the fact that the questions were answered beforehand in my letters of introduction. Finally the Sheikh's Arabs withdrew and I was left alone with Ali in a room only dimly illumined from a petroleum lamp.

The decoration of the room is simple but carried out with greater precision than is usual. The Persian rug, at one end of the room, is where I am to spend most of my time and receive visitors. The whitewashed walls have on one side a row of windows, unglazed of course, but having iron gratings and wooden shutters.

The ceiling is of the regular, lower Mesopotamian and east Arabian kind, a row of thin beams supporting mats made of plaited palm-leaf. Above the matting is a layer of firmly trodden clay.

The following morning I am awakened by the Abyssinian slave bringing the morning meal of tea, hot milk, bread, honey, and various sweetmeats. Soon afterwards Mohammed arrives to announce that the Sheikh is ready to receive me and we follow him at once over a bridge, about five metres above the street, joining Mobarek's palace to the well-built *serai* or government house.

Here, with a view over the sea, and protected by a fully armed bodyguard of about sixty men, who lay picturesquely sprawling on the floor at a respectful distance, I found the ruler of Kuweit, an energetic old man of seventy-three. He was sitting in an armchair and observing keenly the strange sight of a European, in Arab dress, who, though neither English nor German, yet journeyed under the special protection of the Turkish government. My reception was formally polite; but the Sheikh's questions were marked by mistrust and reserve. It is clear that he is in great uncertainty how to treat me. The questions were the same as those he had ordered Mohammed to put to me the evening before and he now makes determined efforts to involve me in self-contradiction, especially in regard to my political standpoint.

It is evident to me that this is the crucial matter and easy to see that my position in this respect is become very difficult indeed. After the hearty friendliness and powerful protection extended to me everywhere in Turkish quarters, I could only express the most friendly sentiments towards the Turks, while at the same time I declared myself distinctly Anglophile. In the present political situation in the Persian Gulf, my singular attitude raised an almost insuperable objection in Mobarek's mind, for the ultimate removal of which I am deeply indebted to England's diplomatic agent in Kuweit, Captain W. I. I. Shakespear.

Several very unpleasant days elapse, however, before we succeeded in getting to this point. My first audience of Mobarek ended with his promising to send a messenger after some Ajman bedouin, who, provided they will accept the responsibility, may conduct me to Katif and Hofuf. Since, however, there are no men of the tribe mentioned in Kuweit at the present moment, some days must pass before anything further can be done. Mobarek gave Mohammed orders that he was to be at my disposition in all things, and first and foremost to show me the town; and after the expression of a desire, ending with a husky, deep-mouthed *inshallah*, that the bedouin might soon appear, the first of a long series of audiences, by no means all encouraging, though always interesting, came to an end.

Mobarek's town, bone of contention in the struggle for power between England and Germany in the Nearer East, lies on a coast which sweeps south-west by north-east and rises only very gently from the Gulf of Kuweit with its rich deposit of Shatt-el-Arab mud. Quite apart from the great political importance of the town, it claims no ordinary interest because, with the exception perhaps of Makalla, on the south shore of Arabia, it is the least disturbed by foreign civilization of the few 'independent' Arab coast towns of any importance.

The town's greatest extent, somewhat over two kilometres, is along its water-front, while inland it is hardly one kilometre in depth.

At about the centre of the sea-face lies the Sheikh's Palace, a large and very irregular complex of buildings with dependancies built at various times in various styles. Thus Arabian, Mespotamian and Persian architectures are all represented.

It is divided into three parts in the uses to which it is put, namely: the Sheikh's private residence with the harem, on the rise from the beach; quarters for the bodyguard, male servants, slaves and guests, on the slope behind; finally the *serai* or government building, on the beach itself.

The Sheikh's residence is a large, fortress-like building round a square court. Its high walls have no windows giving outwards, only loopholes at certain points and the whole building communicates with the outer world directly only through the little door into the very narrow lane which separates the two upper blocks of the palace, the residence and the quarters for guards and servants. At a height of about five to six metres above the lane, there is, however, a bridge, blind on both sides, which connects these two parts of the palace.

Finally there is a wooden gallery, through whose multicoloured panes is a view over sea and town, joining the rest of the palace with the *serai,* above a broader street which otherwise separates them.

The *serai* is built in the Bagdad style, in burnt yellow brick, two storeyed and having on the second floor in the middle two audience halls surrounded by airy arcades. These halls are lavishly supplied with windows, whose panes are partly of coloured glass; the floors are covered with Persian carpets; along the walls stand broad seats and sofas of a hybrid Oriental–European style and the ceiling is divided into panels by wooden fillets. Each panel is occupied by a polychrome lithograph, representing a young and appetizing, including European, female beauty, the whole forming a considerable collection selected with doubtful taste and comprising all hues from the North Cape to Cape Matapan, with particular preference for plump examples.

In the morning after Mobarek has eaten his first meal, he betakes himself, accompanied by a couple of specially trusted servants and a score of bodyguards, across the covered bridge to the central part of the palace and thence over two more roofs and wooden bridges, all strongly guarded to his destination in the *serai*. The guards of the various bridges and doors have meanwhile fallen in behind him, and at the moment when he reaches the *serai,* he is attended by something more than half a hundred well-armed men. If the weather be fair – and it is so generally – Mobarek takes up his position on a seat in the arcade on the side facing the sea, and there for an hour occupies himself with his correspondence, hearing letters read to him and dictating his own and replies to a secretary.

When he has finished he leaves the *serai* and while his bodyguards cluster still more tightly round him than they did within the palace walls, he proceeds to a varnished black barouche, drawn by a couple of black horses with satin coats, which is to carry him to one of the buildings in the bazaar. Here he has to receive visits and decide business matters and law-suits; for only particularly trusted and favoured individuals are granted access to him in the palace itself.

Before the carriage marches the bodyguard; behind, on a white horse, comes a gigantic negro in blue livery with bright Mauser carbine ready for use. Off goes the procession through the longest street of the bazaar, where stray shafts of sunlight falling through a loosely-woven roof of palm leaves, fleck the picture. All business is arrested for a moment in order that everyone may make his respectful *salam* to the Sheikh.

In the innermost corner of the great market place, by the bazaar quarter, are two two-storied buildings from the glazed windows of whose second floors there is a view and here, sometimes in one and sometimes in the other, Mobarek gives audience. As soon as he quits the carriage and is come safely by an outside staircase into the building the guards, now further strengthened, scatter over the market place. So, amid the motley confusion of bartering and eagerly gesticulating Arabs, of groaning camels, bleating goats and children, all to be seen in the market at any time, one keeps coming upon groups of five to ten armed men sitting in a half circle on the ground and small groups of riflemen at the nearest corners of the bazaar.

While the Sheikh is in the market place, the guards left in the palace give their attention to exercises, that is they shoot at marks, naturally not at any regular target set up for the purpose, but some chance mark or other, or indeed any spot – for example, the lowest part of the wall of the *serai*. Bedouins with Martinis and Mauser carbines lie on the roofs of the central palace and fire across the street and gigantic, sweating negroes reach out as far as they can over the slender iron railings of the wooden bridges to get nearer to the mark, and empty the contents of their revolvers so close that the whitewash flies off the walls. When the time approaches at which the Sheikh usually returns, the firing is silenced, and the watchmen automatically take up their wonted places at the entrances, which, however, have, of course, never been left quite deserted, even during the most animated shooting match. If Mobarek has got through his business in the bazaar so early that some time is still free before the midday meal, he betakes himself once more to the *serai* in order to enjoy from the arcade, or from a balcony on the seaward face, the view over the changing, many-hued waters of the bay, sometimes a grass green, sometimes ultramarine, now a storm-lashed grey or a sluggish sheet, clear as a mirror. On a stool by his side there lie always a diamond-studded cigarette case, containing long, 'Bagdad' cigarettes and a pair of field-glasses, with which he watches the white lateen sails that now and then put out over the sea, or looks for the British mail steamer.

Then comes meal-time. Slaves hurry about the small courts and across terraces and roofs, with large metal trays and steaming dishes on their heads, carrying in their hands large round, palm-leaf mats of various patterns on which the meal is served. In the middle of the mat is set the dish of rice boiled with *ghee,* around it heaps of round flaps of bread and smaller dishes of mutton and fish.

During the half-hour while it is being eaten the courts and roofs are absolutely deserted. Then come the slaves again to carry away the remains of the meal and bread crumbs in the folded mats.

'A quiet hour' follows the meal and it is a long one, lasting from midday to about three o'clock. The sun beats steadily down; the clay walls crack; on the earth-coloured town the listless sleeping sea reflects blinding light. The Sheikh sleeps, the palace sleeps, the greater part of the town sleeps; the only creatures not asleep are the flies, which seem to buzz louder than ever, gathering in black crawling clusters on the corners of the eyes of sleeping man and beasts.

At last the midday siesta is interrupted by some few ringing blows, at first intermittent, then falling into a marked rhythm – a dull thud, then a broken clang, and finally the ring of pure metal; then the rhythm is repeated in rapid, rising tempo to the accompaniment of a negro song sung in hoarse falsetto. It is a black slave, who is pounding coffee in a brass mortar to the tune of some ditty of his native land. To this sound the palace gradually wakens; sluggish footfalls pad courts and roofs, carbine barrels gleam by doors and bridges, and soon everything is ready for the Sheikh to pass once more from his harem to the *serai*. Here he takes his place on a sofa at the end of one of the reception rooms, while guests of the palace and notables of the town who come to pay their respects, seat themselves on divans along the sides.

A lusty black enters with a stack of little, handleless porcelain cups in his left hand and a brass coffee pot, of Hasa make and peculiar east Arabian form, in his right. Coffee is served to all in turn, a quarter of a cupful at a time, and Mobarek offers a cigarette to anyone he particularly desires to honour, carrying on the while a series of guarded conversations with the most part of those present. After the lapse of an hour, Mobarek drives again to the bazaar and does not return till near sunset, to take the day's chief meal, served immediately after prayer.

When darkness has fallen and a chill begins to be felt, the guards light small fires by the doorways and in snug corners of flat roofs; coffee is drunk and by the gleam of slowly dying fires bedouin sing in chorus simple melodies far on into the night.

RIYADH IN 1912

March 28*th* – In the course of this afternoon I am to have an audience of the Imam, i.e. not Abdul-Aziz, who is really gone off on a raid but his father Abderrahman. All necessary measures for the protection of an unbelieving dog in this city of the fanatically orthodox are to be observed.

Surrounded by armed guards I go along with Ali, swinging out on a great curve round the outermost gardens of the oasis, while armed men scout ahead and on both flanks to keep off chance wayfarers. After walking through sandy hollows and over stony ridges we arrive at an isolated date grove with a well-kept wall about it, a good half kilometre east of the town wall of Riyadh. Here we are in another of the Imam's gardens, larger and even better tended than that in which I am living myself. We are led on among the palms until we reach a small clearing, where a Persian carpet is spread and a negro is busy preparing tea and coffee. I take a place on the carpet, and an instant later Abderrahman came with his retinue from among the palms. After greetings we both take places on the carpets, each reclining on his cushions; Ali seats himself on the ground before us, and the retinue take up stations further away.

Abderrahman is a marvellously handsome old man, whose whole appearance bears the mark of adventure and splendour. He suggests a living episode of the 'Thousand and One Nights', – this amiable but austere old man with eagle eye and white beard. While we drink coffee and tea alternately, we engage in lively conversation about

Kuwait, about the Imam's expedition, about the interests of England and Turkey in Arabia, about the Turco-Italian War and finally about the relative power of the European States. On the last subject, especially in the matter of Africo-Asiatic politics, I could do no more than confirm the chieftain's deep-rooted belief in the hegemony of the British Empire.

Finally Abderrahman promises to make arrangements for me to join company with a caravan which is departing tomorrow for Hasa, and I then took leave of the old Wahhabi ruler, who went off with his retinue into the depths of the date grove, while I myself returned with my companions to our quarters. On arrival there I received a visit from the leader of the caravan which is going to Hofuf and see unmistakably, by the man's attitude, that he only allows me to accompany them because he has been forced to do so. I expect various happenings in his company to Hasa, but since the Imam has arranged the matter thus, I will not set myself against it. Moreover, Abderrahman has let the caravan leader know that it will go ill with him should he come to Riyadh again without a letter from me to his credit.

A TRIO OF POETS

Walter de la Mare
(1873–1956)

James Elroy Flecker
(1884–1915)

Rupert Brooke
(1887–1915)

Three poets who knew each other prior to the 1914–18 Great War and who wrote imaginatively about the Near East were Walter de la Mare, James Elroy Flecker and Rupert Brooke. The two latter, though much younger than de la Mare, were both to die early in 1915.

Rupert Brooke, who knew that Flecker, like himself, was not strong, became aware by the end of 1914 that Flecker was seriously ill in Switzerland. J. C. Squire, who wrote the memoir on Flecker in the issue of his collected poems, says '*Then in the first week in January, 1915, he died. I cannot help remembering that I first heard the news over the telephone, and that the voice that spoke was Rupert Brooke's.*'

Flecker and Brooke had first met at Cambridge, where Flecker had gone from Oxford to pursue his study of Oriental languages, and they were especially friendly; they continued to correspond in the last year before the war, when Rupert went travelling to America and the Pacific, and Flecker was in the British Levant Consular Service.

In spite of the unforgettable poem *Arabia* by de la Mare, and Rupert's strong expression of pleasure when ordered to go to the war in the Near East, it is evident that the most persistant addiction to the East was Flecker's. J. C. Squire says of him and various influences on his writing, '*An influence still more marked was that of Sir Richard Burton. When still a boy, he had copied out the whole of his long* Kasidah *and its rhythm and turns of phrase are present in several of his Syrian poems. It was in the* Kasidah *that Flecker found* Aflatun *and* Aristu, *and the refrain of the camel bells of which he made fine use in the* Golden Journey .*The verse form of the* Kasidah *is, of course, not Burton's; it is Eastern, and the use Flecker made of it suggests that an infusion of Persian and Arabic forms into English verse might well be a fertilizing agent.*'

Flecker had been christened Herman, the family called him Roy, but he
changed to James when he went to Oxford.

Continuing to describe Flecker's reading and the influence of others,
Squire says that '*he learnt from them but was seldom mastered by them. Flecker's
vision of the World was his own: his dreams of the East and Greece were born with
him. He knew the streets of Stamboul and the snows of Lebanon, and the caravans
departing for Baghdad and the Gates of Damascus, and the bazaars heaped with grapes
and coffee tables botched with pearl and little beaten brass-ware pots, but his hankering
long ante-dated his travels.*'

The play *Hassan* by Flecker, introducing the Caliph Haroun al-Rashid,
begun by him early and worked on until his death, was finally put on by
Basil Dean in 1923. Delius wrote the incidental music for it and attended
rehearsals. Miss Cathleen Nesbitt was the heroine, Yasmin, and the setting, as
Squire said, was gorgeous. The illustrated edition of the book of the play was
brought out in 1924. Flecker's wife, a Greek lady, had helped him to keep up
his work on it until his end in Switzerland. His death preceded that of his
friend Rupert Brooke by only three months, though Rupert was three years
younger and still only in his twenties.

Walter de la Mare's poem that follows is less closely restricted to realities
than was Flecker's work.

ARABIA

Far are the shades of Arabia,
    Where the Princes ride at noon,
'Mid the verdurous vales and thickets,
    Under the ghost of the moon;
And so dark is that vaulted purple
    Flowers in the forest rise
And toss into blossom 'gainst the phantom stars
    Pale in the noonday skies.

Sweet is the music of Arabia
    In my heart, when out of dreams
I still in the thin clear mirk of dawn
    Descry her gliding streams;
Hear her strange lutes on the green banks
    Ring loud with the grief and delight
of the dim-silked, dark-haired Musicians
    In the brooding silence of night.

They haunt me – her lutes and her forests;
  No beauty on earth I see
But shadowed with that dream recalls
  Her loveliness to me:
Still eyes look coldly upon me,
  Cold voices whisper and say –
'He is crazed with the spell of far Arabia,
  They have stolen his wits away.'

WALTER DE LA MARE

JAMES ELROY FLECKER

Rupert Brooke and T. E. Lawrence are mentioned in some *Letters from Abroad* of James Elroy Flecker, in which Mrs Flecker says about their life in the Lebanon in 1912. '*The heat was very trying in July and August and the journey down and up at the hottest hour of the day, there being only one afternoon train that left Beyrut at 2 P.M., reaching Areya at 4, was very exhausting. On the whole, my husband bore the heat very well, what he again missed was the lack of intelligent society. One day T. E. Lawrence turned up early in the morning. As we enquired how he had got to Areya, there being no train at that hour, he quietly explained that he had arrived by the night train, but not wishing to disturb us had slept on the floor in the station to the scandal of the station-master. My husband was delighted to be able to talk literature and Oxford again and to hear of the "amazing boy's" astonishing adventures in Asia Minor. The photo given in the frontispiece, of J. E. F. in Arabic dress, was taken by Lawrence on the three-arched balcony, and that of the "amazing boy", as Roy sometimes spoke of him, by my husband.*'

In a letter in June 1912, from Beirut, Flecker wrote that his wife had caught a slow fever just as they had found an idyllic house on the Lebanon. She was beginning now to recover from the fever, but, '*except Hogarth and his two fellow archaelogists intermittently resplendent on the way to or from Carchemish we never see a civilized soul*'. He mentions again how admirable he found the poem *Arabia* by Walter de la Mare. Once more he makes it clear that he is hankering for England and the Western literary world. To Edward Marsh he sends his thanks, in October 1912, for offering to include him in the company of his old friend Rupert Brooke in his anthology. He hopes de la Mare's *Arabia* is to be included and subscribes to the dedication of the anthology by Robert Bridges.

HASSAN

ACT 3, SCENE I

*The garden of the Caliph's palace; in front of a pavilion. The Caliph: Hassan
in fine raiment, a sword of honour at his side.*

CALIPH: Yes, what the chief eunuch told you is all true, my Hassan.
Our late host, the King of the Beggars, was captured hiding in the
gutter of his roof. This evening I shall judge him and his crew in
full Divan. And in the divan shalt thou appear, O Hassan, clothed
in thy robe of ceremony, and seated on my right hand.

HASSAN: Alas, O Serene Splendour, thy servant is a man of humbler
origin and limited desires. I am one who would obey the old poet's
behest:

> Give all thy day to dreaming and all thy night to sleep:
> Let not ambition's Tyger devour contentment's sheep.

I am not one to open my mouth at divans, or to strut among courtiers
in robes of state. Sir, excuse me from these things. Dispose thy
favour like a high golden wall, and protect the life of thy servant from
the wind of complication. But at evening, when God flings roses
through the sky, call me then to some calm pavilion, and let us hear
Ishaq play and let us hear Ishaq sing, till you forget you are Lord of all
the World, and I forget that I am a base-born tradesman; till we
discover the speech of things that have no life, and know what the
clods of earth are saying to the roots of the garden trees.

CALIPH: Have no fear. You shall inhabit the place I shall assign you in
untroubled peace, and meditate till your beard grows into the soil
and you become wiser than Aflatun. But in this case you are a
witness and must be present at my Divan, be it but for this once
only. And you shall call me Emir of the Faithful, Redresser of
Wrong, the Shadow of God on Earth, and Peacock of the World.
But in this garden you are Hassan, and I am your friend Haroun,
and you must address me as a friend, a friend.

HASSAN [*Kissing Caliph's hand*]: O Master, you speak gently, but I must
fear you all the more.

CALIPH: But why? I am but a kindly man. I love single heartedness
in men as I love simplicity in my palace. There you have seen
floors with but one carpet – but that carpet like a meadow. You
have seen walls with but one curtain – but that curtain a sunset, on
the sea. You have seen white rooms all naked marble: but they await

my courtiers all clothed like flowers. If, therefore, I avoid com-
plexity in the matter of walls and floors, shall I not be simple in the
things of heart and soul? Shall I not, Hassan, be just your friend?

HASSAN: Master, I find thy friendship like thy palace, endowed with
all the charm of beauty and the magic of surprise. As thou knowest,
I am but a man of the streets of Baghdad, and there men say 'The
Calpih's Palace, Mashallah! The walls are stiff with gold and the
ceilings plated with silver, and the urinals thereof are lined with
turquoise blue.' And hearing men say this, many a time hath
Hassan the Confectioner stroked the chin of Hassan the Confectioner saying, 'O Hassan, thy back parlour is less ugly than that,
with its tub of boiling sugar, and one Bokhara good carpet hanging
on the wall. And twelve months did I work at the tub, boiling
sugar to buy the carpet.'

CALIPH: What a man you are for poetry and carpets! When you tread
on a carpet, you drop your eyes to earth to catch the pattern; and
when you hear a poem, you raise your eyes to heaven to hear the
tune. Whoever saw a confectioner like this? When did you learn
poetry, Hassan of my heart?

HASSAN: In that great school, the Market of Baghdad. For thee,
Master of the World, poetry is a princely diversion; but for us it
was a deliverance from Hell. Allah made poetry a cheap thing to
buy and a simple thing to understand. He gave men dreams by
night that they might learn to dream by day. Men who work hard
have special need of these dreams. All the town of Baghdad is
passionate for poetry, O Master. Dost thou not know what great
crowds gather to hear the epic of Antari sung in the streets at
evening? I have seen cobblers weep and butchers bury their great
faces in their hands!

CALIPH: By Eblis and the powers of Hell, should I not know this,
and know that therein lies the secret of the strength of Islam!
In poems and in tales alone shall live the eternal memory of this
city when I am dust and thou art dust, when the bedouin shall
build his hut upon my garden and drive his plough beyond the
ruins of my palace and all Baghdad is broken to the ground. Ah, if
there shall ever arise a nation whose people have forgotten poetry or
whose poets have forgotten the people, though they send their
ships round Taprobane and their armies across the hills of Hin-
dustan, though their city be greater than Babylon of old, though
they mine a league into earth or mount to the stars on wings –

what of them?

HASSAN: They will be a dark patch upon the world.

CALIPH: Well said! By your luck you have saved the life of the Caliph, O Hassan; but by your conversation you have won the friendship of Haroun. Indeed – but at what are you gazing as if enchanted?

HASSAN: What a beautiful fountain, with the silver dolphin and the naked boy.

CALIPH: A Greek of Constantinople made it, who came travelling hither in the days of my father, the Caliph El Madhi (may earth be gentle to his body and Paradise refreshing to his soul!). He showed this fountain to my father, who was exceptionally pleased, and asked the Greek if he could make more as fine. 'A hundred' replied the delighted infidel. Whereupon my father cried, 'Impale this pig'. Which having been done, this fountain remains the loveliest in the world.

HASSAN [With anguish]: Fountain, dost thou never run with blood?

CALIPH: Why, what is the matter, Hassan?

HASSAN: You have told a tale of death and tyranny, O Master of the World.

CALIPH [In a sudden and towering rage]: Do you accuse my father of tyranny, O, fellow, for slaying a filthy Christian?

HASSAN [Prostrating himself]: I meant no offence. My life is at your feet. But you bade me talk to you as a friend.

CALIPH: Not Ishak himself, who has been my friend for years would dare address me thus. [Bursting into laughter] Rise, Hassan. Thy impudence hath a monstrous beauty, like the hind quarters of an elephant.

HASSAN: Forgive me, forgive me.

CALIPH: I forgive you with all my heart, but, I advise you, speak in conformity with your character and of things you understand, and never leave the Garden of Art for the Palace of Action. Trouble not your head with the tyranny of Princes, or you may catch a cold therein from the Wind of Complication. Keep to your poetry and carpets, Hassan, and make no reference to politics, for which even the market of Baghdad is an insufficient school.

RUPERT BROOKE

Edward Marsh wrote in his memoir at the beginning of the *Collected Poems* of Rupert Brooke, published posthumously in 1918, words that show how the young poet, still in his twenties, felt on hearing that the Royal Naval Division in which he had become an officer, was bound for Turkey.

On January the 29th, he came to London to recover from a rather bad attack of influenza, staying first at Gray's Inn and then at 10 Downing Street. I saw him for the last time on February the 25th, when the King reviewed the Naval Division at Blandford before their departure for the Dardanelles. The secret of where they were going was just out, and everyone was wild with excitement and joy. 'It's too wonderful for belief' Rupert wrote to Miss Asquith. 'I had not imagined Fate could be so benign. I almost suspect her. Perhaps we shall be held in reserve, on a choppy sea, for two months . . . yet even that! . . . But I am filled with confident and glorious hopes. I've been looking at the maps. Do you think perhaps the fort on the Asiatic shore will want quelling, and we'll land and come at it from behind, and they'll make a sortie and meet us on the plains of Troy? It seems to me strategically so possible. Shall we have a Hospital Base (and won't you manage it?) on Lesbos? Will Helen's Tower crumble under the 15" guns? Will the sea be polyphloisbic and wine dark and unvintageable? Shall I loot mosaics from St. Sophia, and Turkish Delight and carpets . . .

'I've never been quite so happy in my life, I think. Not quite so pervasively happy; like a stream flowing entirely to one end. I suddenly realize that the ambition of my life has been – since I was two – to go on a military expedition against Constantinople.' This, he added 'was what I really wanted. This is nonsense. Goodnight. I'm very tired with equipping my platoon.'

He and a brother officer had both become ill when they were in the Aegean. *'We were turned out rather quickly'* he wrote later. *'On Friday morning, April the 9th, we were ordered to be aboard that evening if we felt well enough which of course we both said we were.'*

Writing to Miss Asquith again, he said *'But while I shall be well, I think, for one first thrust into the fray, I shall be able to give my Turk, at the utmost a kitten's tap. A diet of arrowroot doesn't build up violence. I am as weak as a pacifist.'*

On 17 April they went ashore for a few hours at Scyros Island. Rupert Brooke was fairly well until the 20th when he began to sicken again and soon had a temperature of 103°. He was transferred to the French hospital ship where everything possible was done for him, but he died on the afternoon of 23 April, St. George's Day. He was buried that night by lamplight, on Scyros Island, with an escort and firing party of his brother officers and men, his grave being covered by them with small boulders of the white and pinkish-white marble.

On 26 April Winston Churchill, apprised by cable, wrote an obituary in splendid language for *The Times*.

In the notebook used by Rupert in the last days of his life was found the following *Fragment*.

I strayed about deck, an hour tonight
Under a cloudy moonless sky; and peeped
In at the windows, watched my friends at table,
Or playing cards, or standing in the doorway,
Or coming out into the darkness. Still
No one could see me.

I would have thought of them
– Heedless, within a week of battle – in pity,
Pride in their strength and in their weight and firmness
And link'd beauty of bodies, and pity that
This gay machine of splendour 'ld soon be broken,
Thought little of, pashed, scattered . . .

                            Only, always,
I could but see them – against the lamplight – pass
Like coloured shadows, thinner than filmy glass,
Slight bubbles, fainter than the wave's faint light,
That broke to phosphorous out in the night,
Perishing things and strange ghosts – soon to die.
To other ghosts – this one, or that, or I.

April 1915

SOURCES

Itinerary of Rabbi Benjamin of Tudela Translated and edited by A. Asher
(2 Vols) London and Berlin, 1840

Cathay and the Way Thither, being a collection of Medieval Notices of China
Translated and edited by Colonel Henry Yule, C. B.
Hakluyt Society, 1886

*The Navigation and Voyage of Ludovico de Varthema, Gentleman of the City of Rome
to the regions of Arabia, Egypt, Persia, Syria, Ethiopia and East India, both within
and without the River of the Ganges, etc. in the Year of Our Lord 1503 ...*
Translated by Richard Eden, 1576
(This extract from 1884 edition, privately printed by The Aungervyle Society
of Edinburgh)

*The Travels of Sig. Pietro della Valle, A Noble Roman, into East-India and
Arabia Deserta ... Whereunto is Added A Relation of Sir Thomas Roe's Voyage
into the East-Indies*
Printed by J. Macook for J. Place, London, 1665

'Verses written in the Chiosk of the British Palace, at Pers, overlooking the
city of Constantinople' by Lady Mary Wortley Montagu from *Miscellany*
edited by Anthony Hammond, London, 1720

'Travels in Arabia' by Carsten Niebuhr from *A General Collection of the best
and most interesting Voyages and Travels in all parts of the world* Translated by
John Pinkerton
(10 Vols) London, 1811

The History of the Caliph Vathek by William Beckford
Paris and Lausanne, 1787
(This extract from 1901 edition, Methuen, London)

'Lalla Rookh, An Oriental Romance' from *The Poetical Works of Thomas
Moore*
Edinburgh, 1875

Notes on the Bedouins and Wahabys collected during his travels in the East, by the late John Lewis Burckhardt
Published by authority of the Association for Promoting the Discovery of the Interior of Africa
(2 Vols) H. Colburn and R. Bentley, London, 1831

Narrative of a Residence in Koordistan and on the Site of Ancient Nineveh with a journal of a Voyage Down the Tigris to Baghdad, and an account of a visit to Shirauz and Persepolis by Claudius James Rich
J. Duncan, London, 1836

The Spirit of the East. Illustrated, a Journal of Travels through Roumeli during an eventful period by David Urquhart
(2 Vols) H. Colbourn, London, 1838
(This extract from Vol. 1, Chap. XIII, p. 224ff.)

Narrative of a Journey Through Parts of Persia and Kurdistan undertaken by Commander J. F. Jones, I.N. in company with Major Rawlinson,
Government of Bombay, 1849

Punch in the East from *Punch or the London Charivari,* part IV/V of five articles from 'Our Fat Contributor', W. M. Thackeray, Feb. 1845

Ninevah and its Remains – with an account of a visit to the Chaldaean Christians of Kurdistan, and the Yezidis, or devil worshippers . . . Austen Henry Layard D.C.L.
(2 Vols) J. Murray, London, 1849. Popular edition, 1861

Personal Narrative of a Pilgrimage to Al-Madinah and Meccah by Sir Richard Burton
(3 Vols) 1855, 1856

Northern Najd, A Journey from Jerusalem to Anaiza in Qasim by Carlo Claudio Guarmani
Translated by Lady Capel-Cure. Introduction and notes by Douglas Carruthers
The Argonaut Press, London, 1938

In Arabia Deserta by Charles M. Doughty
Cambridge University Press, 1888. Introduction by T. E. Lawrence. J. Cape, London, 1921

A Pilgrimage to Najed, The Cradle of the Arab Race, A Visit to the Court of the Arab Emir, and 'Our Persian Campaign' by Lady Anne Blunt
(2 Vols) J. Murray, London, 1881

The Desert and the Sown by Gertrude Lowthian Bell
Wm. Heinemann, London, 1907

Divan of Hafiz Translated by Gertrude Lowthian Bell
Wm. Heinemann, London, 1897

Through Wahhabiland on Camelback by Barclay Raunkiaer. Introduction by
Gerald de Gaury
Routledge and Kegan Paul, London, 1969